# of Digital

Success stories from leaders in advertising, marketing, search and social media

Paul Springer & Mel Carson

KoganPage

LONDON PHILADELPHIA NEW DELHI

Publisher's note

Every possible effort has been made to ensure that the information contained in this book is accurate at the time of going to press, and the publishers and authors cannot accept responsibility for any errors or omissions, however caused. No responsibility for loss or damage occasioned to any person acting, or refraining from action, as a result of the material in this publication can be accepted by the editor, the publisher or either of the authors.

First published in Great Britain and the United States in 2012 by Kogan Page Limited

120 Pentonville Road
London N1 9JN
United Kingdom
www.koganpage.com

1518 Walnut Street, Suite 1100
Philadelphia PA 19102
USA

4737/23 Ansari Road
Daryaganj
New Delhi 110002
India

ISBN 978 0 7494 6604 6
E-ISBN 978 0 7494 6605 3

British Library Cataloguing-in-Publication Data

A CIP record for this book is available from the British Library.

Library of Congress Cataloging-in-Publication Data

Springer, Paul.
Pioneers of digital : success stories from leaders in advertising, marketing, search, and social media / Paul Springer, Mel Carson.
p. cm.
ISBN 978-0-7494-6604-6 (pbk.) – ISBN 978-0-7494-6605-3 (ebook) 1. Internet advertising. 2. Internet marketing. 3. Social media. I. Carson, Mel. II. Title.
HF6146.I58S67 2012
658.8'72–dc23

2012013049

Typeset by Graphicraft Limited, Hong Kong
Printed and bound in India by Replika Press Pvt Ltd

Dedicated to Andrea Springer, Ashley Seffernick,
Maggie Carson and Dave Stobbs

CONTENTS

ACKNOWLEDGEMENTS

Writing a book like this is a huge collaborative process, so we owe a huge debt of thanks to many people across five continents.

There are a crowd that have drip-fed us leads and material throughout. They include: Zhang Yiping and Le Jianfeng (both Beijing Normal University, Zhuhai), Tang Lei (iMag Interactive Shanghai), the team at CKGSB Beijing, Antony Robinson (World of Advertising Research Council), Olivier Rabenschlag (TBWA\Chiat Day LA), Mark Middlemas (UM), Mark Egan (Havas Digital), Phil Mahoney (PhD), Santosh Padhi (Taproot India), Kaswara Al-khatib (Full Stop, Saudi Arabia), Mohammad HA Abudawood (P&G Middle East), Dr Abdullah Dahlan (CBA Holdings, KSA), Tim Stephens, Robert Urquhart, Matt Smith (The Viral Factory), Peter Hadfield (Universal), Nick Lawson (MediaCom), Jon Buckley, Vic Davies, Stephen Partridge, Richard Jones, Justin Luker, Tang Hi Yi, Shadi Elemar and Mohammad Kazeroun (all Buckinghamshire New University), Tamara Ramach, Dominic Lyle and the team at Edcom, the European Institute for Commercial Communications Education.

There's also a crowd that made the interviews possible, most notably: Ajaz Ahmed, Bob Cianfrone, Liisa Juola, Alex Bogusky, Hannah Hickman, Katy McKegney, Thomas Gensemer, Jane Austin, Nigel Vaz, Malcolm Poynton, Rafael Rojas, Gurbaksh Chahal, Jeremy Barbour, Denzyl Feigelson, Jon Winsor, Ashliegh Buck, Angel Chen, Kyle MacDonald, Martha Lane Fox, Vanessa Fox, Danny Sullivan, Andrew Sampson (SamFry.com), Stephen Fry, June Cohen, Qi Lu, Jaron Lanier, Jess Greenwood, Avinash Kaushik and Carolyn Everson, Ronda Carnegie (TED), Andrew Ellis (WeAreLikeMinds), Andy Beal (Marketing Pilgrim), Judy McGrath, Matt McGowan (Incisive Media), Sheryl Sandberg (Facebook), Guy Phillipson (IAB UK), Jim Sterne (Target Marketing), John Battelle (Federated Media), Jonathan Beeston (Efficient Frontier), Lee Odden (TopRank Online Marketing), Matt Cutts (Google), Rand Fishkin (SEOMoz), Richard Eyre (Eyre Supply), Shari Thurow (Omni Marketing Interactive), Sheryl Sandberg (Facebook), Karen Adams (Kraft), Steve Clayton, Shelby Healy, Nickie Smith, Stefan Weitz, Mari Kim Novak, Marc Bresseel, Sandra LeDuc and Kaila Lightner (all at Microsoft).

For the pioneers material online – filmed interviews and much more fun, content and chat – we have our team of Kelsey Powell, Laura Robinson, Sander Saar, Becky and Dave Naylor (Bronco), Kean Richmond (Bronco), Bryan Schaeffer (SINTR) and Jess Slaney and Andrew Goddard (CherryUK.com).

We owe a debt of gratitude to our cottage-industry editing and transcribing teams: Andrea Springer, Ashley and Aubrey Seffernick, Colleen and Josh

LaBelle, Trinitie Kedrowski, Chason Hendryx, Anne Evans and James Carson. And, of course, our patient employers, Buckinghamshire New University and Microsoft in the UK and the United States, who have been supportive throughout this rather large project. We would particularly like to express our thanks to Matt Smith, Jon Finch and Helen Kogan at Kogan Page for keeping the process smooth – true pros.

Introduction

The internet as we know it today would be nothing without key people. An Englishman, Tim Berners-Lee, shaped the free network we now call the world wide web. Microsoft's Bill Gates sought to put a PC on every desk and in every home. Google's Sergey Brin and Larry Page set out to organize the world's information and make it universally accessible and useful. Mark Zuckerberg, co-founder of Facebook, now strives to give people the power to share and make the world more open and connected. And of course, the late Steve Jobs did much to put the digital revolution into people's hands (and ears) and show how technology could enrich lives through simple but brilliant design.

True pioneers of digital, these innovators have pushed the boundaries of what's possible through the internet and created compelling, entertaining and useful experiences that have touched millions around the world.

But they're not the only ones. Far from it.

When we sat down to discuss writing this book, we wanted to tell the stories of pioneers of digital that you might not necessarily have heard of. We wanted to write about people who had explored new areas of the internet, people who had developed groundbreaking technologies and businesses, people who had discovered new ways to reach new audiences, people who made the web look like it does today. These are the people who had inspiring insight and have great stories to tell.

Having communications backgrounds and an avid interest in digital media, we narrowed our focus to discovering pioneers in the fields of advertising, marketing, search and social media, to showcase individuals who had excelled in embodying an entrepreneurial spirit by creating captivating connections with consumers in a multitude of different ways.

Our voyage of discovery led us around the world, from the UK and Europe to the United States, India, the Far East and Middle East. We had conversations with pioneers of digital who helped us understand where they had 'the big idea', what drove them, how they accounted for their success and what they think we can learn from their experience.

The result is 20 stories that span multiple disciplines, platforms, campaigns and industries across the digital space. Each of our pioneer's stories begins by explaining their digital discipline, and then their journey unravels in their words.

With analysis of why their work has succeeded, each ends with sound bytes that echo the main takeaways from their cases. From big brand advertising to search engine optimization, from political campaigning to virtual reality, from social activism to digital creativity, from online video to celebrity social media – it's all in these pages.

Pioneers of Digital also includes some of digital history's more unusual stories. For instance, how did a political campaign have 80,000 unread e-mails? Why does the father of virtual reality now question the technological ideology he helped create? What do you do when your website's a global success but your client wants it taking down? Who went on to generate a billion video views online after being turned down by the BBC? From dilemmas to innovation, the stories behind digital's most consumed and followed content are told by the people who helped create it.

As this project progressed, themes started to emerge: cross-cultural themes, attitudinal themes, inter-disciplinary themes and astonishing themes. Would it surprise you that most of our pioneers had little idea, back in the 1990s, that two decades later the web would have become quite so huge and all-encompassing in our daily lives? Could one of the secrets to success truly be to simply love what you do? Is it really best to avoid originality and focus on agility 'in the moment'?

We've identified the pioneering territories of the world that are taking up the digital challenge. How have China and India – the world's biggest countries – developed digital communications? How has the Middle East, with the largest proportion of youth buying into digital, been shaped for their brave new world?

In the final chapter we've reflected on the main issues, views and, in some cases, counter-logic from the cases that defines these pioneers' views from commonly held assumptions about digital.

Many people have asked us how we chose our pioneers. They are people who, to industry insiders, are synonymous with digital innovators, early adopters, real-time adapters and entrepreneurs. In the main these are the people whose contribution to the digital ecosystem we could do little without. We wanted to cover stories and themes that explain the bigger picture of digital communications today, through the words of the opinion shapers, games designers, crowdsourcers, knowledge givers, celebrity social media power-users, digital advertisers, cause campaigners, network coordinators and trading pioneers who have all done so much to set the standard.

Our aim with this book is to inspire; to reveal and to make these pioneers' histories accessible. You might learn about a new technology or best practice. You might discover new ways to approach a problem or choose a new path. You might be surprised, motivated, or you might disagree.

We want you to apply what you read in this book to help you be the next generation of pioneers of digital. The pioneers profiled have helped us to tell their stories and, in some cases, reflected on their achievements for the very first time.

These inspiring stories don't stop at the end of this book: we want you to connect with us and give us your thoughts at our website, **www.PioneersOfDigital.com**, and through our Twitter feed and Facebook page.

This conversation is just beginning. As many of the pioneers pointed out when we spoke with them, when it comes to digital space we've only just scratched the surface; there is so much more to come, but these are the people who first set out to do something new and ended up pioneering.

Thomas Gensemer

MyBO and Obama's 2008 Presidential Campaign

Digital discipline

Pioneered cause-related community building. He came to international prominence during Barak Obama's first run for president where his agency organized the campaign's web activities and introduced digital methods for servicing active communities.

01

Rallying the troops

The role of the internet during Barak Obama's 2008 Presidential Campaign was as significant as broadcast television was for JFK during his face-to-face debates with Nixon in 1960. Thomas Gensemer and Blue State Digital have been widely credited with propelling Obama's online push with myBO.com. Some pundits tagged Obama For America as 'the best use of digital channels yet' in the months following Obama's presidential win. A British newspaper, *The Guardian*, even ran a feature on Gensemer under the headline, 'Is this man the future of politics?'

Gensemer's unique shaping of digital is informed by keen interest in entrepreneurship, technology and politics, and his trial-and-error experiences of these ultimately took him to a position where, aged just 28, he masterminded online funding activities for a Presidential election, raising over $600m and mobilizing over 13.5m people on the way to the White House.

Gensemer's story, through politics, entrepreneurship and technology

Gensemer never intended to stay in politics long term: 'Although I'm interested in it I never thought that it would mesh with my business interests. If you had a rationale at the end you'd see it planned, but there was no plan – it was just serendipity and an interest in online community.'

Gensemer was raised and schooled in rural western Pennsylvania, though two days after finishing school he went to New York City: 'That was in 1995 at a point when the first dotcom boom was just beginning. I found the good fortune of meeting my mentors – a family involved in manufacturing and early-stage investments with start-up companies, mostly into marketing-related digital businesses.' This family and its ventures had ties with the Clinton family, so when Gensemer worked with them he

> got exposed at an early age to an entrepreneurial circle in Washington and New York, and saw a number of early digital companies across the states – early-stage publishers turning to digital and core technology investors. So we started a ventures' fund in the late 1990s and invested around the world... I got exposed to business fundamentals – early stages of business growth and management, and business technology – usable technology. I'm certainly not a technologist by any means, but we were focusing on usable technologies for particular business needs.

It was the digital organizing platforms, including an investment in Meetup.com, that made the biggest impression on Gensemer, from 'puppy owners to political causes, people were coming together online for different interests. As Robert Putnam identified in *Bowling Alone*, the book that inspired the creation of Meetup, technology gives you the capacity to isolate yourself or bring people together in a society.'

After briefly working at the cutting edge of digital commerce, Gensemer worked from 1997 onwards, while finishing his degree in politics from New York University. After graduating he went straight back to start-up investments at the height of the dotcom boom in 1999. Then, in 2004 'the bubble burst. Broadly speaking, all of us were then looking for good technology stories, like "what had happened with all this creation and sudden loss of wealth?"' Then the Howard Dean (Presidential) campaign was one particular campaign that was 'using technologies in smart ways early on'.

Howard Dean's run for the US Democratic nomination for president in 2004, although short-lived, was the first campaign to coordinate fundraising and grassroots activities through the internet. Initially Gensemer became involved with fundraising and organizing on a voluntary basis after relocating to Los Angeles, initially on a volunteer basis. Then he received a call from General Wesley Clark's campaign office

> Family and friends were organizing the campaign, and General Clark was – literally – drafted in online. There were a couple of start-up grassroots groups that thought he was the one to beat George Bush. I thought it a fascinating challenge. I relocated to Arkansas – the city that gave birth to the Clinton efforts eight years earlier – such an interesting political dynamic!

Gensemer enjoys the irony, as his grandfather, a butcher, became a state-level Republican politician after the Food and Drug Administration introduced strict guidelines on meat packing (Gensemer himself is vegetarian). Gensemer's particular fascination is centred around politics 'as a cultural exercise – the back office is more interesting because you learn a lot of business lessons. Although the aim in campaigns is to raise and spend as much money as possible! However, that nimbleness to move against a tight timeline was one of the lessons we learnt that we (later) applied to Blue State Digital.'

Learning from losing

Despite not winning elections with Dean and Clark's Presidential Campaigns, they provided valuable lessons. One such lesson included keeping all correspondences up to date. After one campaign Gensemer discovered a mailbox full of unread e-mails that were responses to a feedback link: 'they thought they should have it but no one was responsible for it. So we dug in one day and found 80,000 unread e-mails.' From this Gensemer learnt not to create opportunities for people to engage if you can't service them, and more besides:

> Don't create a random e-mail if it doesn't have a clear end and, similarly, if you're sending out an e-mail, Facebook page or tweet, make sure you can absorb the responses that you're getting; make sure that it's instructive so that you can shape that data. It's not good customer service if you don't get a response – and certainly not a good way of raising money!

As a result, Gensemer would advise companies to manage a smaller online relationship first 'and grow it from there'.

Another lesson Gensemer learnt was to have access to customer data where possible. 'We never had the desire to replicate Facebook but had desire to capture data. When I worked on the Dean and Clark campaigns, I had people showing up at a Santa Monica pub that was organized through [the network service] MeetUp, so we didn't have access to the data. That segment of data would have been on our most loyal supporters because they were turning up offline. And because the tools weren't owned by the campaign and we didn't have data rights, there was this big black hole (of information). So the creation of myBO was about maintaining that integrity of and access to data.'

Blue State Digital: meeting of curious minds

Another consequence of the campaign was the foundation of Blue State Digital (BSD), formed with staff from Howard Dean's campaign team: 'Little did I know that, now, I would be working with the people I was opposing! We only knew each other personally after the campaign, when we all moved to Washington to continue the fight in different ways.' They shared a mutual curiosity for how online channels could be leveraged during campaigns: 'The organizing possibilities of new technology – that's what sparked our interests... What was strange for the Democrats, when rallying to beat George Bush, was that there were remarkably few technology platforms that could service a campaign. They neither had the scale to process as many contributions, nor [ability to] send as many e-mails as was were needed, nor [were] nimble enough to meet the rapid response needs of a campaign. So if I was having a big fundraising day for General Clark all the other candidates were compromised – it shouldn't work that way in 2004–05. We all got to realize early on that there was a play here for a technology provider in the political context.'

During this period Gensemer also discovered the cost of creating content: 'I was working for an organization called America Come Together [in 2004] – a shadow campaign for [John] Kerry, and I did a viral video with actor Will Farrell impersonating George Bush on a ranch. It became a liability for me because I had to pay for streaming video sources. So in the first couple of days we had 200,000 hits and I'm getting a bill that wasn't in the budget, because YouTube didn't exist...'

Despite this, the team still spotted the potential in channelling communications online: 'It was never about the wonders of technology for me. It was the potential for digital platforms in making cause fundraising possible.

'When you see the possibilities of content and people responding to it, we all just felt that we'd just scratched the surface. [When] the second wave of IT investment started, more people expected that scalable relationship with organizations. [At the time you had] responses to direct mail declining while more young people wanted to engage in specific interests [online]. So it was all of those things together – plus our own political desires to make an impact – that led us to think "let's do this".'

Spotting opportunities in a world of new communications

BSD spotted that their digital methods for politics had wider commercial potential. 'We realized that there was a "play" to be a technology provider to organizations that don't have creative muscle to put online tools to work. With technology we needed creative to give the appropriate level of service to the clients we wanted to go after. So we continued in politics working with a lot of candidates and trade unions, then we slowly moved into non-profit areas – so many of the same tactics apply.'

It took plenty of persuasion to get prospective clients to realize the opportunities online in 2004. Back then, many now-familiar platforms – Twitter, Facebook, YouTube – did not have the reach, so 'it was more database management – how do you talk to and activate these supporters to give them a seat at the table and get more money out of them. At that point – and even today – so many companies were still applying the lessons of direct mail to digital efforts – in the tone and the copy as well as in the cadence of things. They were trying to plan, three months out, as if they were going to hit the printing press! We needed to teach them rapid response...' This approach, with an emerging track record of political projects, helped BSD acquire clients, from corporates to non-profit charities. However, their political experiences meant that their stock value remained especially high in politics.

Ten days to create Obama's platform

In 2005, with Howard Dean and BSD having now built up their online tools offering, we were brought in to largely replace the other technology providers. So we built a supportive community that went on to serve the Democrats.

Then on a cold February day in 2007, Barack Obama announced his intention to run for president. Obama knew the organizing ride would need to be in place very quickly.

'Because of our reputation with the DNC and Obama's experience with community organizing, their camp realized that they wanted to keep traditional organizing tactics at the heart of their campaign, but that the use of the internet would really allow these person-to-person interactions to take off. He came to us two weeks before – we signed a contract just 10 days before that [announcement] rally in Chicago', so Gensemer's BSD team had just 10 days to get the site operational – which they achieved with one hour to go! 'Fortunately the tools were already in order. It was more about making sure it was scalable enough because it was a widely anticipated event – we knew it would be a battle against Hilary Clinton. We anticipated a lot, but it exceeded even the bold expectations because people responded to Obama's message to get involved in the campaign so early on. It was a "bottom-up" effort.' From the beginning, BSD set about using digital tools nationally to ignite local action. 'From the call-to-action from Obama's podium in that Springfield,

Illinois, announcement address, it was "start creating your local organization now". Suddenly everyone was using our tools in a way that had never been done before. So that was a nail-biting experience for sure, for all of us.'

Obama's team knew it would be the main coordination tool for followers, but had no idea it would be so significant in raising funds – 'you couldn't have estimated that'. 'Because everything had to go through that platform – not just using digital as an add-on but as a fundamental approach to involving millions in the inner workings of the campaign. From that early stage, 22 months into the campaign, it exceeded all expectations. But it took support of the campaign management, from the candidate [Obama] down to other traditional power-brokers, to realize this was the prioritized channel.'

What made MyBO work

Blue State Digital and the campaign needed the flexibility to adjust strategy and respond rapidly to the ups and downs of news cycles during the testing primaries. During the primaries and the final Presidential campaign there were lines of communication that didn't take off, which Gensemer attributes to the trial and error of real-time campaigning. 'The biggest lesson,' according to Gensemer, 'was not to ask people for money but engage them in other forms of valuable activity before asking for funds... we've applied that principle to the world of corporate brands too – it works for subscription sales, membership sales, everything. Ask them for stories first, then involve them in something deeper. Such actions were informed by what we'd learnt.' In practice this was the approach that led to the campaign raising $600m. It could be claimed that an even bigger achievement was in creating fluid working conditions where fresh thinking, quick responses and a collective voice meant that the campaign was consistent and supportive of offline activities: '... having the communications team, the fundraising team and the field team all working under the same platform – that's where the creative energy flew'.

Right wing–left wing approaches to digital

As Gensemer is now experienced in US, Brazilian and UK election campaigns, what are the differences between left and right wing uses of digital? 'It's hard to generalize but the right wing tend to want to control the message a bit more. Left wing groups tend to be happy with digital communities, the right wing have a stronger voice through press and television. The Republicans have certainly not embraced digital in the same way. They have interest groups, but from a campaign perspective not as grassroots messaging; it's more top-down although this may evolve... I do think there's a progressive and conservative approach to campaign messaging that transcends borders... a progressive party can embrace certain interest groups – getting people to respond to messages. For instance, the Democrats have had women's movements, gay rights, against a more unified conservative approach. It comes down to how comfortable they are about devolving power [and losing message control].'

Gensemer identifies US politics as being different from other countries – 'it's a relentless campaign cycle! In most countries party structures transcend the candidates – you subscribe to a political party: in the United States candidates can transcend their parties [so] you rely on the next great candidate.'

With hindsight learning: lessons taken from Obama's Presidential campaign

When asked which 'Obama tactics' were the most important, Gensemer is very clear: 'having digital at the core and not just reporting to the Communications Manager or Fundraising Director was significant'. This meant that the energy of the supporters featured prominently in the site's content: 'When you see a video submitted from a field event – that the Campaign staff had nothing to do with, how do you re-broadcast and spread it to supporters to keep the momentum going? It's a piece of campaign energy you can then share, so you can have people shaping their behaviours off it. That two-way relationship was something new.'

Lessons from the Obama campaign extend way beyond politics too. Sending timely e-mails to voters and donors (Ryan and Jones, 2011), newsletters and user content all made the dialogue richer than simple messaging. 'When it comes to brands – especially big traditional brands, where we operate is in this grey area between communications and PR. And often when working with organizations big and small these departments don't collaborate at all. The things we build require a daily investment in content and a clear point of view and driving point action by the audience. We say "no – this channel needs to be vibrant every day". It's not just a Twitter strategy... you need to look beyond your milestones of media campaigns and product launches to realize these are relationships that people want, ongoing.

'I think a lot of chief marketing officers over the past couple of years have spent a lot of money to get lots of fans on Facebook. And they're realizing now that they've no idea who these people are, and they have no idea what to do to drive them to action. They may have got them through a contest or giveaway, and then they are just there, with low engagement rates...'

So what principles carry through from political to corporate brand communication?

'Not using separate media, but looking at how it all hangs together: a relationship that starts on Facebook can become part of your storytelling experience – and the actual experience of engagement.' Gensemer's other key principle concerns the organization of communications: 'You can't wait for three weeks to get a message out. Your Facebook calendar can't be built six months in advance down to a granular level of "this is the message of the day". Because if you're not responding to the news of the moment – even if it's not about you, but about your sector, then you're not servicing the relationship and people will look elsewhere. Changing bureaucratic tradition is often the first step.'

One crucial lesson Gensemer is keen to share is how technology needs to support core business, rather than dictating how it works. 'Just giving people new technology doesn't do it.'

> *In organizations, if all decisions are by a technology officer, you tend not to be going in the right direction...*

'With due respect to technologists, it (should be) prioritizing the content above the delivery channel – that's where the conversation should be. Even today many chase the latest technologies – the latest application. Unless you have an audience ready to engage that way, you need to keep the barrier of entry low – make it really easy to be involved. Technology should service that relationship – not dictate.'

These days Gensemer finds he's dealing with a different 'unknown' in political campaigning. 'We're learning tactics for how to organize tone and approach when in power. Opposition is easier to rally power; when a party is out of power there is undoubtedly a stronger drive. In both situations, you still need to drive people into the infrastructure of a campaign.'

While his situation may be different from previous campaigns, Gensemer hasn't lost his passion for politics. 'The beauty of politics is that people really take responsibility for getting behind a specific cause... while there's still difference in approaches to politics, we've proved time and time again that the same organizing effort can exist.'

Sound bytes

- Don't set up formats for engagement if you can't service them. Be realistic about what you can maintain and only set up correspondence you can support.
- Don't let the head of IT dictate policy; remember what the function of IT is for – and consider how it will work in the eyes of the end user.
- Get involved in campaigning and try an under-resourced way of working! 'It will be incredibly valuable – whichever side you work on.'
- Learn on the job, and don't expect to have a granular grand plan. Several years later, BSD is 'still learning our way'.

Further reading

Putnam, R (2000) *Bowling Alone: The collapse and revival of American community*, Simon & Schuster, New York

June Cohen

HotWired and TED.com

Digital discipline

Creator of cutting-edge digital media experiences since 1991. Early adopter of digital storytelling at Stanford's pioneering student newspaper; at HotWired during the birth of the web, created unusually useful sites like WebMonkey.com; led the team that brought TED to the web in 2006.

02

Hopelessly interested

Since 1984, the organizers of the TED Conference have been bringing people together to share their work and spread ideas. Since 2006, they've been sharing the conference talks online. And this year, they expect to reach one billion video views.

One of the leaders behind this milestone is June Cohen. Cohen's own digital story began on the Stanford University campus, where she was editor-in-chief of the school newspaper, *The Stanford Daily*. Journalism, she says, was the perfect career for someone 'hopelessly interested in everything'.

Immediacy of video

One of the givens, Cohen remembers, of being a student at Stanford and living in California's Silicon Valley is that you 'breathe in technology along with the air'. So, in 1991, when computer giant Apple announced it was launching the video application QuickTime, she and her newspaper team sat in a pub after putting the day's issue of *The Stanford Daily* to bed, and imagined how this new multimedia tool could work for journalists.

Pre-web (internet browsing software had not been invented yet), they 'started scribbling on cocktail napkins and getting very excited about the idea of delivering news over a personal computer and including not only text and photos, but also video', Cohen remembers. Over those few beers, they pondered the question: 'What would happen if you could combine the immediacy of video and broadcast journalism with the in-depth reporting of newspapers?'

The potential they saw that night meant that, as the clock struck 12, they had already decided to build one of the first multimedia publications.

Cohen assembled a team of writers, photographers, designers, filmmakers and computer programmers, and together they imagined what this new publication could be, and what content might suit it best. The publication was built using an application called HyperCard, and made available as a downloadable 'Special Edition over the Stanford University network. About 18 months after the idea first sparked, the digital edition was featuring videos of Stanford athletes training for the Olympics along with news stories on the topic.

Crucially for Cohen, the experience exposed her to a whole new process and series of questions that would prove invaluable in her career:

> It was my very first collaboration with a programming team, and it got me thinking not only about storytelling and design, but also about technical architecture and how you could bring all those elements together to craft a new kind of news experience. It was a cross-disciplinary challenge: Programmers, designers and writers all think very differently – and at that time, they had very little contact with each other – but it was clear we needed all of those perspectives to succeed. I loved finding a way to bring everyone's talents to bear.

> I was also so curious to see how the medium would evolve. Would it let us tell new stories in a new way? Or old stories in a new way? Would it change what it means to be a journalist? Would it change the nature of the newspaper? I was completely fascinated by these questions the first time they ever came to mind – in this bar in Palo Alto at in 1991. And I'm still interested in the same questions.

With a thirst for a career in journalism, the bright lights and purring printing presses of New York seemed the obvious next move for Cohen after graduation, but the experience of launching *The Stanford Daily*'s multimedia news meant she simply wasn't interested in paper-based journalism anymore: 'Once I worked on this project, I became enchanted by the idea of working in what we then called "multimedia". So that's what I decided to do.'

She started searching for a company that was 'hiring people to work in this new emerging discipline'.

Thinking differently

In 1994, *Wired* magazine announced the launch of a new digital publishing company called HotWired. Cohen became one of the first employees at the new venture, one of the first commercial web magazines. HotWired.com was unveiled on 27 October of that year. An early distinction: Cohen remembers it was the first website to carry banner ads, as well as the first site with a membership and commenting system built in:

> We were the first website to use most of the new technologies that emerged. The founders of *Wired* were really visionary that way. They decided to throw resources against this new medium, and they committed really courageously to developing things that were experimental and native to the web. From the beginning, they encouraged us to think differently. Not just to think about what we would do on TV, or what we would do in a newspaper, or what we would do in a magazine, but to think about *the web*, and what actually works on the web.

Thinking about what works on the web has become a fundamental discipline that Cohen has kept with her throughout her career. Back in 1994, she says, there were some serious technological constraints on what you could actually build on the web. 'We were constantly thinking about how to get around the limitations of the technology to deliver the experience that was waiting to be born.'

Cohen spent six years at HotWired, where she had a 'front-row seat to the dot-com boom'.

Those years were ones of learning for Cohen, especially in the area of usability and user experience. She learned to listen, understand and respect what HotWired's audience wanted, and was 'continually surprised' by the way people used the website:

> It took us a really long time to get our heads around what people wanted to do online. We originally thought of the web as an immersive, playful, entertaining medium. But we came to understand that what people wanted out of it most of all was utility. They wanted things to be fast, and they wanted them to be intuitive, and they wanted them to be super useful. And the more useful something was, the more people used it. That seems really obvious, but it's not as obvious as it sounds.

One of Cohen's early projects was to create an online toolkit for web surfers, a kind of reference guide that included a roundup of e-mail services and search engines. Shortly after it launched, HotWired's president, Beth Vanderslice, came over to Cohen's desk, holding the site's visitor statistics. The traffic numbers in Vanderslice's hand showed that Cohen's Online Toolkit had become the most popular thing on the site, and she was asked to invest time in figuring out why it was so popular and how she could expand the idea.

> Our big learning from the Online Toolkit was that useful tools succeed. So I started focusing with my team on content that filled an obvious need.' In what must have been one of the first examples of content optimization, Cohen's team took their learnings from the toolkit and applied them to create WebMonkey, a collection of resources that taught people to design and build websites. It became one of the most successful projects at HotWired in terms of page views, viewership and revenue.
>
> WebMonkey succeeded because it filled a real need: there was a lot of interest in creating websites, but there wasn't a lot of good information out there. And technologies were evolving so quickly that books couldn't keep up.

But Cohen says its success was also driven by the way the information was presented:

> There were two things that really defined WebMonkey. The first was that it was accessible: we avoided jargon and we used a lot of humour. We loved the fact that the web allowed anyone to be a publisher, and we wanted to help as many people as possible take advantage of that. We tried to demystify the process of creating websites. The other defining factor was that it was personal. Each tutorial was written by an engineer or a designer, in the chatty, informal blog-like voice that was popular online. We included their photos with the tutorials, and really celebrated them. We turned geeks into rock stars.

Unusually useful

After leaving HotWired in 2000, and moving back to her home state of New York, Cohen set out to complete a pet project: writing a website owner's handbook. 'It was the manual we always wished we had in the '90s. We would hire new employees, and we'd need to bring them up to speed quickly on web design and technology. But there was so little documentation in those days; everything was passed down as an oral history. We always wished we had a book we could just hand people, and say "Here, read this. It's everything we've learned so far."'

Published in 2003, *The Unusually Useful Web Book* contained excerpts from interviews Cohen had conducted with more than 50 people in the industry, extracting tactics that helped make websites succeed. And while the book was released during a 'distinctly quiet' time in the industry (between the dot-com boom and the rise of Web 2.0 and social media), Cohen said the book helped propel her into her next adventure. She had learned so much from talking to so many people in the industry that she 'was quite fortified with a really wide range of best practices on everything from usability testing to leading brainstorming sessions'.

And her next adventure came calling in 2005, when she received an e-mail from Chris Anderson, who ran TED, inviting her out for breakfast.

Up to the world

Cohen had been attending the TED Conference since 1998. The conferences were held annually in Northern California, and she describes being 'in heaven' when she attended them because she could go to one place and hear from the best teachers in the world on a broad range of topics, one after another. 'I've always had a really wide set of interests, and TED is the perfect place for polymaths. You really get to feed your hunger for learning.'

In other words, it was another natural fit for someone who was hopelessly interested in everything.

2005 was the first year she hadn't signed up and bought one of the $2,000 seats. Chris Anderson, who had taken over the running of the conference a couple years before, had noticed she wasn't on the attendee list and suggested they meet. The two had struck up an e-mail acquaintance over the years: 'I was always sending Chris speaker suggestions (this is a very common thing among TED attendees; we all feel some ownership over the programme!) and it turned out we had very similar ideas and interests.'

During the meal, Anderson let her know he'd been thinking of opening TED up to the world. Previously an elite event founded by Richard Saul Wurman and Harry Marks in 1984, TED had been for many years a small exclusive affair. 'It was a closed system. What happened at TED stayed at TED.' But Anderson had purchased TED with his foundation, and turned it into a nonprofit; now he wanted 'to open TED up to the world.'

Cohen remembers:

> At that first breakfast, Chris shared with me some of his vision for the conference. He wanted TED to have a broader role in the world. And one way he wanted to do this was by making the talks accessible to a wider audience. I found that such an inspiring vision, as well as a risky one: It wasn't clear that you could open TED up, and still retain the magic that made it what it was. It was a courageous idea! And in the seven years I've worked for Chris, I've never seen him back away from that vision. He's been bold, unapologetic, consistent and generous in his determination to spread ideas.

The result of that breakfast was a job offer. Anderson asked Cohen to help him run the speaker programme and pursue his idea of bringing TED out into new media, beginning with television. But TV proved a non-starter. 'At that time, networks just weren't interested in TEDTalks, as we envisioned them. The talks were such a departure from typical television content that they couldn't imagine them succeeding on TV. When the BBC told me that TEDTalks were too intellectual for them, I realized it was time to change strategies.'

Packaging up for the web

The answer, of course, lay in Cohen's past. One of TED's sponsors – Cohen remembers it was Chris Fawcett of Sony – had suggested that one way to initially finance the television series might be by packaging up the talks for the web and releasing them as podcasts. This made intuitive sense to Cohen: The web would allow for a global audience, free access and easy sharing – all qualities that would help further the mission. And the moment seemed right: Online video was just taking off, and the buzz about podcasting was building. In the autumn of 2005, Anderson and Cohen decided to take the leap and launch TEDTalks on the web.

The move happened to coincide with the launch of the fifth-generation iPod by Apple, which included a video screen. YouTube was still in its nascent stage, and online video was starting to play a more and more important role on the Internet. In hindsight, the conditions may seem perfect. But at the time, 'almost no one I knew thought TEDTalks could succeed. Taped lectures just didn't scream "big idea" to anyone.' The potential audience seemed very small. And could a camera truly capture the magic of the live event?

For the talks to succeed, Cohen knew they would have to be expertly filmed and edited by someone who understood the constraints of the online environment. So she hired an old friend, Jason Wishnow, whom she believed to be the smartest person in the industry when it came to online video. (Wishnow had created one of the first online video sites in 1996, and was himself an accomplished film director.) Together, they set about working on best practices for editing for the small screen so the talks would have maximum impact on the viewer.

Cohen and Wishnow were convinced they could capture the power of the talks they so believed in. If they could film them correctly and bring 'the lens of modern filmmaking to the process of bringing them online', they felt they could succeed.

High school musicals

Wishnow used to joke that most videos of lectures were shot like high school musicals, with one camera turned on and forgotten at the back of the room. Cohen says it was crucial to work in other angles and get the editing right:

> Most of us don't necessarily have a great sophistication when it comes to video editing, but we know with our eyes. We expect it. We can't remain interested in something that isn't edited well. So we really paid attention to that in TEDTalks, shooting with several cameras so we could produce a dynamic edit. We paid special attention to getting close-ups of the speaker, so they could communicate with the user emotionally, even though they're peering out through this 2-inch portal.

Cohen and Wishnow believed TEDTalks should 'start strong':

> We don't include the host's introduction or even the speaker's opening remarks: 'Thank you ... It's so great to be here ...' We start where their speech really *took off*. And we do this because people online are extremely vulnerable to distraction. If you hesitate even a moment with a rambling introduction, for example – they'll start writing an e-mail, or doing a web search, and you've lost them.

By throwing the viewer straight into the talk, they hoped, people would keep watching all the way through because they got hooked right at the start. There was nothing to distract the viewer or let their attention wander. Cohen and Wishnow wanted the online user to feel they were sitting in the best seat in the house.

How to spread ideas

In addition to these filming and editing techniques, the team had to think hard about how to make the videos accessible and help them spread:

> Different people watch video in different ways at different times. So to reach the widest possible audience, we released TEDTalks across multiple platforms. At launch, they were available as a podcast on iTunes, as streaming video on TED.com, as an embeddable player that could be integrated into blogs, and also on YouTube. (This was an unusual strategy at the time.) Today, we've extended that strategy. So TEDTalks are available not only through online platforms like YouTube and Netflix, but also on mobile apps, through cable systems, through set-top boxes like Roku and Boxee; even on airplane in-flight video systems. And we just launched a radio show with NPR. We try to remain very adaptable, so as media habits continue to change, we remain as accessible as ever.

Six years on, Cohen believes the success of TEDTalks comes down to sticking to the task they had set out to accomplish:

> Our entire mission was to spread ideas. And because we had such a clear mission and such an inspiring one, it really allowed us to make a very good set of decisions around how to bring these talks out into the world. It was very clear to me that all of our decisions had to be geared around giving these talks every chance at success, to be used as widely as possible. But this goal

> was also important because it gave us a shared purpose with our audience. From the beginning, TED inspired curiously passionate responses from our audience. Not only were people inspired by the talks themselves, but they were moved to help us with our mission.

And that cuts to the heart of Cohen's strategy: exploring the user's desire to share:

> When you think of viral videos, you tend to think of kittens and college pranks. These videos go viral because they're funny or surprising. And that makes you want to share them. But there are other contagious emotions: like awe or elevation; when you're lifted above yourself, you want to share the moment. Also when you're touched – when something brings a tear to your eyes – you want someone by your side. Or when you've learned something new, and you have an 'Aha moment' ... you're dying to pass it on.

On the future of TEDTalks, Cohen is philosophical:

> Six years on, we're no longer a conference or even a media company but a platform for spreading ideas. This evolution began when we stopped thinking of ourselves narrowly, as a conference, and started aligning ourselves around a much broader mission of spreading ideas. It accelerated as we invited our audience to become part of our team. And, like any interesting story, we don't know exactly where it will take us. But we do know how we'll find our way: by listening to what people want, by trusting in open models, and by continuing to ask the question: How can we better spread ideas?

When June Cohen looks back on her career so far, she's most proud of creating environments where 'madly creative people can thrive', creating experiences that help to define new media, and building teams from the most talented, hard-working 'and nice' people.

TEDTalks are on their way to their billionth video view, and that's due in part to a New Yorker who spent time in Silicon Valley and remains 'hopelessly interested in everything'.

Sound bites

- Don't assume you know what your audience wants. What works for other media might not work online, so survey, test, learn and optimize.
- Stay curious and adopt early. Think about how new technologies can be adapted and stretched within your field to generate maximum engagement and return visits.
- Build content that creates an emotional connection. Think about not only why your audience might take part, but why they might tell their friends too.

Denzyl Feigelson

iTunes Advisor and Artists Without A Label

Digital discipline

Online music pioneer with a remarkable story. He has contributed to getting the music industry online twice over. Feigelson created a format for unsigned musicians to promote and sell their music without a record company's backing. Then he advised Apple on music projects, which led to an integral position within the iTunes ecosystem: this role ultimately resolved a number of issues and took commercial music online.

03

Feigelson's story: right person, right time

Life stories are rarely as interesting as Denzyl Feigelson's. In 1996 he left the music industry after 20 years, and ended up becoming the first online florist business in Hawaii. Yet six years, two ventures and one eureka moment later, Feigelson's music know-how helped to shape the way commercial music is sold online.

It's hard to overstate Feigelson's contribution to online music. He helped define how music is priced, how artists are profiled, how music buying can be tracked and how acts get networked online. In the nineties Artists Without A Label – AWAL – gives musicians scope to distribute music independently and with guidance. Then, in March 2003, iTunes Store launched in the United States, which meant that authorized music could be sold online. Feigelson's story therefore explains some of the rationale behind online music, and why iTunes became bigger than most existing record labels.

Feigelson thinks that he just happened to be the 'right person at the right time', and he's right. When the web took off in the mid-1990s, others could have got there before him, but he was the person to come up with formats that caught on, using his connections at the right time. Three other factors also made Feigelson the right person: his approach – quietly spoken but incisive and driven; his reputation; and his experiences of the music industry, which have involved the biggest names in US and African music since the 1980s.

Originally raised in South Africa, he moved to the United States alone in the early 1970s. Feigelson studied music and psychology in New Mexico and then music therapy at California State University, while playing as a musician across the central US states. He returned to South Africa during the political tensions of 1982 and landed projects producing prominent black musicians, including the legendary Steve Kekana. When US singer-songwriter Paul Simon expressed interest in working with African musicians, Feigelson helped host him in South Africa. They clicked, and Feigelson went on to work on Simon's seminal *Graceland* album and tours that followed. *Graceland*'s worldwide success introduced prominent black African musicians to a global audience. Paul Simon was keen to support the musicians showcased on the album, so he facilitated a New York office allowing Feigelson to manage artists that featured on the album. Feigelson moved to Los Angeles in the late 1980s, and his management remit grew as he took on more artists. Although he didn't know it at the time, such hands-on experience was perfect priming to move entertainment online.

Eureka #1: simplifying the business of music

After a decade of constant travel and 24/7 work, Feigelson was in need of a change. So in 1996 he took some time out and bought a remote farm in Hana, Hawaii: 'Completely off the grid. It took a four-wheel drive to reach the farm, which had no phone, no fax.' The property was an abandoned flower farm and

Feigelson simply grew flowers there, but didn't know what to do with them. This, in 1997, coincided with the rapid growth of the world wide web, so he created an online business called The Hana Flower Company, *hanaflowers.com* (still going), and posted pictures of flowers so that people could see what they were ordering. Hana Flowers' first clients were people he had known through his work, from Quincy Jones and Oprah Winfrey to people he known at North West Airlines and Jeep. With their endorsements it wasn't long before he had a successful internet business on his hands.

This is when the penny dropped for Feigelson: 'I thought, wow! This could be interesting for music.'

At the time Feigelson was visiting friends in New Mexico:

> A friend of mine gave me a cassette and said: 'Would you listen to my boyfriend's band?' His name was Forest Sky. It looked to me like a nice cassette, and I plugged it in and said, 'This is great. Does he have a record label?' He was unsigned. And a ping went off in my head. I thought... Artists Without A Label... internet... put a picture and stream of the band on the internet – you could listen to the band and order it. So that was the early version of AWAL. It was 'Give me your CDs, I'll put them up on online, people can order from it, we can split the difference – we'll charge $10 plus shipping, I'll take $4 – you take $6, I'll do some marketing and advertising.' Simple.

From the outset, Feigelson only took artists that he knew and admired. He was keen to make the venture less onerous than he had found it previously. To start with he changed the industry-standard artist contract – a '180-pager', and introduced a one-page agreement to make signing less protracted. The non-exclusive agreement had a clause allowing artists to leave with just a short notice. Consequently, many artists soon incubated with AWAL before moving on to bigger labels.

By 1998, AWAL had an independent artists' community with over 100,000 subscribing to its newsletter. It helped musicians manage their own marketing and provided trade links plus industry knowledge. However, the footfall became greater than AWAL's server could handle. 'When Napster featured AWAL, it nearly shut us down because we got too much traffic.' AWAL's growth was limited by the capability of the internet. So too was its music distribution online:

> By 2000 we were desperately trying to sell downloads but it was too early. Technology then was too clunky and it took too long to download – bandwidth wasn't there; people still used dial-up; the idea of paying for music online wasn't understood; people weren't that interested on spending money on artists they didn't know. So we kept physical distribution going on one side, but we desperately wanted to get into digital distribution. We knew it was the future.

It was some years before the technology could service Feigelson's AWAL ambitions, and it took the iTunes Store years later to pave the way.

Problem 1: selling music, but not as hardcopy

The idea of paying for downloading content was a hurdle for Feigelson. Consumers were used to buying a physical object when they bought music. From shellac 78 rpm records early in the twentieth century to vinyl singles and albums in the 1940s, each innovation sold music as a physical artefact. Developments in sleeve packaging during the 1960s reinforced music as a luxury product. Even through formats such as the Super-8, cassette tape and compact disc, with its 'jewellery box' case and scaled-down artwork, music was predominantly sold as a retail experience. Downloads were more practical because music could be bought immediately, but it still required a leap of imagination for consumers to buy music without the hardcopy packaging.

Problem 2: challenging expectations of free downloads

The other problem was that many internet users expected to download music for free, and the music industry seemed reluctant to engage with the issue. The music industry was late to move its activities online, so was unprepared when websites and net users shared music without paying. 'It was scary because, being a song writer and a manager and someone on the end of royalty cheques, we all saw a generation of young people growing up thinking that music was free, because they could get it so easy.' The music industry campaigned against piracy on grounds of morality, which had little impact on digital's early adopters. The industry needed to move its business activities online or risk losing its core means of income.

Conversely, at the same time, the internet created opportunities for budding musicians. They could use social networks to get their music heard without needing traditional record label support. If they could attract enough followers they could build a fan base. They still needed expertise that only industry experience could offer – how to promote, distribute and earn from their music, which is where Feigelson identified a new need for the digital age.

Music for the digital age

With AWAL's potential stalled and waiting for technology to catch up, Feigelson applied his expertise. He created licensing opportunities, approached brands, produced compilations and consulted with fashion and sports industries on music sourcing and licensing agreements. This was how he came to work with Apple.

One contact, Academy Award-winning director Bill Couturie, made the videos that Steve Jobs used for his keynote Apple addresses. 'When Apple produced a new product and Steve Jobs needed a presentation, Bill approached me in 2001 to see if I could take over the role of sourcing, licensing and clearing the music.' In early 2003, Denzyl was invited to become part of the initial iTunes team. 'It was such a small team of people, very dedicated... There were engineers in the background, but very small considering what we were doing. We were doing it all – label relations, we were talking to artists, record labels. I was one of a very small and powerful team.'

At the time, Apple had launched the first-generation iPod which, in 2002, enabled users to transfer music between their iTunes library and the portable Apple device. Most Apple and PC users already had iTunes downloaded on their desktops. Apple's first iTunes activity encouraged users to *Rip, Mix, Burn,* and migrate their music collections to digital. Much of iTunes' early success was due to its ease of use. If you were online while uploading music, iTunes added the names of tracks through Gracenote software (which matched online metadata with music previously recorded to vinyl and CD). This simplified importing music and, in some cases, it became slightly addictive. Before joining the team Feigelson had been an evangelist – 'I was a huge Power iTunes user for my licensing work. I had a room almost three metres square with shelves full of CDs and I had imported all those CDs into my iTunes application and had them all categorized.' Being a user of iTunes and a fan, Feigelson realized its potential online – and also the hurdles it faced in tackling problems that the existing music industry couldn't crack.

Addressing issues, one by one

iTunes could easily have been seen as just another opportunity, another format – just like the mini-disc, a format that 'the music industry had pushed hard'. However, Apple's advantage over other music-selling formats was that its brand was familiar. It had grown a reputation for being easy to use and, through its iconic advertising, its products were both desirable and trusted.

Keeping user functionality simple in the iTunes Store was key, as it needed the same sense of fluidity that customers would find in using other Apple products. The developers' challenge was to make the iTunes interface work fluidly on PC software as well as on Apple's operating system, but still use the same interface. At the time, this involved negotiating 64-bit versions of Windows XP and Windows Server 2003, which the team managed to accomplish without having to compromise on content.

Feigelson's challenge was more to do with the online store's content. His experience in building AWAL's community taught him how to make iTunes Store continually worth visiting and he became the first iTunes editor. 'It was like "what are we going to do?" Every Tuesday we're going to refresh iTunes Store with somebody who's into music – we needed to know what to feature and present. So from early on I was more of the editing part of the team.'

Thirty-second clips and 99c tracks

One innovation was to let people hear tunes before buying – 'how brilliant was it to hear a 30-second clip of a song and then have it immediately?' This was akin to online window shopping, and being able to buy tracks impulsively made iTunes Store more of an online leisure activity. Feigelson saw the potential of this at the time: 'Before this, artists needed marketing to lead people to record shops. Now you're leading them to something they already have – a computer, and they're already on all the time.'

The pricing of tracks also posed problems. While some expected music for free, the industry was used to selling pre-packaged products and was unaccustomed to dropping prices. Feigelson's music industry knowledge paid dividends for iTunes. He was known and trusted within the music industry – and he knew how to meet vested interests in the most economical way.

The price structure had to be simple and one that record labels and music catalogue owners would agree on. So why 99 cent tracks? 'It was common sense. If you add up the number of tracks on an album, what the publishers need, what the collecting societies need, after the publishing mechanical royalties and the record label share and the artist share... someone had to come up with a price that everyone could agree on.'

With these key elements in place, Apple was able to launch iTunes Store online in April 2003.

iTunes Store splash – how they moved the music industry

When Feigelson helped Apple with the roll out of iTunes in Britain, Germany and France the market was ready to take up music vending online. Within several years the iTunes Store had become the number one music vendor in the United States – outselling hardcopy music purchases. By 2012 iTunes had sold over 16 billion songs. 'The team had no idea how big iTunes would become. It blew us away when we sold one million tracks in the first five days. We didn't expect it. At the next meeting we said "something's going on here".'

Online music sales soon started to affect music-buying trends. If consumers wanted to buy two or three songs from an album they could do exactly that, rather than having to buy the entire album (as you had to with the previous pre-packed hardcopy formats). Yet it took a while for the music industry to come to terms with this change: 'Being able to buy two or three songs from an album rather than the whole album was a big issue. Music managers tended to think of long-term A&R (artist and repertoire) whereas with iTunes there was the need for short-term hits. So labels said "you can make your album, but make sure you give me one or two or three radio hits".'

The iTunes team were surprised when they saw one or two tracks way outselling others on an album. But albums always sell in any format, so when people realized that there were three to five good tracks they continued to buy the whole album. 'You could tell when people were picking out songs from an album. Although data analytics helped, these were early days. This was before songs were protected by Digital Rights Management (DRM), which is what most in the music industry wanted.'

AWAL reborn

iTunes Store's success was a revelation to many new distribution and aggregation companies. It is a little known fact that AWAL artist Bret Dennen became iTunes' very first *Single of the Week* in 2003. Feigelson has learnt much from the experience: 'Simplicity, giving a constant simple message of clarity – don't give too much, don't confuse the public, that's what I learnt from working with Apple.' According to Feigelson, iTunes Store's capability helped many upstart labels to grow:

> It gave labels the ability to come up with new forms of distribution, with independent artists. Yet these are artists who can compete with major recording artists who don't do TV advertising, they're not on the radio. How else would they be able to do that? AWAL could train its artists on how to become self-marketers. That was an innovation. Artists who are independent have the ability now. It can be more of a level playing field.

Another legacy has been to enable making commercial music a cottage industry – home-made music finding its audience with self-driven marketing. Data capture can inform artists of which tracks sell and where in the world they're selling. AWAL made a simple log-in system where this data was made available to artists through their account. This for Feigelson was the 'game changer': 'artists' managers were never able to get their hands on immediate sales data. We got rotary boards every three months, which were organized poorly. Now we were able to get data on a daily basis and see our sales.'

In 2005 Feigelson partnered with two UK record producers, Kevin Bacon and Jonathan Quarmby, and set up the operation with an office at the iconic Rak studios in London, with another in Sheffield.

By 2012 AWAL had over 6,000 artists, a catalogue totalling 150,000 tracks and over 20,000,000 downloads. Without AWAL's simple art of connecting, acts such as the Arctic Monkeys, the Klaxons and the Editors might never have found their worldwide audiences.

Being of the moment, not ahead

> *As an independent recording artist, AWAL makes it possible for my music to reach my fan base from all over the world. But it's not just about releasing new music. It's all about creativity, innovative ideas, and thinking outside the box – adapting to the ever-changing shades of today's music industry... AWAL is all about empowering up-and-coming talent.*
>
> (Karen May, a *power AWAL Artist* and iTunes Store Artist of the Week, 2011)

According to Karen May, 'AWAL is an extension of Denzyl's vision', and the stories of AWAL and iTunes Store are intertwined through Feigelson. Yet he remains modest about his contribution in producing both platforms: 'Things become culminations of what you know. In everyone's life, the more knowledge you gain, the more you know. Everything then culminates into repositories where you can place that knowledge. AWAL certainly has been that for me.'

Feigelson remembers how significant it was to enable tracks to be bought online: 'To be able to get a track now, in real time, was a real breakthrough moment. "I want that track now. Download it now – in my library." Before it was "get my car, get to the store, buy a £20 CD for that one track".'

Advice from Feigelson: learn on the job

What advice would Feigelson offer to those following his example? Hard work, focus and clarity of message. 'Simplicity's the key, giving a constant simple message as to what it does – don't give too much, don't confuse the public, that's what I learnt from working with Apple. As the internet grew and access to social networks grew, it has become easier to achieve.'

He would also advise against shaping businesses around traditional lines: 'We only needed a small staff base [AWAL have just 10 staff in London and Sheffield]: We wanted offices in LA and other countries, then we realized this is a digital business – distribution is a low-margin business. You don't need a digital presence everywhere, just online.'

Feigelson also reckons the best of digital is yet to come:

> Digital presents this wonderful opportunity called discovery. To discover something new that enhances your life or inspires you. If you've been into one kind of music and you find something you never thought you'd like and you enjoy it and consume it; I think that music, visual arts and communication have come together. Technology's brought us to a liberating point, but we're all still building blocks of this new modern lifestyle which allows us to discover so much more. And we can push boundaries to live a more exciting life.

Sound bytes

- It pays to be of the moment – not ahead of time.
- Keep your business model simple, and don't base it on traditional lines.
- The real potential of the internet is still to be harnessed, and presents a wonderful opportunity.

Further reading

www.AWAL.com

Kot, G (2009) *Ripped: How the wired generation revolutionized music*, Scribner, New York

Vanessa Fox

Google and Nine By Blue

Digital discipline

Ex-Googler and celebrated online marketing and business strategist. Most revered as a search engine optimization expert, programmer, author, tech columnist and the driving force behind Google Webmaster Tools. Now founder of Seattle-based web consultancy Nine By Blue.

04

Global 'go to'

When Vanessa Fox picked up the phone to a Google recruiter in early 2005, the English major turned computer programmer was confident her track record would be a good fit. Fox already had a reputation for considering the user experience (UX) in her work and making websites more intuitive to use. But in 2005, when Google were seven years into realizing their target of becoming *the* No 1 search engine, not even the tenacious Fox could have imagined the enormous impact her influence was to have on thousands of businesses around the world. Fox created the tools by which people can legitimately optimize their websites for Google – she made it a global 'go to' for businesses trying to harness the power of the web.

Relevancy and revenue

Eighty-five per cent of internet users around the world start their day typing in keywords below the 'Google Doodle' to find whatever product, service or piece of information they're looking for. The United States alone sees 12 billion searches being conducted every month. For hundreds of millions of consumers around the world, Google is their window onto the web. For millions of business owners, Google is their lifeblood, the constant source of footfall into their virtual stores and offices, and revenue into their coffers.

Ever since 1996 when the then Project 'BackRub' was first incepted, founders Sergey Brin and Larry Page have been driven to realize the company's mission statement, *to organize the world's information and make it universally accessible and useful.* Their ambition was always global, and to work, it needed to be an easy-to-use commercial tool.

By the time the Google name was registered in 1998, they had already assembled an army of software engineers at their HQ in Mountain View, California, capable of pushing the boundaries of internet technology to make the internet more commercially relevant and usable, by crawling the web, indexing billions of web pages and ranking them against searches, almost in real time.

By the time Fox approached them in 2005, Google's advertising business was well on its way to generating over $6bn annually through its AdWords platform, where advertisers could submit their sites and pay every time a user clicked on the ad that related to a keyword search.

But not everyone was willing to pay for success with Google. Many saw the 'organic' listings just below the paid-for advert listings as the Holy Grail. If website owners could get their products to surface at the top of those results, not only would their company get more visibility, but they'd sell more and make more money... for free.

With so many competing websites aiming to top Google's free listings, it became more and more difficult to get those top spots, and some search engine optimizers (SEOs) began using shady tactics to get ahead.

Google didn't like this. These tactics led to web spam, irrelevant results and – ultimately – unhappy searchers.

By the start of 2003 Google were so concerned that they even posted a web page to spell out their guidelines for what kind of site behaviour they would accept and, more to the point, what they wouldn't.

World-leading SEO Dave Naylor remembers, 'For years, webmasters would spend hours and hours trawling through web logs looking for insight and trying to spot crawling errors. What the industry needed was an intelligent geek from Google to listen and communicate with us.'

Evolution of an information 'UX' junkie

Born in Long Beach, California, during the early 1970s, Fox's first love was the written word. But she was also smart with numbers. Encouraged in junior high to represent her school at the state 'math decathlon' one year, she spent every lunchtime for two months in the library learning advanced methodology so that she could participate.

It was this self-application early in her education that set a tempo and template for Fox's career of not just solving problems, but being able to articulate the answers to anyone.

Ever the tinkerer, she'd play around with her grandparents' Commodore 64 at elementary school and when she started college in 1990 got hold of her first PC – an 8086. Although it was seldom turned on until midnight (because the northern Californian climate was too hot for the hard disk), late-night computer sessions still held no indication of what was to come: 'I was always interested in the technology side but it never crossed my mind that that would be something that I could potentially ever do for a living', she recalls.

After graduating from the University of the Pacific, Fox's first job was to use a word processor to write company operational memos, print off 500 copies and put each of them in staff pigeon holes. In order to utilize her skills and passion for writing with more profitable results, Fox turned to marketing and engaged with tech companies as a way of quenching her burgeoning programming inquisitiveness.

Spending so much time with programmers, documenting their work and making the information accessible meant that she started to pick up her first computer languages. Fox soon learnt to write her own code simply by applying what she'd seen from those around her.

Fox then took this a step further and started to build what she calls a 'unique set of experiences'. By combining her love of writing with her new-found technical know-how, she was able to start improving user experiences by helping make connections which today might seem so obvious, but in 1995 didn't exist because most programmers simply didn't think that way.

A traditional offline staple like printing collateral to take to an event was elevated to a whole new level by digital: 'Some of us started thinking there was so much more we can do. We could host conference brochures online just in case we run out at an expo. We could make it so you could link between different ones and maybe you wouldn't need to print them at all.'

So simple now, but so radical back then. Fox spent the next 10 years working in roles that let her push the parameters of online information exchange until, while working for AOL in Seattle, she spotted a job opening at Google's Kirkland office for a technical writer.

Google jobs were so sought after that, at the time, job interview processes took anything up to nine months, so it seemed that Sergey Brin and Larry Page had missed their chance to discover Fox, who had already snapped up a role at another company when Google's recruiter finally called. Fox explained her predicament, and was on a plane the next day to Mountain View for an exhausting interview marathon. 'Now I realize that was absolutely ridiculous and I can't believe that happened. I spent nine hours interviewing, but I had what they needed.' She was offered the job days later – probably then, and certainly now, a record hiring of sorts.

The Sitemaps project begins

Working out of Google's new and small Kirkland office was a strange gig, as everything and pretty much everyone were in Mountain View at the time. Fox was asked to work on a number of developer projects that weren't really ready to launch, although she did work on a few items such as the API (Application Programming Interface) protocol for Google Talk.

The Kirkland office was run by Shiva Shivakumar, whom Fox describes as a visionary engineering director: 'He wanted the Kirkland office to come up with new innovative things that were totally different and really change the way people thought about things.'

One of his ideas was the initial 'Sitemaps' project and he asked Fox to start working on it. Sitemaps involved reimagining how Google could work with website creators to submit their sites to their index. Little did Fox realize at the time that this project would be just the beginning of a fundamental shift in the way internet search engines worked with site owners.

Until this point Google had been so successful because its raft of smart engineers had built technologies that 'crawled' the web quickly, indexing billions of website pages and presenting relevant search results every time a searcher typed in keywords to their search box.

But the driving factors behind Google's popularity were relevancy and speed of search results, and it cost money for all those servers and crawlers to be up and running, generating so many connections between consumers and website owners. This is where the Sitemaps project came in. Instead of Google just coming to the website and hoping to find everything, the website owners could submit their sitemap – literally a list of all the pages on their site and how they interconnected – which would connect the dots and ensure that the Google crawlers had a comprehensive list of what the site owner wanted indexed.

Shiva blogged in June 2005: 'It's a beta "ecosystem" that may help webmasters with two current challenges: keeping Google informed about all of your new web pages or updates, and increasing the coverage of your web pages in the Google index.'

Fox is very philosophical about how the idea developed: '... but this is very common, right? This is what happens. You iterate and you change. His idea was to do the opposite of what people expected. People could just submit a list of URLs. Done! Let's shake things up and see what happens.'

Help me help you

So Fox started to shake things up: 'I could already see that there were tons of other things we really should be doing.' She talked to site owners at search conferences and realized that Google had all kinds of useful information that could help them create better websites for their (and Google's) audiences. She travelled to Mountain View a lot, talked to engineers from all parts of Google and started asking them what information they needed from site owners to make their jobs easier.

Her approach was to ask Google's engineers how she could help them. So many people in Fox's position would have embarked on a project like this with a 'help me' attitude but she knew she had to kick it off by saying 'help me help you'. She was a nobody from the Kirkland office, she had no computer science degree and she was touting a project nobody knew or cared about. She had to find a positive reason for other teams to collaborate with her.

One person she ended up collaborating with most was Matt Cutts, then, and now, head of Google's web spam team. Cutts had made a name for himself at conferences and in online marketing internet forums as a spokesman for Google on what webmasters shouldn't be doing – how they might be contravening Google's guidelines and run the risk of getting banned from their search results. Given Google's reach and ubiquity, this was enough to give any website owner sleepless nights and so people would hang off Cutts' every word.

Even with Cutts' support, Fox still needed to get some full-time help, so she started making friends with new Google employees to generate interest in the project.

Choosing the right team

'Unique to Google culture was the idea that you can choose what project you wanted to work on. A lot of new Google engineers got confused because they weren't sure what project they were interviewing for. But they weren't interviewing for a project. It's just that when they got there they could choose one. You basically spent your first month at Google learning about all the different projects and then you chose one to work on', she remembers.

Engineer Amanda Camp worked on the project from the beginning. She built the submission process for Sitemaps and even helped spread awareness of its innovation by regularly speaking at conferences.

As Fox canvassed other Google teams, she realized that within Sitemaps' mode of operation there was a wealth of data that could benefit site owners. 'There is way more information that people wanted to know. It wasn't about just submitting their site, but how Google crawls their site, how they discover URLs, how they index them and how they rank them.'

The value exchange

This kind of data proved to be crucial in helping webmasters stay competitive and the Google engineering teams started to understand how helpful it was in reducing their workloads too.

A mutual exchange of information led to quicker resolutions of issues on both sides: information Google provided in the growing set of Sitemaps-related tools reduced support requests significantly – Fox was helping the company save money! Fewer technical conflicts meant quicker and more relevant search results for consumers. More people coming back to Google because they found what they wanted quicker was profitable for their advertising business and helps explain their massive year-on-year revenues.

When senior management – in the form of Google co-founder Sergey Brin – finally came asking questions about the project, a bet was made as to how many sitemaps would get submitted by webmasters. The prize was an all-expenses-paid holiday in Bermuda (and they could take a friend too)! What better impetus to start getting creative about how to influence site owners to part with their website DNA than a free 'busman's holiday'?

The early days, however, were not easy. Some SEOs were scared. They thought it was an elaborate ploy by Cutts and Fox to have sites submitted so they could investigate and uncover shady practices that contravened Google's policies.

Fox says one thing SEOs didn't realize was:

> When we first launched Sitemaps, the infrastructure wasn't yet hooked up to anything. We first built the submission and parsing system and only once that was tested and working correctly with a steady stream of sitemaps did we begin hooking it up to the crawling and indexing system. I would hear these stories where people would say 'I submitted my site to Google and got taken out of the index!' But the connection was impossible because the search team didn't even know the site owner submitted a sitemap yet. I was the only person that could see the sitemap because I was able to see it in my system but no one else could.

Google Webmaster Central is born

So Fox's team embarked on a trust-building exercise of providing more information in the user interface, and making themselves available at conferences and online. They set up their own blog and their own forums and started to engage with the search engine marketing and optimization community in an open and authentic way. They provided them with motivational reasons to engage in a different way to help build a thriving community and, ultimately, a better, less shady web.

To be fully supported by Google, Fox and her team needed buy-in from the established search industry – which had a vested interest in maintaining the exclusiveness of systems already in place. However, Sergey Brin's 'user hurdle' was reached and passed quickly – 'if you compare that goal to how many are using it now it's a tiny number that would not even be considered a drop in the bucket!'

Fox took Google Webmaster Central, as Sitemaps was renamed once it included tools and education well beyond simply the sitemaps protocol, out of 'Beta' (dry run testing) in the spring of 2007 at a search conference in London, where Fox says confidently, 'It became a legitimate product because I made it one.'

When the team blogged that they had passed a million users, Fox noted they'd actually had significantly more people engaging with them, although we may never know the exact number.

Today **www.google.com/webmasters** is one of the website addresses on the internet most visited by businesses. It's eagerly pored over by even the most expert of experts like Dave Naylor, though he notes that: 'Even though in the early days Webmaster Central wasn't polished or even close to being a full product, Vanessa and her team listened to us and slowly we saw the product evolve into an invaluable piece of SEO software.'

Other industry commentators look back at the bearing Fox had on legitimizing SEO, as Lee Odden, CEO of TopRankMarketing.com, remembers:

> In the early days of Google, communications with webmasters was a bit of touch and go through mysterious personas on SEO forums like the 'Google Guy'. Then along came Vanessa Fox. I've always found Vanessa to be helpful, approachable and sincerely interested in helping website owners better understand search marketing. She's been a tireless pioneer and advocate for search engine and webmaster communications which has advanced the search marketing industry in immeasurable ways. Her work providing analysis and insight through industry articles, speaking at conferences around the world and developing Google Webmaster Central has helped define how search engines overall relate to the webmaster community. She's been a significant influence towards elevating how search marketing is viewed: from a mystical bag of tricks to a high-impact channel for strategically attracting and engaging customers.

Two years and three months after joining Google, Fox left to pursue other projects and now runs her own consultancy Nine By Blue, ironically just off Pioneer Square in Seattle, and has published a book called *Marketing in the Age of Google*. Dixon Jones, marketing director at Majestic SEO and one of the industry's most seasoned incumbents, reminisces about Fox's tenure at Google and her subsequent influence:

Often controversial, but certainly one of the go-getters of this world, her husbandry in developing the Google Webmaster Tools project made a significant impact on the industry, as it opened up lines of communication between webmasters and Google. This ultimately led to similar initiatives from Microsoft and other digital giants which probably saved the SEO industry becoming outcasts within the digital marketing age. Her wings would always have been clipped in an organization the size of Google – but she has remained a worthy ambassador for them ever since moving on. Vanessa's presentations at conferences were always among the 'must see' set and, as often as not, they were used to announce new features within Webmaster Tools. Post Google, her presentations continued to test the preconceived perceptions of SEO marketers, by looking at data in ways that were not always that obvious.

OK to admit the ability to fail

Any seasoned internet marketer will tell you that one of the secrets to success is to, in the words of *New York Times* bestselling author, Bryan Eisenberg, 'Always be testing!' Bryan and any number of Fox's industry peers spend a huge amount of time expressing the importance of optimizing your digital marketing by trying different things, testing, analysing and then refining based on results.

In the same blog post in which Shivakumar had announced the Sitemaps project back in 2005, he recognized that this idea was a gamble of sorts, writing that it would 'either fail miserably, or succeed beyond our wildest dreams in making the web better for webmasters and users alike'.

Seven years later, there is no doubt that thanks to Fox and her team picking up this incredible project and approaching it from the point of view that it was necessary to provide a value exchange between Google and its now millions of business users, the search industry and billions of consumers alike have benefited from their doggedness, drive and openness to listen and understand.

Matt Cutts, who is still guarding Google's index from the scourges of spam, agrees:

> Vanessa always had an outstanding ability to bridge the world inside Google with the world outside Google. She could dive into deep technical details with engineers, and then translate those technical details into plain language for regular people. Likewise, Vanessa took comments and feedback from the webmaster community and made sure that the right people at Google heard that feedback. Vanessa was always a pioneer in terms of pushing Google to be more transparent and to surface useful data to site owners.

So the next time you have what seems to be a crazy idea, remember that even the 'wildest dreams' can be achieved if you have the right pioneering attitude.

Sound bytes

- Spend time with colleagues and partners in different departments. Really try to understand what they do and how to speak their language. It'll help when it comes to communicating ideas and having empathy with their thinking.
- Understand how information you have could provide value to your customers and how a mutual exchange could, in turn, benefit your business. What's in it for you? What's in it for them?
- Learn to listen authentically, be as transparent as you can and respond effectively. At least if you don't have all the answers, go back to your teams and discover them. You'll build trust with your customers that way.

Further reading

http://www.VanessaFox.com
http://support.google.com/webmasters
http://www.ninebyblue.com
http://Twitter.com/VanessaFox
Fox, V (2012) *Marketing in the Age of Google, Revised and Updated: Your online strategy IS your business strategy*, John Wiley & Sons, Hoboken, NJ

Gurbaksh Chahal

ClickAgents and BlueLithium

Digital discipline

Pioneered performance-based online advertising when the world wide web was in its first flush. He went on to perfect the approach using the most up-to-date technologies available at the time, and by addressing the challenges that each era threw up. In the process he championed profiling data systems to help advertising find the right customers online.

05

Man who made digital advertising first click

In his first digital venture, ClickAgents, Chahal tracked the click-through habits of users and developed per-click pricing structures for online ad space. His second company, BlueLithium, ensured that banners and column ads found relevant web users, based on their web habits. Chahal's third company, RadiumOne, was the first to use real-time social data to inform the matching of advertising to web users. Chahal's story therefore runs in parallel to the timeline of digital innovation. His mark as a pioneer has been to harness the capabilities of each new technology for advertising.

> *Social has come to mean everything on the internet. Sharing has become the most important signal and no one has tapped into that as an enhancement of data.*

Blueprint of an internet pioneer

Gurbaksh Chahal is *the* model internet pioneer. He first rose to prominence when he created the successful web advertising companies ClickAgents and BlueLithium, which were eventually sold for a combined $340m. He's as famous beyond the digital world for the speed of his success. Chahal amassed a personal fortune of over $200m in 13 years, before he reached the age of 30. Those that know Gurbaksh Chahal – they tend to call him 'G' – say he's remained work-focused throughout his career. His life story so far – the son of a US Green Card Lottery winner now resident in California, who found success through his own ingenuity – has not escaped press attention: in the US press Chahal is characterized as the epitome of the American Dream and in the Asian press he has been described as 'Punjab's most eligible bachelor'.

Chahal's story: stepping up to business online

Chahal was a hands-on learner, hard-wired to the fledgling internet and also keen on making money very early on. His first business involved buying and reselling printers on eBay when he was just 14 – 'Nobody questioned how old you were online. So I learnt by doing at an early age.' This generated enough capital for Chahal to consider a more ambitious business venture. In 1998, when pay-first advertising was the norm, Chahal identified click-based advertising while researching cheap software to sell on.

So, at 16, he convinced his father to let him leave school to set up ClickAgents. He ran the company out of his bedroom, convinced he could emulate market leader DoubleClick's method of selling ad space. He even invented co-workers – 'Gary Singh, Head of Sales' – to make ClickAgents seem more than a one-person operation. To Chahal at the time it didn't seem that bold: 'being 16, you just do it and don't put too much thought around it'.

His self-belief was well founded. Chahal's natural curiosity in seeking out customers and researching online suited this venture. He monitored the click-through rates of online advertising – banners and columns – and worked out rates of effectiveness. He channelled this evidence to put advertisers on the most relevant sites, then charged based on performance. This meant that advertisers paid only for what was viewed. Advertisers had click-through evidence that ads were being watched, while Chahal was being rewarded for his research and application. This made the process of advertising online transparent for the advertisers.

While Chahal wasn't the first to come up with this idea, he made it work for his clients. Making his practices easily understood was, for Chahal, as significant as being relevant. 'Many people think you need to start something that is completely innovative, different, completely groundbreaking. I think differently – I think you need to have something that's a business that people understand, you can out-execute your competition by being agile, being more nimble. As soon as you've gotten traction and have reached a stage of competitiveness you can innovate and pivot your business.'

Driving click-throughs at the right time

Being an online businessman enabled the young Chahal to disguise his age. He was able to negotiate deals for ClickAgents, test software before buying it, sign up and get domain names and start the company without meeting suppliers face-to-face – everything was online. He could pick up a phone and dial for customers rather than having to meet with them.

However, once ClickAgents was registered he could not always avoid face-to-face meetings. As a young Sikh (then) with a beard and a turban, he was able to disguise his youth at business meetings. He routinely took cabs for meetings so that prospective investors would not know he was too young to drive. Because the internet was still new, Chahal reckoned that more people were prepared to give him a try. He did well by doing what came naturally to him – researching customers, technologies and opportunities online – but in business he received knock-backs despite doing well, which started to shape his view of business and his approach. 'I became more outgoing, shaped largely by the experiences I encountered. I was basically an introvert at 16 becoming an extrovert.' While he didn't always get clients or the rates that he went for, he learnt to 'treat every rejection as a challenge'.

The company soon grew way beyond a one-man operation – by 2000 Chahal had amassed 34 staff, though it was still driven by Chahal's ability to strike a good deal while continually researching on many digital fronts. Then in November 2000, little more than two years into ClickAgents, he sold all its assets to ValueClick, a much larger company. Chahal realized that far greater resources were needed to take ClickAgents' ambitions further. Chahal found that he was still trying to micro-manage each project as he had at the start – 'It wasn't a real structure. I had to grow, become a delegator.' At this stage the entrepreneurial Chahal had identified newer methods of mapping customer habits, which made him want to start afresh within a new paradigm. He had to wait three years – the length of his 'non-compete' sign-off with ClickAgents – before he could launch his next venture.

Company #2: BlueLithium and behavioural targeting

In January 2004 Chahal launched BlueLithium. Its activities centred on behavioural targeting, which was becoming more established in 2004. However, Chahal's unique twist was that he could apply data on users' web habits to inform the placement of advertisements.

> *Behavioural targeting is such a wide category but BlueLithium was able to nail it a few ways: one game-changing product we launched was called 'selective inventory partnership'. Publishers [of web data] formed a non-binding relationship with BlueLithium to show ads only to specific customers, rather than on rotation. Advertisers could cherry pick the audiences that drove the highest ROI to them. Keep in mind this was back in 2007.*
>
> (Krishna Subramanian, co-founder of BlueLithium, 2004–08)

In organizing a larger company from the outset, Chahal got his first taste of bureaucracy: 'I realized I had to vet the process and get people to collaborate on a solution, rather than just choosing to do something on my own.' This was a hard habit to break, especially as he had achieved a great deal by himself. BlueLithium was more of a team effort from the outset.

As a larger venture than ClickAgents, BlueLithium rivalled other advertising media. Chahal found traditional advertising business models harder to dislodge in the eyes of clients, despite offering better returns, because the wider sector had already formed stereotypes about online advertising: 'We were up against a traditional model, and there was a preconceived notion that every ad was the same. The way we disrupted the model was to say that traditional is great, but it is no longer *the* model that all ads were equal.' Chahal explained to clients that advertising worked in a deeper, consistent way: 'We could say that it's based on "how do you leverage someone's personalized experience of the web and incorporate that into behavioural targeting?".' Behaviour filled the void. Leveraging a closer understanding of customers swung many clients towards BlueLithium, and enabled them to become established in the United States.

The market catches on

The year 2006 proved to be pivotal for BlueLithium. The company grew at a faster rate than its competitors and expanded operations to the UK and France (with over 175 staff). This required Chahal to change the way he led. 'I had to hire people that I thought were smarter than me. When you are 16 and younger I didn't think about that. Now I had to – even if it meant paying $500k a year to hire someone. I didn't let the cost steer me away from hitting the best people. The best talent costs.' As co-founder Krishna Subramanian remembers, even with new talent on board Chahal was still very much the leader. 'Gurbaksh has an uncanny ability to see the future, make the gut calls on product, and never allows failure to stand in the way of reaching his vision.'

Chahal's gut calls helped BlueLithium establish a dominant market presence within two years, which had not gone unnoticed by the larger web search and service providers. As with ClickAgents, BlueLithium's scope to grow was limited by the data they could draw on. Chahal's BlueLithium model informed the placement of advertising by mapping customer habits from data that were freely available. As the search industry grew, data that had been freely available became protected, a commercially valuable asset. Eventually only large service providers had access to behavioural mass-data, because they could micro-track customers and restrict access to third parties. BlueLithium had limited scope to expand without being attached to a larger service.

BlueLithium's rapid rise also reverberated in other ways. It inspired rivals to copy their mode of doing business, so with more competitors and a larger workforce, growth began to slow down. BlueLithium's boom-and-plateau was typical of many companies that were successful very quickly. As Chahal notes, 'A lot of businesses realize their eureka moment isn't just when one thing goes right. I think a lot of companies say "it's when one thing happened". But it's really a mixture of all the right product decisions, sales decisions and marketing decisions. The Big Eureka Moment is when you realize there is a hockey stick in growth, and the revenue speaks for itself.'

Chahal was familiar with being a sector leader from a small base. By applying new technologies and customer data insights he had been able to operate faster than the larger digital corporations. So working in a now-crowded market with slower growth brought personal and professional challenges. This stage marked a crossroad in the company's development. 'When we started BlueLithium, behaviour-targeted advertising was unique and no one paid that much attention to it. But when it started working and on a large scale, that's when everyone started to jump on that bandwagon. Our business evolved from disrupting conventional advertising to something completely different – a "business process" business. I realized it would be a bigger asset with a larger company – that's when I realized that I needed to sell the company.'

BlueLithium attracted interest from a number of major search companies and, given the need for a bigger partner, Chahal and his board decided it was the right time to sell in 2007. They chose Yahoo! Inc, who paid an estimated $300m to develop the platform further. 'They had the bigger data set at their disposal and were in a better position to take BlueLithium to the next level. I realized through BlueLithium that the next business [I did] had to have barriers of entry, so even though it could be a "disruptive play" and brand new, as soon as performance and data come into play I could hold the barriers for my own data.'

Company #3: RadiumOne and owning real-time audience data

Chahal knew that owning his own data set was crucial to take advertising to the next level under his stewardship. Without this, there would be a limit to how far he could take advertising platforms, because he wouldn't have the data reach of digital multinationals to make systems work outside a limited market.

After BlueLithium and his 'non-compete' abeyance, Chahal researched the potential of audience-tracking technologies – the territory he next needed to crack. Within months he had figured out how to own enough data on customer habits and how to motivate digital advertising practices, by sourcing new technologies available and applying them in a unique way for advertising. Although his web user data were not of the scale that Google, Microsoft or Yahoo! had at their disposal, it was the 'nimbleness' he described in linking technologies to the task at hand that propelled his next venture, RadiumOne.

RadiumOne was able to make an immediate impact because it gave advertisers far more up-to-date information to make value judgements. RadiumOne's platform runs and generates data in real time. Its agility comes from being able to continually adjust content to match the changing social web demands of web users – a first for online advertising. With RadiumOne's own tools to map user behaviour – they labelled it their Dynamic Audience Platform – they can apply lessons learnt from statistics based on live interaction. This lets RadiumOne's analysts segment and then match advertising to the most appropriate users, with a stream of real-time information to constantly inform their positioning. The technology can also identify new audiences from first-time site visitors. Being able to scale new and existing audiences in this way gives RadiumOne an advantage because, in having granular detail on web users, they can accurately predict footfall and response rates for advertising. RathiumOne are, therefore, making online advertising less of an art, more of a science, with clearer returns on investment.

In many respects Chahal's objectives have been consistent through each company he founded. Modelling advertisements around customer habits has been a constant. The changes in online habits and the sheer growth of user numbers have been a moving challenge. In each case he has risen to the challenge, applying technology to give advertisers an informed competitive edge.

Advice to precocious digital pioneers

Although Chahal made digital ad formats work three times out of three, would he have done things differently given his time again? 'There was a benefit to not having a stereotypical education – I was pushing ahead with my own frontier. There are many ways of learning – the societal way through degrees, then there was the way I took, which was growing the street-smart way, and building a logic around it.' As Chahal's was an uncharted journey during the web's early pioneering years, he had to learn on the job. There were no forerunners aside from those in the internet bubble that burst when Chahal was starting out. His methods come from good business practice rather than anything tailor-made for the world of digital.

The upshot of learning through experience is that Chahal has homed in on aspects that work, and learnt to ignore the headline-grabbing trend for the next big thing: 'I learnt through the different businesses that the biggest asset available was data. It's not the perfect algorithm that will break new ground; it's the perfect data set.' How you apply data, argues Chahal, is the key to forming a successful business that works online. Yet software journalists get wowed by new technologies and techniques, and have not learnt the lessons of the internet's brief history:

> *Anytime during the good times some people just don't learn. I remember March 2009 when the Dow hit 6600, people thought it would go to 5000. Fast-forward to now, just after the bleakest period in memory, and you have a birth of companies trying to do what the original dotcom companies did in the first boom – and their valuations are staggering. But, they have no idea how to even generate revenue let alone profit.*

'It's incentivizing the wrong type of entrepreneur and creating the wrong type of business. It's basically trying to go ahead and flip to the greater tool, and that is not a real business. In good or bad times, you need to have a real business with a CEO that understands how to generate revenue – not just generate losses. Just because it's trying to figure something out – that's not a business.'

Chahal's experiences have drawn him to see facts before the dazzle of media hype. Concentrating on the product and the market is what really matters – not what the pundits say. This approach is essential to lead innovation, rather than be caught up in its wake.

Lessons learnt

Chahal urges people to see through the hyperbolic language used to sell products that, in truth, are essentially the same as their predecessors. 'When I had my "non-compete" [contract] with Yahoo! and I was looking to see what to do next, I came back into the market and I realized that, holy crap, everyone was still doing the same thing!'

> *Everyone was using big words to describe what they're doing, but when you peel the onion you realize that 'oh, it's the same thing we were doing in 2005, but with a long adjective around it'.*

RadiumOne, Chahal's third venture, made its mark by using social data. 'When I started RadiumOne, people were saying "what's social?" Now they are doing the same thing – adding the word "social" to make it relevant. The entire business of display advertising grew leaps and bounds because behavioural targeting resurrected it and added an element of performance that only search did before.'

Chahal reckons that positioning has been crucial in all his ventures:

> The way to think about it is that there's a sense of noise in the marketplace. First there's the big guys, Facebooks and Googles are dominant in their space. Then you have a bunch of companies that are doing something cool but don't have defensibility around their space. Thirdly and lastly you have the small group of companies with a layer of defensibility that are truly doing something unique. You want to be part of the group that is unique and getting the attention of the big guys.

Lessons for future pioneers: protect your business!

> The projects I'm launching from now on are based on what I've learnt from my last business – which is, if you have a great disruptive model and business, protect it. And add a layer of defensibility (around the data and technologies you're using) that prevents others getting into it.
>
> You can say that the business of behavioural targeting, the way it was launched, there wasn't the ability to make it defensible long term because the power was in the advertisers' hands, because the pixels were on their sites. We're changing this power shift – we're becoming 'first party' to data and sites ourselves, so think of it as a very strategic way we're building this business: it becomes hard for others to enter and replicate it. They can use the word 'social' and the vocabulary, but the assets won't be easy to copy.

Whatever Chahal's earlier objectives – to get customer reach or owning the data, he has consistently pinpointed the issues that matter for advertising networks. As Chahal notes, 'Every one of my businesses fulfilled a promise of being an ad network. And then it layered behavioural, then social, then first-party data. That's how I've envisaged each business.' While he has followed customer trends he has also followed his gut instincts and not been swayed by press opinion. Perhaps that defines an authentic online advertising pioneer above others. In his wake Chahal has left a string of good decisions through periods of boom and recession. Like the technologies he's applied to inform advertising placement, the business acumen Chahal learnt on the job has made clients confident in shifting from the familiarities of traditional advertising to a fluid online environment, and the certainties of better returns.

Sound bytes

G's rules

- Do not forget the general principles of building a business: a business revolves *not* around ideas of 'futures', but around revenue and growth.
- Don't get carried away thinking that, because it's online, it's different from any other business.
- If you want to go ahead and disrupt a market, don't necessarily go after something brand new. Go after something that people are already doing. Once you've scaled that, incorporate what you want to bring (new) to market.
- To grow a successful online business 'you need traction on what people are already doing – existing behaviours, existing products'.

Further reading

Chahal, G and Fenjves, P F (2008) *The Dream: How I learnt the risks and rewards of entrepreneurship and made millions*, Palgrave MacMillan, London

Jaron Lanier

Virtual reality and Microsoft Research

Digital discipline

An internet visionary, creator of virtual reality technology, bestselling author, musician, composer, industry pundit and social media cautioner, who now questions the very technological ideology he helped create in the 1980s.

06

Striving for somatic

When Jaron Lanier took to the stage at the 2011 *IAB MIXX* event in New York, the father of 'virtual reality' spoke about realizing human potential through technology. His audience was a crowd of senior advertisers and marketers eager to tap into new and enthralling ways to attract and engage consumers in the digital age. Speaking for 30 minutes without slides or prompts he succeeded, as Randall Rothenberg (CEO of the Interactive Advertising Bureau in the United States) said afterwards, in representing 'thought-leadership at its zenith'. With a few flicks of his trademark waist-length dreadlocks and some customarily excited high-pitched squeals, Lanier – partner architect at Microsoft Research's eXtreme Computing Group – shared the science of avatars and how his team is probing the most intimate and creative parts of people by bringing the human body into computing, a development he calls 'somatic computing', *somatic* being a Greek word meaning 'of the body'.

Lanier had every right to be excited about what he was saying. Work he'd begun in the 1980s, creating computational experiences where the human form could take on a different guise and be used to dive deep into other worlds, had set the scene for the future of interactive entertainment. A future that had been realized a year earlier, in November 2010, with the launch of Microsoft's Kinect for Xbox 360.

Codenamed *Project Natal* during its development, the Kinect device was to be a peripheral add-on produced to enhance the Xbox 360 video gaming experience. By transcending the old category of webcam motion-sensors, Kinect enabled gamers to turn into *avatars* as they played games, and interact without the use of a hand-held controller. As the adverts all over the media proclaimed: 'You are the controller!'

Deemed then the fastest-selling electronics device in history (source: *Guinness World Records 2011*) after Microsoft shifted 10 million units in the first four months of release, Lanier's 30-year-old vision began to take on other forms as third-party developers started researching other ways of using the technology that Microsoft had not thought of. Whether it was helping children with autism, creating virtual instruments that could be played by just the movement of arms or fingers, operating theatre and other medical applications or advanced robotics, within one year Microsoft was able to release an inspirational video talking about the 'Kinect Effect' and challenging the scientific community to see what they could come up with next.

In March 2011, at Microsoft Advertising's Imagine conference, Lanier described Kinect as something he'd been waiting for, for decades:

> I can't tell you how exciting this is, because prior to Kinect, in order to turn into a full body avatar, you had to put on a whole motion capture suit. Those suits are fine if you're working as an artist in science fiction special effects and you want to turn into a creature, but if you're a person just wanting to experience being an alternative avatar it was a non-starter and Kinect broke through that. The most important thing about virtual reality isn't the idea that

> you're seeing this dramatic 3D thing, it's that you yourself change and you're experiencing yourself in a different way than you ever have before, that you can experience being a creature or do things like fly, so this ability to input yourself bodily using Kinect is something fundamentally different from what we had before, and fundamentally really beautiful and exciting.

Kinect wasn't actually invented by Lanier, though. It was developed by a team set up to design innovative and disruptive products in Microsoft's Interactive Entertainment Business to recognize gestures, faces and voice. Lanier's work on virtual reality applications at Atari and his company VPL Research in the 1980s has, however, enabled commentators to draw comparisons, although a July 2011 article in *The New Yorker*, titled 'What Jaron Lanier thinks of technology now', describes him as 'a technology expert who dislikes what technology has become'.

Imagining and tampering

Lanier was born in New York in 1960, but spent a difficult childhood firstly near El Paso, Texas, and then Mesilla in New Mexico. His mother had died in a car accident when he was 10 and he and his father lived in tents for seven years while they built a geodesic dome home to live in based on his designs. It was tough going for the grieving young man as he tried to negotiate his teenage years.

He was always building things and remembers creating a 'crazy haunted house' using lissajous patterns from TV sets which was 'sort of like a virtual reality system'. If the tools were available he'd be tinkering with them and if technology broke down, like the telephone system in his area that did one day with the result that everyone could hear each other at once, he'd be finding provocative nuances in those disruptions that would help shape what was to come.

A neighbour of the Laniers happened to be Clyde Tombaugh: he was head of optics at the White Sands Missile Base at the time and the man who discovered the planet Pluto. Dropping in on Tombaugh now and again had Lanier learning how to make telescopes, and by the age of 14 he was writing computer programs using punch cards, thanks to the proximity of New Mexico State University and a grant from the National Science Foundation to explore 'digital graphical simulations for learning'.

Paying his way as an 'independent goat milk and cheese provider', Lanier's path eventually led him to a research job at Atari in California. 'Atari was the first video game company, and it was actually an important company. It was big enough to have research, and it was growing like crazy. Interestingly in those days when the Silicon Valley Company grew like crazy, it was based on revenues, not on investment. So it actually was really growing', he recalls.

The department, run by Alan Kay, who had been the leader at Xerox PARC (who Lanier claims developed the 'modern sense of the computing interface including clicking on icons, and browsing for things'), included cognitive scientist

Marvin Minsky and had a branch by MIT in Cambridge on Kendall Square. Lanier's gig was to 'build all sorts of really strange ideas for the future of interactive entertainment including very strange haptic things, and strange displays.'

Youthful vigour

When asked whether the experiences that were strange then would still be strange now, he reflected that his perspective was shaped at the time by his experiences of life to that point: 'You have to remember I was maybe 21 or something so a lot of them were sort of very sexual in their qualities. Like, we designed this lingerie that made music when you touched it. And the cords would only resolve in erogenous zones. So you would play music by stroking the other person. We actually made a prototype. I still think that could be like this huge multi-billion-dollar thing if somebody wants to sell it.'

In those days, Lanier remembers, there was 'an eternal quest to get females to want to play digital games', so the team worked on a haptic broomstick that you'd ride like a witch that has been 'done now a number of times for Harry Potter type things and what not'. Fast-forward 30 years and women do play digital games more than ever, as a result of 'going social'. Perhaps this is because of the audience-broadening effect a product like Kinect has had, by creating gaming storylines and experiences that women actually want to get involved in. Back in the 80s though, Lanier admits 'it was something of a big mystery'.

Back then, Lanier describes himself as 'this weird kid' that's now come full circle to work as a senior person in a Microsoft lab that has its own 'weird kids'. Being that young and full of sexual energy, he had an eye on the 'big picture issues of where the species was going', but can't honestly say that he was thinking about new markets for products and services connected to the work he was doing.

He thought about it more in terms of the drama of our times. With the situation of our human species changing, in some part for the worse, with natural resources starting to run out, Lanier saw a 'Malthusian picture' developing against a background of technical progress with science opening up other areas of our existence. The question he sought to answer was how it all linked together. How could he discover bridges across those realities using technology? When one door of our existence closes, how could his research help smooth the way towards others that were just opening?

Building a business

Well-meaning idealism became more difficult when he was working off his own clock, however. Lanier's first company, VPL Research, came about in 1984. Not coming from any money or connections, his 'flaw as a start-up person was thinking too much about survival instead of success'.

On his time running his businesses and being an entrepreneur he muses:

> Sometimes, just the immediate claustrophobic fear of making it through can close you off to the bigger things. And I think I've succumbed to that a few times; it's a very tough discipline. So for me, it was month to month. I noticed a few times with my competitors, they seemed to be able to relax a bit just because they always knew they had a home to go back to or whatever, and just that sort of backup plan B in their lives made it easier for them. So the start-up thing is very hard psychologically if you're really depending on it.

Visual Programming Language (VPL) was an exciting time despite survival concerns. His website records that he and his colleagues 'developed the first implementations of virtual reality applications in surgical simulation, vehicle interior prototyping, virtual sets for television production, and assorted other areas'. He spearheaded the effort to create the 'first widely used software platform architecture for immersive virtual reality applications'.

It was this groundbreaking work that not only caught the attention of larger companies looking to start creating VR experiences on a large scale, with Sun Microsystems buying up VPL's patents in 1999, but also the glitz and glamour of Hollywood.

Hollywood comes knocking

In the early 1990s, Lanier got a call from movie director Brett Leonard saying he'd got the film rights to Stephen King's short story, 'The Lawnmower Man'. Lanier remembers that Leonard told his reluctant celluloid subject that he'd leverage the King story option to get the project funded but then do a 'weird science fiction biography of you and your company.' All the director needed was some explanation of how virtual reality kit worked and some old prototype gear from the era that ended up actually being used in the film. Lanier's entrepreneur character was played by then unknown actor Pierce Brosnan, and real life appears to have mirrored the outlandish plotline as Lanier claims 'it turned out VPL was part of a justice department investigation later, on the French Intelligence Service using the investment arms of French companies to do industrial espionage on American start-ups in Silicon Valley'.

Although *The Lawnmower Man* debuted at the US box office at number two in March 1992, it's not an experience Lanier reminisces about fondly. 'I honestly don't think anyone involved in that movie on any level was particularly proud of it, or particularly cares to promote it these days.'

Not so Steven Spielberg's epic *Minority Report*, starring Tom Cruise, which he advised on in 2002. Part of the multi-day creation process with the director and screenwriters, he helped conceptualize scenes and storylines, specifically most of the interactive gadgets, the rolling eyeball scene and segments involving Tom Cruise running away with the advertisement security lens notifying the police of his whereabouts. Those, and the now famous glove interface, were all technologies that Lanier was working on at the time as chief scientist at Internet2, where they'd also done the first facial feature tracking to reanimate avatars, similar to Microsoft's Avatar Kinect, and were researching the possibility of recasting old movies, exchanging actors' faces and replacing the entire performance.

Roles and social tribulations

In the 1990s Lanier had many different scientific roles, sold four start-ups (one to Google) and, after a spell as visiting scientist at Silicon Graphics Inc where he worked on solutions to core problems in telepresence and teleimmersion, he joined Microsoft in 2006 as scholar at large and since 2009 has had the role of partner architect in the company's research division.

At Microsoft he was a subject of 'intrigue', as the company's storyteller, Steve Clayton, puts it. The Englishman, now living in Seattle and tasked with writing about What's Next at Microsoft and evangelizing all the new innovation pouring from different Redmond labs, has been aware of Lanier's work for 15 years and was 'surprised' to see him on campus one day, unaware he was working at Microsoft Research. Such is the mystery and secrecy surrounding some of the father of VR's work.

In 2010 Lanier was named among *Time Magazine's* 100 most influential people in the world. The same year his book, *You Are Not a Gadget: A manifesto*, was released to critical acclaim. Heralded as one of 2010's best books by Michiko Kakutani in the *New York Times*, she described Lanier's thoughts on the 'enshrinement of the wisdom of the crowds' as illuminating, provocative and impassioned.

In the introduction to the paperback edition, he describes the book as not anti-technology but 'pro-human'. He tells the story about how he was warned that his talk at the South by Southwest conference in Texas in March 2010 might be greeted with some negativity by people not happy with his views on where the internet and technology were taking the human race. On stage, he asked the assembled throng to delay tweeting or blogging about his talk until after he was finished, not out of respect for him, 'but for themselves'. Encouraging them to give themselves the chance to completely listen to, weigh, judge and filter some of what he said, even if 'it was to register violent disagreement', he wanted to inspire the audience to grant themselves time and space to think and feel, luxuries he does not think social media in particular afford the human race much these days.

To his pleasant surprise, his request was greeted with applause – applause not echoed by those in Silicon Valley to whom Lanier refers as 'cybernetic totalists', an influential sub-culture of technologists whom Lanier sees as putting too much emphasis on the importance of the network effect of connecting millions of people through computers and the cloud. He feels that 'emphasizing the crowd means deemphasizing individual humans in the design of society'. Concerned that we're creating a world where people have to define themselves as being part of some category on a networking site's drop-down menu, he fears that future generations will cease to desire to grow and reach their potential because of the limitations laid down by the very ideology he and his peers helped create.

That ideology is the one that all information on the web should be open, free and accessible:

> If we want to move to a world where the machines are really good, and we take care of technology at a maximum advantage, but we still want people to have jobs, then we have to value what people do in an information space. If we make everything free, then we impoverish them. I'm convinced that part of the current global recession is simply people not benefiting properly from the effects of information technology because we've conceived the remaining human role is being worthless, when in fact, it's absolutely essential. And so the problem with free is that free sounds good if you cast yourself as sort of like this child who has parents to take care of them, and all you want is free, free, free. But if you cast yourself as somebody who is responsible, and needs to earn a living, then free doesn't sound so good anymore.

Liberty or artistic return

Ultimately, Lanier has a problem with 'free' because it gives rise to the need for paying for services like Google and Facebook through advertising 'spy networks' that need to bucket users into interests or behaviours in order to target relevant messages and recoup revenue from marketers. It's a cycle that sits uncomfortably with him as he feels that smaller players are squeezed out. He suggests that because big companies like Google and Facebook are competing for the same set of advertisers, they should think about identifying customer bases that are distinct from one another. Facebook could become the peer-to-peer commerce platform for intellectual property, for instance, by creating an easier way to sells good and services between people: 'To really have growth in an economy, you need to have the network effect of that economy, and so you need to allow the smaller players as well to be able to jump those boundaries, and that's not going to happen the way things are going where we're trying to benefit from putting up these walls. We need to have vastly less friction, and vastly more cross-access between these online stores and these online ecosystems, in order to have economic growth for all of us', he urges.

Lanier's perspective is that we as a society need to take a step back and take stock of where the internet is taking our economy and our individual selves. He fears that we're on a path dominated by bigger players, who in their desperation to increase market share are hoarding the most valuable information and access to information in return for advertising dollars attracted by the dumbing-down and over-simplification of civilization. This, claims Lanier, is a situation that is made worse by the growing emphasis on social networking within our world. 'People are pack animals basically, and we are hopelessly fascinated by this question of social ranking, and politics, and who's up, and who's down.' But, he says, he's observed that really smart venture capitalists and companies do the opposite of engaging the algorithms of the mob by hiring high-performing individuals or CEOs, recognizing a role for intuition and risk-taking and rejecting automated decision-making or group consensus on key strategic points, saving them for more tactical gestures.

Lanier's view is that there is much contradiction within the digital space. Companies hire brilliant individuals to create huge networks, the success of which is determined by algorithms that attempt to mine the connections ordinary people make with the web and with each other. Is he being a curmudgeon when he rails on the very industry he helped create? Is he right to despair that a PhD from Cal Tech is spending their time on an app that distributes discount coupons for hamburgers instead of doing something more valuable for humanity?

Curmudgeon, no. Well-intentioned cautioner, yes.

Lanier is not anti-advertising. He praises the industry for 'romanticizing' the production and progress he sees, but smarts at the 'dry practice' of targeting ads online. At the end of his talk at IAB MIXX 2011, he encouraged the audience to use technology to realize human potential, he implored the assembled throng to build beautiful things for our children, because although the 20th century was an anomaly, where we spent too much time absorbing media and not interacting with it, there is no such thing as passive perception, he warned. Young people today will 'remember our media as quaint, cute but not quite fully engaged'.

There is time, he thinks, to change course and make beautiful things a reality for individuals and individual brilliance to shine within.

We just have to start now.

Sound bytes

- When building a business, try not to get suffocated by the need to survive. Have a plan, understand what success looks like and aim for that. Know who your competitors are.
- Don't always think about making your content free and advertising driven. Push the boundaries and create new business models in which consumers are willing to pay something for their experience.
- Retain a sense of individuality in everything you do. Social media has its positive side, but try not to get swept up by the wisdom of the crowd. Be you and make beautiful things for others being them.

Further reading

http://www.JaronLanier.com
http://www.Microsoft.com/Next
http://Research.Microsoft.com
Lanier, J (2010) *You Are Not a Gadget: A manifesto*, Vintage, New York

Angel Chen

OgilvyOne China

Digital discipline

The strategic brains who marshalled advertisers and clients to push the potential of digital in advertising in China. Angel Chen was a key figure behind the rise to prominence of OgilvyOne Beijing before becoming president of OgilvyOne China in 2012. She introduced tailored processes that help clients make best use of digital media.

Hidden persuader

Angel Chen is one of the world's most significant behind-the-scenes managers of digital advertising. In a land that has the fastest uptake of mobile media, Chen has driven the agency to produce advertising in the most relevant formats of the day – from augmented reality (AR) to social networks. It was Chen's methods, which included reshaping her agency's working environments and wooing clients with digital demonstrations, that persuaded clients to take risks in digital for the first time. This allowed OgilvyOne to pursue the types of project that their rivals dreamt of undertaking. Chen's contribution to pioneering digital is, therefore, mostly what the customer does not see – devising processes that get the most from creative teams and clients. In taking digital advertising forward, Chen devised campaign structures that made using digital media commercially viable.

Angel Chen is credited as the driving force behind OgilvyOne Beijing's pioneering digital work in China. The agency's winning formula has led to consistent recognition – it is the most awarded digital agency in China, picking up numerous 'Digital Agency of the Year' media awards. Its reputation goes far beyond China.

With OgilvyOne since 2000 and managing director of OgilvyOne Beijing from 2009, as of 2012 she is president of OgilvyOne China. In the new China Chen is the very model of a dynamic 'can do' businesswoman – a passionate digital marketer with strong business acumen and an instinct both for what clients want and for what they need. Debby Chuang, president of Ogilvy & Mather Group, Shanghai, knows Angel as '... a tireless and passionate innovator. She has been a fundamental part of the OgilvyOne successes in the past decade. With her at the helm, the agency will prosper as a global hub of creative excellence.'

In many respects Chen is one of the digital era's great hidden persuaders – it is not her creative work that end users get to see, but it is her digital know-how and vision in using technology to convince clients to try the new that make Angel Chen the champion of digital creatives and China's most successful leader of a large digital hothouse.

> *... what we've come to rely on most are recommendations based on their insights into the dynamics of our industry, China and global business. Some of our campaigns have even won awards as a result of insights they've uncovered,' says Mark Wang, marketing director, commercial BU, Lenovo China.*
>
> (Source: Campaign 2011)

Angel Chen's route into digital

Before she joined Ogilvy, Chen had no experience of advertising. Instead she arrived at Ogilvy's via a digital journey that started in the early days of internet commerce in China during 1996. Chen's first digital job was with a company called IHW.com, which was one of the first commercial internet service providers in China. 'It lasted for just two years, but gave me a very good starting point. They started before anyone else in China, so they were real pioneers in 1996.' Then she joined China.com as marketing manager in 1998, 'so basically that time was when China.com went to IPO on the NASDAQ. We still had no ideas how we were going to do the marketing – we just tried to get more visitors. Basically there was no overarching strategy – just pieces of ideas. Pieces of tactics.'

She started to make a name for herself in the emerging digital marketing field, so much so that she was approached by Joe Chen (CEO and owner of RenRen.com) at an industry conference, who outlined his plans for a new start-up dotcom in China. 'After two months he approached me again with Yang Ning and Yun Fan Zhou, the two owners as well, who had by then started ChinaRen.com – so at that moment I was their marketing director – and their first employee for ChinaRen.com.' It proved to be a fantastic opportunity. 'After one year I had helped them to set up the entire company, and also helped it to become a top-ten dotcom company in China – all within one year. This was at the start of 2000, when we were all going fine and everyone was very happy.' This was during the global internet market's first flush of activity. However, the first internet crash during 2000 led to the first big shake-up within China's first generation of digital companies.

Moving within digital – from search to creative agency

'When the internet bubble crashed the entire company went to a very nervous situation because cash became a big issue. So Joe and his partners decided to sell the company to Sohu.com – Charles Zhang. By the end of 2000 the deal had almost finished. At that moment I was thinking that I should change my job because I had been in the dotcom industry for five years. I just felt I had been taken through a quick development period with a lack of systematic approach or methodology – we had been too much into tactics. We had been doing lots of very good events, but no structural thinking.'

This marked the point when Chen received her first big break. TB Song, the CEO of Ogilvy China (now the chairman of Ogilvy Greater China and chairman of WPP China), invited her to join OgilvyInteractive.

'He said, "we are looking for digital talent – why don't you just try to work in our agency?" So that is the first time I tried to work in the agency. I came in with my digital experience, but I had to learn how to operate as an agency. I started as the business director in OgilvyInteractive, then by 18 December 2000 it became OgilvyOne Beijing – I remember the date very clearly!' In total, Chen was there for 11 years before bigger opportunities came her way within the Ogilvy network.

Chen's innovation: processes that make digital work

Since being at Ogilvy, Angel Chen has carved out a reputation as a formidable behind-the-scenes operator.

She joined OgilvyOne, then a one-to-one marketing agency, within a year of its first being established in China during 1999. Chen was instrumental in the agency specializing in digital – it is widely regarded in China as being the first big digital advertising company. It has subsequently become the largest digital and one-to-one marketing network in China. The group's presence in China is now vast, with more than 500 digital specialists working from six offices in Greater China. They are also the most awarded agency, becoming the first Chinese agency to win a Cyber Lion in Cannes in 2004 for their work on China Mobile M-Zone. However, it is not her work leading creative designers that makes Chen a pioneer of digital. It is her strong business sense, understanding of the digital landscape (she is an avid researcher), plus her acquired management skills and strategic planning that make her unique. Without her input, Ogilvy's creative teams simply would not have the scope to use new technologies in uncharted ways.

Chen famously regrouped the personnel in her agency to make the structure of the agency more appropriate for digital work. This required new ways of working, to allow for creative and technological experimentation. It enabled Chen to develop the structures, methods and systematic approach to work that she identified as lacking during her previous jobs.

Tools for planning, specialist research and nurturing clients through the process were top of Chen's agenda. Under her leadership the agency developed a range of methods, using digital technology, to inform their brand, consumer and media planning operations. To stay abreast of opinions on their brand accounts, the group introduced an 'online listening tool' called OBuzz, a blog-tracking device to monitor the range of net conversations that were related to their clients' brands. 'OBuzz was developed by our in-house team – we have very strong strategy and planning skills [at OgilvyOne Beijing] so I was able to develop them. We have a consulting team with over 40 people to work on strategy and unpack the research.'

Ogilvy's OBuzz system began development in June 2008 with a team of three staff. By 2012 Chen's 10-strong team had developed the format to monitor over 300,000 Chinese social media channels. OBuzz has been used to generate more than 50 internet word of mouth studies for Ogilvy's brand and given 13 of its key clients in China long-term Social Media Listening services. This makes Chen-managed advertising strategies well informed with up-to-date consumer data.

OBuzz was able to provide the current thinking on brands so that the content of campaigns would be informed by up-to-date opinion. To support this, 'Innovation Teams' – specialist researchers whose job it was to identify the latest technologies and trends of use – were introduced to make the latest digital innovations available to their clients. Staff were brought in to identify strategies for clients in e-commerce, user experience, business acceleration, market entry and marketing technologies. One method Chen championed, called Customer Fusion, was a five-step process for client engagement, which was eventually rolled out across all Ogilvy's operations in China. Although the OBuzz fusion tool was invented by Ogilvy Global, it was Chen's application of it in planning the full Chinese consumer experience that made the difference. In China, with the biggest mass market and most media platforms at her disposal, Chen ensured that the tools of analysis underpinned the right choices of media and right tactics for each of their clients.

Showing clients state-of-the-art technology and picking the right strategies did not necessarily mean that clients would want to make the leap into digital, so perhaps Chen's biggest challenge – and her biggest success to date – was to devise ways of inspiring clients to become early adopters of new technologies. Chen had to be innovative with client engagement processes for her clients to understand the imperative need for digital – and needing to be different with digital to have an impact. Chen pioneered the notion of having a space to 'brief up' clients in the potential of digital media, in what became known throughout the global Ogilvy network as Digital Lab.

Digital Lab – finding the pulse of technology in China

Digital Lab was a global initiative initiated by the Ogilvy group, and it became a concept that Chen embraced because it showed clients the potential of embracing digital promotions. Part of the problem Chen faced when she came to Ogilvy was to convince clients that their money was best invested in the potential of new formats – not the traditional modes they had been used to working with.

'Because we had very big difficulties when we wanted to sell new innovative ideas to the client, they would say they wanted more mature technologies and media, because they just couldn't imagine how their products would come out [when communicated through newer media].'

Digital Lab was a space that showcased the most current media technologies, featuring examples of how to play to the strengths and unique features of each current media type. Chen was really motivated by the impact of what for her was 'a small room filled with all the most advance marketing technology in it. For example, we have multiple touch screen, AR, 3D and a lot of mobile apps... so basically we put all our best cases – our best practices in the world – into the facilities, to give visitors a real experience, to see real examples.'

Chen's Ogilvy Beijing was one of the first five Ogilvy agencies in the world to implement the Lab idea, and the first in China. In China both the agency and their clients embraced the potential of newness more than anywhere else in the world. 'We started in 2007–08 and we invested funds in people early on.

It gave us a quick identity for digital innovation within the industry and also it really does bring with it a lot of innovation cases – it brings fresh creative ideas to our clients, which is really valuable.

'If we invite clients to our labs and they visit, it tends to be like "wow", they're so inspired. When they see the new technologies they may have only heard of before, it turns words into something real, they can imagine how this could be beneficial to their marketing. They tend to say "I'm going to try this".

'Sometimes we would simply do "demos" in the Lab – they see my brand and how it would help their consumers to engage in the conversation.'

And the impact? According to OgilvyOne's figures at the end of 2011, they had a 75 per cent win rate for new business pitches, and in terms of inspiring existing clients, five out of eight accounts handed to OgilvyOne Beijing were without a pitch. The agency also claims that its client relationships average 8.4 years, compared to the industry norm of 2.7 years. So client relationships and a carefully managed relationship with technology appear to be paying off.

Digital lab has also proved to be good at generating publicity. It has won awards at Cannes and the One Show (USA) and drove the use of Augmented Reality, mobile coupons and large-scale digital retail in China. According to Chen, it brought the first ever mass-audience events game to China, which won the first MFWA media foundation awards, and has attracted worldwide press attention.

Bringing new technologies into advertising

One outcome of this, in 2010, was that they were able to produce one of the world's first original augmented-reality advertising campaigns for Tsingtao beer, China's bestselling beer brand, with their client's full backing.

The AR work for Tsingtao ran during the FIFA (football) world cup between April–September 2010, and used the technology as it was becoming a much talked about format.

By scanning the AR code printed onto special-promotion bottles of Tsingtao beer using the video camera in a laptop or smartphone, the user triggered the animated Tsingtao beer i-Cheerleaders. These were miniature virtual characters in 3D form, who appeared to spring out of the containers before launching into a repertoire of dance routines with an upbeat soundtrack against a variety of backdrops, mixing pre-recorded virtual and real footage from the user's environment. It was certainly novel and captured a much wider audience through the world's technology press.

'Digital Lab certainly inspired the marketing managers of Tsingtao beer and the campaign really worked. It was for a cheerleader competition. You can play the game and see the cheerleaders compete with each other.' It was an integrated campaign supported by a TV campaign and a lot of retail events. The aim of the interactive game was to get the cheerleaders to catch the virtual bottle. The aim was simple and typical of early computer games, but the interactivity against pre-recorded and real-time environments seen through the video camera made interacting a much more personal experience. The strategy fitted with Tsingtao's objective, which was to find a fun way of engaging their consumers while reinforcing the brand's sponsorship of NBA basketball.

Later on the agency pushed AR technology further to bring a print campaign for Volkswagon Scirocco to life. Using AR, a virtual dashboard of the car sprang out so that those testing the format could have their own virtual Scirocco driving simulation, in what became a much-awarded first for the agency in making the animation a full-on real-time experience. The platform attracted 35 million unique visitors and over 2 million user interactions.

Although many rival agencies could have delivered creative work for new digital platforms, Ogilvy were able to be first because their clients bought into their approach. Therefore getting clients to buy into formats before they became widely known was a great achievement for Digital Lab. It meant that they could produce formulas for client inductions to new media and, in a short space of time, produce a body of work that helped them become synonymous with digitally innovative advertising. Digital Lab therefore helped OgilvyOne Beijing – and Ogilvy branches across China – position itself as the agency to go to for big-brand advertising online.

Difference of online advertising

The press coverage for such campaigns tended to pick up on the 'wow factor' by profiling how it worked and the experience it generated. The actual purpose of the experience – for Tsingtao it was to reinforce the message of Tsingtao's NBA sponsorship – could have been lost but for the fact that Chen's planning processes ensured the strategy was embedded at the heart of the campaign. The subject, game content and style of interaction all pointed to the brand–sponsorship association. Chen acknowledges that a balance needs to be struck between using media innovatively and ensuring that the actual communication is delivered in the right way. 'I think that in the past, the advertising message was mostly in a headline. We use the technology to turn it into a real experience – but it is still an elaboration of the advertising message.'

Recurring difficulties of being new

With a string of successful digital campaigns behind them, have Chen and Ogilvy in China created the perfect method for producing digital campaigns? Not at all! 'A lot of technology is still quite new. Especially in China, the technologies used for marketing are not as mature as in other markets, so it is very difficult to find stable reliable companies to produce [our ideas as we want them]. So there is always some crisis in each project we do – always some surprises. You might be able to produce many brilliant ideas, but there is always an issue with the execution.'

Often the speed at which communications need to be produced – and the eagerness of clients to get work out – means that achieving the ideas of Ogilvy's creative team on time is a challenge: 'They want to do innovation and be seen as leaders, but in terms of their knowledge, understanding and skills they might not be ready to do that. The problem is, they cannot wait: the market is developing quickly so you cannot wait. This is the problem in China. Everything needs to be rushed, quick. So you have to find a way. It's not about how innovative it is but how you can find a new way, somehow. Just not rely on new technology too much.'

The challenge it seems, is as much in the process of production – short cuts, devising ways around problems – as it is in making big ideas work digitally. For all the difficulties of realizing ideas through new means, Chen reminds us that the purpose of digital communications should not be lost: 'Technology is not the core – it is support. Communications is still at the core.'

The pioneer of organizing digital

What makes Chen's growth within the Ogilvy network so intriguing is that she has developed methods that are very well known throughout the agency network, but not outside. As an Ogilvy insider, her rise to MD of OgilvyOne Beijing and then to OgilvyOne China makes sense. Her career started during the first internet boom, and the fact that she cut her teeth on creating digital businesses before going into an advertising network meant that her view of work was very much rooted in the delivery of results. To deliver, she realized, she would need methods and structures that would work. For a network with ambitious growth targets, Chen was the right choice because she could make infrastructures that worked for employees and clients. Chen is therefore highly respected in Chinese advertising circles, and throughout the Ogilvy network, as one of the few women to have made it to the top. Her methods of leadership have been less to do with people-management than by being innovative with structures. Chen has mastered the art of organizing teams specifically for the challenges of new technology, and her approach has been both envied and emulated by rival networks.

Innovation in digital

In a career spanning the full period of digital communications, and in an agency that has often been awarded throughout Asia over an 11-year span for the way it has used new technologies, what has been the biggest innovation Chen has been party to?

'Actually, I would say that we have had a lot of different innovations at different stages of digital technology's development. [Consumer] Fusion was a global initiative and methodology that went to all Ogilvy offices and Ogilvy disciplines around the world to use. It was a methodology for integration and also applied to all client planning. So Fusion is not only specifically for digital – it was a good way to think about projects from the starting point of being a business issue, and use it for engagement planning and execution. So it was a big global thing. If you are talking about impact specifically in China, Digital Lab was for me a very, very big highlight.'

To share with readers

For those looking to work in digital advertising for the first time, and those inspired by the digital work coming from China, what advice would Chen give?

'I think that today, in digital marketing and advertising, you get to see new things. Digital is so dynamic – it changes every day. Change in this industry is very fast. People like me, in terms of age – I'm older than a lot of people in it, but my career, my job, makes me have to be young at heart. I have to re-learn and study to keep updated. This is a pattern that can support you to go a long way.'

For those fast digital-adopting youths in China looking to go into advertising, whose parents often have lofty academic ambitions for their children, Chen has particular advice: 'If you want to do digital marketing in this industry, just go off and do it – don't wait, because I have seen many young people coming to the Ogilvy network with brilliant ideas. I think they are ready now, so just do it.'

Sound bytes

- Consider carefully how you get your clients to buy into digital.
- Using new technologies may make content interesting, but don't forget to make the message that needs to be advertised central to the content.
- If you're really keen on going into digital communications, go try – don't wait. Show agencies your work to get feedback.

Further reading

Sinha, K (2008) *China's Creative Imperative: How creativity is transforming society and businesses in China*, J Wiley, Singapore

John Winsor

Victors & Spoils

Digital discipline

Author and strategic thinker, now best known as the founder of the world's first advertising agency built on crowdsourcing principles. Victors & Spoils is a communications agency that sources creative ideas from the digital community for some of the world's major brands. Winsor, the CEO, had created innovative online publications over a two-decade period. He took a wealth of communications and digital experience, including projects with the acclaimed advertising firm Crispin Porter Bogusky, into a crowdsourcing (ad)venture.

Winsor's story

Jon Winsor is active in every sense and it has rubbed off on his self-determined career to date. He has authored bestselling books on creative communications – including one with fellow pioneer Alex Bogusky; he has created networks around publications and then capitalized on them. Perhaps one of his most telling contributions has been to renegotiate the value-chain between advertisers and digital publishers. He is, however, most significant as a pioneer of crowdsourcing creativity for advertising.

Winsor has consistently been active in the digital communications blogosphere and conference scene, so it is not surprising that he has emerged as a pioneer in sourcing creativity. One major contribution to digital promotion is that he has cracked how to orchestrate the rich pool of talent made possible by Web 2.0. His reward systems and performance-based pay method have become a blueprint for creative firms across the digital community.

Winsor's route into advertising, digital and crowdsourcing is, as one would suspect, not a typical story:

> I've had a circuitous journey through the media more than advertising, so I would say I had a broad lens. My great-grandfather, my grandfather and father were all in the daily newspaper business. When I was born I think I was expected to follow them. Through junior high, high school and college I got to run different functions on the newspaper side at *The Canton Daily Ledger* – a small-town newspaper near Peora, Illinois. I was the reason people could get summer vacations because I would be the copy editor for a week, I'd run the press for a week, then sell advertising for a week. I learnt the business from the ground up.

Winsor earned his MBA from Denver University and then worked in the advertising division of *Cablevison* magazine for a couple of years. Then he quit for two ambitious ventures – he wrote a book, *Fitness on the Road*, and started his own publishing company, called Sports and Fitness Publishing. It grew quickly, from 4 to 120 staff, and sold to Condé Nast in the 1990s. According to Winsor, 'that's where my journey into "what is digital" and "what is digital advertising" started'.

Road to digital

Winsor's route into digital was tied with sports and fitness. With the launch of *Rocky Mountain Sports* in 1986, his first challenge was to make it more viable:

> With two of us working there the magazine was doing $100,000 in revenue but $35,000 of that was spent on typesetting. It was this horrible arduous process of running galleys through the wax machine, using a pen knife to cut things up and on blue lines – back to the era of my newspaper experience. Paying myself $5,000 a year wasn't acceptable – especially as I was getting

> married. So I did this crazy thing – I bought this thing called a Mac Plus and a laser writer, then I bummed some prototype software off the guys at Quark in Denver. That allowed me to work on my Mac and Mac Plus. It cost me $23,000, but I was able to substitute a $35,000 a year annual cost for a one-off capital expense. With one move it allowed me into digital technology and allowed me to be in business.

Winsor was one of the first to attempt digital publishing and, at the time, 'the typesetters just laughed at me and said this desktop publishing thing is a joke, it'll never happen and you'll be paying us way more than we charged you before. It will never work. That was when I realized the power of what disruptive technology can bring.'

Perils and advantages of being too early an adopter

Winsor became fascinated by the potential of digital publishing and was keen to stretch publishing horizons. However, while he could create original types of content he was limited in how far it could be shared:

> I owned a bunch of online skating magazines which I wanted to license around the world. We had this crazy idea in 1996 that we were going to shoot tricks and do a 'How To' website. We put enormous resources in it – digitizing views and getting a magazine company around it online – all the time most people were on dial-up. We were way too early in the idea of creating content. It was fun to play with, but so much of innovation isn't the ideas. It's being in the right place at the right time. Too early and they fail: too late and they fail.

During the course of 13 years, Winsor developed 10 national titles within his publishing company, which he sold to Condé Nast in 1998.

Reworking one advertising model

This became a fresh starting point for Winsor who, inspired by Everett Rogers' classic 1962 book *Diffusion of Innovations*, sought to capitalize on being an early adopter. 'One thing I didn't like about the advertising community is that agencies have all this money and we were at the end of the funnel, getting a small amount of revenue. I wanted to change that.'

Winsor had noticed that one of his magazines, *Women's Sports* & *Fitness*, had a membership containing the top global athletes in the world. Early-adopting advertisers needed access to this community. So Winsor spotted an opportunity 'with us at the top of the funnel', by linking his digital know-how and his digital community of elite sportswomen with advertising.

He formed Radar Communications and introduced his idea of 'anthro-journalism' – 'mashing up anthropology and journalism: a lot of it was film-based. The idea was that we'd got this community of 150,000 women athletes who'd paid to subscribe to our community, and the wider community of women athletes around the world was millions. Instead of attracting advertisers to our magazine, let's take these athletes – opinion leaders in their field – and charge companies to access them for product innovation, market research and strategy ideas. So by inserting ourselves between the client and the agency, instead of waiting for agencies to give money at the end, we flipped the paradigm. We were in charge.'

Winsor's ability to challenge operational norms played out in two books he wrote at the time – *Beyond the Brand* and *Spark*, from which he hit on the idea of co-creation. Alongside this, Radar Communications was working well with clients such as Hewlett-Packard, Intel and General Motors. 'The idea was that anthropologists were good at getting the story but journalists were better at telling the story. If you could mash them up you could make something good.' So Winsor took his team from Sports and business into Radar, based the practice around co-creation and co-created ideas with marketing and production companies.

Spark that led to Victors & Spoils

Winsor was in the process of selling this company to a big holding firm when he met Alex Bogusky, co-founder of advertising agency Crispin Porter + Bogusky. At the time CP+B were a 'pretty small little shop' and Bogusky and Winsor – both keen cyclists – took to riding together. Bogusky was equally keen on a co-creation model and proposed that Winsor's team came in as CP+B's strategy department on pitches – something that CP+B had not done in five years. 'We thought "let's have a whole different prospective of what advertising should be and what planning is", and really blow this thing up.' In 2007 Winsor sold Radar Communications to CP+B. This is when, in Winsor's words, 'we were in the right place at the right time'.

The merged teams went on to produce award-winning work for Domino's Pizza and PC clients, all underpinned by the idea of how to co-create. On one project in 2009, Winsor and Bogusky were considering work for the brand Bramo Motorcycles, an electric motorcycle company. CP+B did not have resources to do their logo, 'so we said let's try this thing called crowd-spring. Having written on co-creation and spent time with Jeff Howe (author of the book *Crowdsourcing*), it was fun to try it in an agency. It caused a huge stir in the industry and results were great. Within a few weeks we had 700 submissions, of which 100 were decent designs.'

> *Alex and I looked at each other and said 'holy shit' this is the end of agencies. All of a sudden people from all over the world wanted to do work for free.*

'It still needed to be well directed but, as Alex (Bogusky) put it, "if I was an art director or a copy writer in the middle of my career I would be scared to death". Out of that conversation and those ideas came the idea for Victors & Spoils.'

They talked to CP+B's holding company about the idea – 'it was too scary a proposition, that you could create a digital offering system for an agency where you don't need a place base. You can just capture social input through these new technologies. You could build technology that allowed for big social conversations globally, to execute ideas and assemble new teams in new ways, all the while getting ideas faster, at a lot lower cost. That's the principle that Victors & Spoils is based on.'

Why the name? 'We liked the pirate theme – the idea we're trying to do something different. A lot of the contests at the time were one winner-takes-all, so that's why the plural of "Victors", coupled with the old saying "to the Victor, goes the Spoils".' They also liked the sense of challenge in the name. 'It's right for the paradigm. I have a feeling, you know, just like the music industry and photography industry that the agency business will be radically changed by technology. You don't need thousands of people in an office in London or New York because it's a super-expensive way of getting things done.'

Victors & Spoils' founding principle

Victors & Spoils was launched from Colorado in 2009 and founded on a simple but fundamental principle, 'that ideas can come from everywhere, there is this radical democratization that social media and technology gives everybody the same right to participate in any kind of thing'. For Winsor it went way beyond advertising – 'You see it in the anti-banking rallies in Wall St (2012) and the Arab Spring (from 2011). These new technologies allow for that kind of thing. The principle in our case was that best idea should win – even if you're an amateur from Lexington, Kentucky. You still have the same ability to win and be awarded the prize as if you're an executive creative director from New York.'

Once they had an accessible creative crowd, they then needed the work. V&S again turned the chain of operation on its head by reinventing the pitch process for Harley – without invitation:

> We noticed, like everyone else did, that Harley Davidson had got rid of their agency for the last 30 years. We just decided to use the power of social media and digital to put our own brief together and launch it. We put our money where our mouth was, threw in $5,000 for the best ideas, launched it into our crowd and told Harley that we were working for them. I wrote a blog post saying "hey enjoy the pitch processes with your agencies and have a good dinners and great meetings. As you guys do that, we'll have 2,500 people working on your business. Give us a shot if you want to talk about it."

Harley Davidson's CMO appreciated the spirit-of-the-age approach and took them on. V&S's work with Harley has developed into TV, press, web and film among others. They have subsequently produced web strategies with Levi's and integrated campaigns with Discovery Channel.

How the creative sourcing systems work

Victors & Spoils' operation has creative direction, strategic direction and account direction at what Winsor calls 'curation level'. Within their 22-strong key team there's a chief creative officer and accounts team head, and a chief finance officer and teams under them:

> Essentially we always have a leader – whether internal or one of 25 creative crowd directors that we vet, and they can run projects on our platform. We decide with clients what the crowd strategy is – is it a private project, something that needs a Non-Disclosure Agreement [NDA], in which case we put teams on it, usually around 10 people from around the world who can lean into it in the best way. We NDA them and pay them up front to do the work.

The team services the huge outsourced V&S membership – some 6,000 people from 130 countries, representing every continent except Antarctica.

The strategy and creative execution are sourced from their crowd and presented to clients like a regular agency. Work is submitted through V&S's 'agency machine platform', and they develop selected ideas for presentation. 'We have a lot of work on our open platform where we'll put ideas out there and anyone signed up to the platform can lean into those ideas.' Winsor estimates that 75 per cent of their work is by 'picked and paid' as clients are sensitive about their strategic direction and where they want to go. Their objective isn't unlimited growth; it's to service a client list of two-dozen.

Their first client, Harley Davidson, was won through an unsolicited pitch – 'In our pirate spirit we went in and blew everything thing up. That worked really well for us. We just went in with a brief and threw it out to the crowd.'

In 2012, V&S were working on a structure to support crowdsourcing for pitches. For Winsor, 'The most important thing is figuring out who's the right person for the project and who's won the most projects.' A ranking system has even been introduced, based on how many times you've entered and how many times you've won and how fast you are at getting back to the creative directors.

A style of growing business

In 2011, V&S created an innovative type of app for Harley Davidson called a Fan Machine. The Facebook-based app enables Harley's fans to create advertising and share their product innovation ideas with Harley, in an online environment that is moderated by V&S's Harley brand specialists. Harley can put up their own briefs, launch it to their own fans. Anything seriously off-brand gets moderated out, those ideas actually go back onto Facebook and it's working well for Harley.

They have developed a range of unusual approaches that certainly work for Harley. Winsor puts it down to their style of thinking – according to Winsor it's 'a style that came from CP+B's – always media agnostic thinking, always big thinking. We don't jump to thinking about ideas as a TV commercial. Instead we go by the saying "this is an event, it could be a global thing". All of our campaigns could be multimedia or media agnostic – it's always thinking it through with the client.'

Their aspirations match their innate left-field people-centred thinking:

> With a community of 6,000 people Victors & Spoils will be whatever those people want it to be. My feeling is that it's going to be a multitude of things. It's going to be a community; it could be viewed as a different kind of holding company; it'll definitely have global presence because we already do, but my sense is that people in the community will start to use the technology themselves, and self-aggregate teams of folks to do interesting things. They may use us for their own brands. Really this brand should be for its people.

Is V&S symptomatic of the digital age?

Given the agency's success rate in getting prestigious accounts and winning creative awards – is V&S the model agency of the digital age? According to Winsor, technologies have reached a point that allows sharing of all kinds to happen. 'Historically, you had to go to the right school and get factual knowledge. Now kids are creating killer things and we all have the ability to express ourselves creatively, through advertising, video or writing a blog. One girl all of a sudden can become a famous writer. It's crazy to see this happening. Democratization is blowing up industry and I love that.'

With crowdsourcing still in its infancy, Winsor is aware that reshaping work from it will, in the fullness of time, represent just one small stage in digital fulfilling its potential:

> Any new technology just fragments and totally destroys the old way of doing things. There are millions of new seeds which are planted that, sooner or later, will get organized in a new way. Things like Google or Facebook are really awesome but are really the plumbing of this new system. They're not the fruits, they're not the creative output, they're just building the simple infrastructure, roadways, sewers and all that kind of stuff in our old way of doing work.

One could argue that the actual content of work at V&S is no less traditional than offline campaigns, it's just that the medium is contemporary and has shaped the style of working. The means of sourcing ideas from a wider global community, which will have been informed by contrasting cultural norms, gives the agency a far broader pool of talent to draw on. The real change is in the food chain, and who 'owns' different aspects – the income, customer data, the creative sources and the brand management on a day-to-day basis.

Winsor also anticipates a revised chain of operation:

> A lot of the old needs to be incorporated into the new. My sense, within this digital revolution, is that agency functions such account management and

stewardship of the brand will reside back with clients. The book value of a company is usually low but the value of the brand is usually high, so what CEO in their right mind would say 'let's outsource all our brand development and production'? They'll want to own and manage it. The idea of an agency doing that out-of-house is a thing of the past. So chief marketing officers are going to rise in organizations.

It works for clients too

Winsor admits to being concerned about the reaction of brands when he explained their working model.

'When you're in the agency business you're indoctrinated that's the right thing that clients really want.' However, he found that the V&S structure intrigued and excited their prospective clients. 'Our biggest feedback at CMO level was "thank god somebody is changing this thing". They understood that it's human nature – you always work inherently the way you're compensated. For instance, if you're in a public company the aim is to raise revenue to satisfy stakeholders on a quarterly basis. The only way to affect that when you have full-time staff and charge one time, is to go slower for your clients and put more people on the work. Those are the two dials that you have control of. That job is going to take twice as long so we're going to charge you twice as much; we thought it would be 5 people on that project but it's going to be 20. That's a thing of the past. There are new ways to do things that don't mean more time or don't mean more money.'

V&S's legacy

Given his role in creating the first crowdsourced advertising company, what would Winsor describe as their greatest achievement to date? 'We've had financial success – I feel like we've done a good job. It was such a hectic first year and a half, it's been nice to have to give a lot of notice to the PR as we had to in the first year. It's nice just to get on with the work and figure out the technology systems, building the technology ourselves. So I'm proud of a lot of things and I'm proud of the folks that are here.'

Sound bytes

- Don't be fooled by those belonging to the old ways of doing work.
- If you're going to consider crowdsourcing, consider the operational structure and rewards (Howe, 2008) – 'you always work inherently the way you're compensated'.
- In charting new technologies, it's helpful to take an holistic view of where your idea fits in the bigger scheme of things.

Further reading

Bogusky, A and Winsor, J (2009) *Baked In: Creating products and businesses that market themselves*, Agate/CP+B, Colorado

Howe, J (2008) *Crowdsourcing: Why the power of the crowd is driving the future of business*, Three Rivers, New York

Rogers, E M and Rogers, E (1962) *Diffusion of Innovations*, Simon & Schuster, New York

Winsor, J (1985) *Fitness on the Road*, Shelter Publications, Colorado

Winsor, J (2004) *Beyond the Brand: Why engaging the right customers is essential to winning in business*, Dearhorn, Chicago

Winsor, J (2004) *Flipped: How bottom-up co-creation is replacing top-down innovation*, Agate, Colorado

Winsor, J (2006) *Spark: Be more innovative through co-creation*, Agate, Colorado

Danny Sullivan

Search Engine Land

Digital discipline

Internationally renowned tech writer specializing in search engine optimization, online marketing and social media. Sullivan founded Search Engine Watch and SES conference series in 1996, leaving in 2007 to set up direct competitors Search Engine Land and Search Marketing Expo.

Thirst for discovery

Sitting in a parking lot, thumbing through the college prospectus of UC Irvine under pressure to decide what course to take, might not have been the most auspicious start to a career as a journalist. But legions of fans and followers in the search engine marketing industry all around the world will be glad Danny Sullivan's outstretched finger travelled no further than 'j' that day.

Now founder and editor-in-chief of news site Search Engine Land and conference series Search Marketing Expo, the decision to 'give it try' stemmed from a desire to ask questions and a tendency to want to organize and improve efficiency everywhere he went. He thought that, as a writer, he could help people by helping dissect issues: 'I just want to understand things. And part of understanding things a lot of times is kind of breaking it down, and then reassembling it in a way that you can explain.'

One of the least understood areas of digital is search marketing. A complex, often very technical discipline dominated by Google's ubiquity but fragmented by their main competitors, Yahoo! and Microsoft's Bing search engine, it takes a lot of explaining.

Acronym-rich – SEO (search engine optimization), PPC (pay per click), SERP (search engine results page), CPC (cost per click), CTR (click through rate), to name but a few – the industry attracts a certain kind of marketer that really cares about structure, research, analysis and technical execution, so for a man that organizes his Lego into 30 different bags, Sullivan was the perfect person to start documenting the industry as far back as 1996.

Many might think that the now ubiquitous 'infographic' is a relatively new thing, but back in 1995, Sullivan was working at the Orange County Register as a journalist specifically tasked with making sense of information and data using imagery, all with the help of an artist. When he saw the world wide web for the first time, he wanted to get involved. But it was obvious that his colleagues at the time were not early adopters and, in his words, they 'were not going to get there any time soon'. So, with a friend – Ken Spreitzer – he set up a web development company called Maximized Online.

Part of the process of getting the websites live and discoverable was publishing them to the web and submitting the URLs (website addresses) to all the different search engines. Way before Google – prototypes for 'Project Backrub' were not demo'd until 1997 – search engines like Yahoo!, Excite, Lycos, Hotbot and Alta Vista all needed to be given the nod that a new website existed.

How to be number one

What got Sullivan's interest was a request from one client who felt that his site should be number one in the search results listings for the term 'Orange County'. The web was bereft of any information as to how search engines ranked sites for particular search terms, so Sullivan set about testing different things over a period of four months. He was looking for common factors that were important in site design and structure that affected how and when the search engines indexed and revisited a site submitted to them. Taking his research online, he published it in what he called the 'Webmaster's Guide to Search Engines'. With a background in journalism, he wanted to 'give back to the web' some of the things he'd discovered. It was designed to highlight what webmasters should be paying attention to with regard to using the engines to send traffic to their sites.

In what must be the one of the first examples of paying attention to return on investment (ROI) in search, he also spent a lot of time working out which search engines it was really worth submitting sites to. Some submission processes were easier than others and Sullivan remembers one for Galaxy being a three-page-long form where he says you 'had to pick a billion different categories'. So, instead of following the wisdom of the crowd, he used rudimentary ComScore traffic data to assess whether a particular search engine was worth bothering with. 'You really needed to know that not all search engines were equal, nor worth the same amount of time that you put into it', he recalls.

Even back then he was encouraging webmasters not to put all their eggs in one basket, saying: 'Don't depend on these search engines. Don't depend on them for all your traffic, and don't run around just trying to spam them. You're probably going to be better off if you are building good content, and doing the things that make your site search engine friendly.'

Although he was dishing out sage advice, his own business was not making enough money to keep it going, so Maximized minimized and Sullivan moved to the UK with his British wife, Lorna, which was part of the plan anyway. Before leaving, he started his own consulting firm called Calafia, after the myth that California was an island ruled by an Amazonian-like queen called Calafia. He'd update the site periodically with news or insight he'd uncovered about SEO and took temporary writing assignments to pay the bills. By the following year, Calafia.com was thriving. He'd opened up a subscription service and was surprised when visitors actually started to donate money by way of thanks to keep the lights on.

Sullivan remembers trying to get more traction from the search engines themselves, but when it came to sneak peeks of new features or interviews with executives it was slow going initially. Bloggers were not taken that seriously and he was asked more than once what 'magazine' he worked for. Many of the PR teams were still a little old school and hadn't realized that what he was saying online was really resonating with a target audience they should really be listening to. But he says 'people like Google were especially good because I think they realized early that here was a publication that was all about search, and it could have an impact on them trying to build up their awareness'.

By July 1997, his writing was so in demand that the guide was getting too confused with his consulting firm and he felt it needed its own brand. So Search Engine Watch was born. His entrepreneurial side chose the name with 'watch' in the title because he'd seen some similarly named start-ups lucratively sold and thought that it 'probably wouldn't hurt'.

It didn't. Search Engine Watch was sold to Alan Meckler's company Internet.com four months later for a healthy, undisclosed sum, and Sullivan stayed on as editor until he left to set up Search Engine Land in December 2006.

So, in the space of a couple of years, Sullivan had spotted a niche that needed writing about. He created useful, compelling content that few people in a fast-growing industry knew about or understood, and in a matter of months built a brand around it ready to be sold.

In essence, though, the work was just beginning. Meckler's team were keen to keep Sullivan writing and not bogged down with the day-to-day running of the site. They teamed him up with Chris Sherman, a Stanford graduate, who had been consulting on web projects and writing about search for a number of years too. Together the pair made an effective partnership, especially when the business wanted them to move into real-world education and evangelism by starting conferences on search engine marketing.

Search on tour

Chris Elwell, now president of Third Door Media – the holding company for Search Engine Land and others in the group – suggested Search Engine Watch go on the road in 1999. Sullivan had been doing some speaking at conferences like Internet World, but at the time search engine marketing and SEO were not featured heavily. An in-depth subject, it was often limited to sideline tracks, or speakers were given just 45 minutes to cover it in its entirety. Having a whole day dedicated to search would allow webmasters and marketers to really gain from the team's knowledge and the other speakers that lined up to impart theirs.

Their first conference started at 8 am and ended at 6 pm and included a smattering of five-minute breaks, such was the sheer amount of ground they wanted to cover. Sessions on search-engine-friendly design and metatags were followed by others on doorway pages and keyword research. It was the last session of the day, however, that sealed the deal for what became known as the Search Engine Strategies conferences.

In an unprecedented move, Sullivan had invited the search engines to participate. Google founder Sergey Brin was there, but given the dominance of Yahoo! at the time, Sullivan tapped up a personal contact who was an editor there – Andy Gems – to 'come out and answer some questions'. The organizers were nervous. Today, 'search engine reps' are expected to attend, speak, and mix with the crowds at internet conferences. Some, like Matt Cutts from Google, now receive a cult-like following and are often seen surrounded in the corridors of convention centres by delegates clamouring for the slightest titbit of information that might give their work the edge over their competitors. But in 1999, Sullivan felt that the large engines like Yahoo! didn't care and that they might receive a frosty reception from the assembled throng. He was wrong. The first to the microphone during the search engine representative question and answer session thanked the companies for being there and listening to their issues and queries. The room responded by breaking out in spontaneous applause. SES was a hit.

In 2005, ZenithOptimedia estimated global online advertising spend to be growing 30 per cent year on year to $19bn. In the United States alone, the Interactive Advertising Bureau (IAB) claimed that search engine marketing generated 41 per cent of the $12bn spent by American advertisers. Search was big business. Actually, it was even bigger because those figures didn't include consultancy fees and retainers for search engine optimization of 'organic listings'; those numbers were just the cash falling into the coffers of Google and other pay per click engines like Overture, Looksmart and Espotting.

With so much attention being paid to search, it meant that Search Engine Watch's audience was growing and growing. It would get visited daily, sometimes more than once, by regular readers wanting to stay ahead of the rapidly changing landscape, and browsed by newcomers who were just getting into the industry and wanting to learn more.

Sold... again

One company impressed with the site and the Search Engine Strategies conference series that was building an international reputation was global B2B publisher Incisive Media who bought the business as part of the ClickZ.com network from what became Jupitermedia for $43m in August 2005. In a post at the time, Sullivan wrote, 'Overall, it's a good thing. Jupitermedia is concentrating on its images businesses, and the deal puts us with a new owner looking to expand the work we do.' All staff would be retained, the conference planned for San Jose that month would go ahead, and 'While the owners are changing, the quality content we aim to deliver to you is not.'

But while the content didn't suffer, over the next year Sullivan's relationship with ClickZ's new owners did. Sullivan knew that they had little experience in search and thought that he should have some kind of long-term stake in the business if he was to help it develop and grow. He told them: 'All I know is that in five years from now you decide to sell it to somebody else and I've built up something yet again, and not had an interest in it.'

Moving on

According to Incisive, a generous offer was made, but Sullivan felt he had nothing to gain from it, so quit on 29 August 2006 after 10 years with Search Engine Watch. The subsequent outpouring of feeling from the search community bordered on hysteria. There were over 100 comments from well-wishers on his personal blog, Daggle.com, all thanking him for the impact he'd made on the industry, their careers and their lives.

One such commenter, Rand Fishkin, now CEO of the Seattle-based SEO software company SEOMoz, remembers Sullivan's generosity towards him earlier in his career:

> In 2004, I'd been contributing to online forums and writing on the nascent SEOmoz.org blog, but had never formally participated in the search industry in person. Seattle wasn't yet a regular stop for conferences or events and I

> had very little income, so buying tickets to a show at $1,000 a piece was out of the question. When I posted on the Search Engine Watch forums at the end of that year, asking whether I should try to sit in the bar during the SES New York conference to meet people, Danny dropped me a private message and said he'd give me a ticket. When I met Danny in person toward the end of the event, it was the most star struck I've ever been. For years, he'd been an online hero to me, and now he'd given me my first chance at becoming more than just a name on a forum. For the next SES conference later that year in Toronto, I pitched to speak on a panel and was accepted. It started a long career in conference speaking that's brought incredible returns for me personally and professionally.

Sullivan followed his resignation post the next day with some words reflecting on the decision and some of the comments made about it, just to make sure his fans were in no doubt that it wasn't just about getting paid more money:

> Incisive repeatedly stressed that they wanted to retain me and that they had no intention of cutting me out of future plans. Such reassurances are nice, but they aren't binding. I simply was unwilling to transfer any further knowledge of the search engine and search marketing space to Incisive on the basis of verbal reassurances. There was absolutely no reason for me to do this.
> It would put me in a weaker position with the company.

So with his inbox already flooded with offers, a niggling desire to write a book and the possibility of expanding his own consultancy, Sullivan sat back and thought about what to do next. Crucially, he had no non-compete clause in his contract. There was nothing stopping him from setting up a competitor site and series of conferences.

So that's what he did.

Becoming a challenger

In December 2006 Sullivan announced that a new company – Third Door Media – would be created to house his new site SearchEngineLand.com and series of search conferences under the name SMX or Search Marketing Expo. His editorial partner Chris Sherman was to join him, as was Chris Elwell, who had been the driving force behind the SES conferences.

Questioned at the time about what was going to be different about his sites or conferences, he'd reply, 'Why would I do something different, what I'm doing is working perfectly fine!' In fact, it wasn't anything really radical that was needed, rather the nice touches that would surprise and delight that seemed to make the biggest difference, like hot food at 'meet and greet' lunches instead of sandwiches out of a box, and the SMX Theatre where people could present or see presentations without necessarily making it to the main stage.

Suffice to say, with search spend set to double to $11bn over the following five years, it appears there was room for competing sites and conferences to exist and thrive. And they have.

While Sullivan's venture has been a successful outlet for him and his team, it's important to point out that Search Engine Watch and the Search Engine Strategies conferences haven't been left in the dust by his new venture.

Matt McGowan, Incisive Media's MD for the Americas, says he's thankful for taking over the businesses and inheriting an extremely healthy and strong brand. 'My predecessors knew what they were doing when they built the SES Conference Series, Search Engine Watch and ClickZ. Together, both Danny Sullivan and the team at Jupitermedia built a trust with their readers, attendees and sponsors that I have had the opportunity to build upon.'

There are now SES Conferences in Shanghai, Singapore, Hong Kong, Chicago and Berlin as well as New York, London and Toronto where Sullivan's SMX events also operate at different times of the year. Incisive welcomes that competition too. In an extremely healthy and growing industry, they recognize that people are hungry for education and networking opportunities and have continued to expand to fulfil that need, but acknowledge there's plenty of room for other players.

Five years on and the Third Door Media team have further expanded their reach with the launch of MarketingLand.com, which hopes to continue their work telling the world news and insight about other forms of online outreach through display advertising, mobile, e-mail and all important web analytics.

Adore what you do!

Sullivan's draw has in large part been due to the way he writes. His research and analysis sometimes runs to a word count well over a thousand for a single article. 'Danny tries to look at search engines, search engine optimization, and search engine advertising from multiple perspectives – giving his readers and colleagues the full picture', says Shari Thurow, author of *Search Engine Visibility*. 'He thinks of things that others might not have considered. Combine his thoroughness with his objectivity, and you have one heck of an expert.'

When looking back on his career, Sullivan is adamant that his accomplishments lie in that he has always really relished what he's been doing. 'If you're trying to be successful, one of the keys in that is whether or not you're doing something you enjoy.' He feels his team's passion also shines through in tandem with his own. They realize that their mission to provide information about search engines and online marketing is something to really take pride in and have fun while doing it.

What he also senses gave him the edge in the early days was fulfilling a need. Really, there was no one else writing about search engines back in 1996. When he broached search to the publication he was freelancing with at the time he says:

> I thought they were missing a huge opportunity because web search was a big giant space that wasn't being covered which is why I started and stayed with it, and I think I was right. I don't even think the magazine I was writing for is in business anymore. So my feeling would be that, if you're trying to break into a space, you pick up an area where people aren't necessarily covering.

He spotted the gap and realized it was growing and needed to be filled. He's not sure he would have started a competing site to Search Engine Watch if he hadn't had so much experience and support, but that doesn't mean that taking on established competition should be discouraged. It's bringing something new and different to the table that's important. It may be as subtle as a hot lunch or a better quality conference giveaway bag, but often it's the little things that get remembered and talked about.

When looking back at his achievements, Sullivan feels his most important contribution is 'to have helped search marketing be a legitimate, valuable activity that people should do'.

Thousands of marketers from all over the world would agree with that, and millions of consumers who use search engines every day should be grateful that he started in 1995 helping webmasters make their sites more relevant for search engines, and that he provided a platform for the search engines to sit up and help webmasters help them.

John Battelle, founder of Federated Media and author of Searchblog, echoes their sentiment:

> For as long as I've followed the space (more than a decade now), Danny has been my go-to source on nearly anything that has to do with search and its impact on the massive ecosystem dependent on search. He's thoughtful, thorough, and a really good person to boot. That combination doesn't happen very often.

Thanks to him, there may now be more than one place on the web to catch up on search marketing and social media news, but there'll only ever be one Danny Sullivan.

Sound bytes

- It's important to love what you do. Thriving in a professional area of expertise is dependent on you actually enjoying being in that space.
- To compete effectively, sometimes it's the small things that help you positively differentiate. A more intuitive website or friendlier, more personable customer service agents. Simple, nice touches can work really well.
- Don't build your business in a bubble. Look at other sectors and see what's working well. There may be lessons from the offline world that will translate successfully on the web.

Further reading

http://www.SearchEngineLand.com
http://www.Daggle.com
http://Twitter.com/DannySullivan

Alex Bogusky, Bob Cianfrone

Burger King's Subservient Chicken

Digital discipline

Viral advertising: the team at Crispin Porter + Bogusky, led by Alex Bogusky, created the most commercially successful viral site ever, with over 460 million hits worldwide. The campaign pioneered the use of leading technologies for advertising and created an aesthetic readily identifiable with digital advertising.

How BK Subservient Chicken worked

Internet users typed instructions for the chicken who acts out their request. This encouraged people to play and share the site and its message, that customers could have chicken burgers anyway they wanted at BK restaurants.

> *We haven't conceived our Subservient Chicken, but at least we're trying.*
> (Mothers of Invention marketing agency, Maynard, MA)

Story of an advertising phenomenon

The short history of digital advertising has been marked by many quirky and impactful instances. From Sega's 'Beta-7' fake game tester to Mark Ecko's supposed graffiti-ing of the US president's plane, some campaigns have made millions worldwide take notice. The most significant of these did not involve elaborate set-ups, just a man in a chicken outfit and suspenders acting out some 500 actions for viewers to play with.

The reason Subservient Chicken became a phenomenon and a key moment for advertising is that it fused new technologies of its day with the most successful types of interaction from other pioneering digital industries – search, gaming, social networks and porn.

Stats on Subservient Chicken

- Filmed in two days.
- Produced in six weeks, from start to finish.
- Total cost $50,000.
- Twenty million hits in first week.
- Fourteen million unique visitors and 396 million hits in one year.
- Weekly 9% sales increase of BK TenderCrisp sandwich during first month of the site launching.

Why a sexy chicken?

The project was devised at the Florida HQ of Crispin Porter + Bogusky, an advertising agency which, at the time, attracted press coverage for their radically creative solutions. The story of the chicken goes back to April 2004 when Alex Bogusky, the agency's executive creative director, first won the chance to work with Burger King in the United States. 'They were a great client that had had several years of declining sales. Their audience was very much like those that beer companies advertise to. So why is your advertising so different?'

Burger King were impressed but wanted to see more. 'We were given a week to come up with some ideas. I was in London, flew straight back and worked really hard. We presented for over three hours before we showed our first television commercial spot [highly unusual for agencies at the time]... At the end they said "we want to give you the account".' Bogusky's radical approach appealed to the company at a time when sales had dipped across the United States.

The duo that devised the chicken idea, copywriter Bob Cianfrone and art director Mark Taylor, had the project 'thrown at them with all the others' in Bogusky's creative department, and they were the first to get their ideas approved by BK. 'They had sold a campaign for television slots early on – no one remembers the commercials, but they were kinda cool...' The fact that the ideas happened early was significant for Bogusky: 'My philosophy is that new business doesn't happen when you're looking around; it happens in those first moments of getting an account. So I tried to create a case history in those first few moments. I knew that it needed to be something special.'

BK had been keen to reach their 18–34-year-old demographic 'with a male skew' through commercial television. Cianfrone and Taylor stretched BK's 'have it your way' line to make it funny, cheeky and referential – the right tone given its audience. As Cianfrone remembers, 'We understood the essence of the brand, the idea, was to let people have chicken their way – and all that that encompassed.'

Subservient Chicken first aired in 2004 to launch BK's TenderCrisp chicken sandwich. The storyline featured two women in their living room. One is ironing while the other, on a sofa, deliberately drops a pencil and commands the chicken, human-sized and clearly in costume, to pick it up. She kicks the pencil again just to see the chicken bend over. The scenario seemed like a role-reversal lap dance, hinting at something a little more risqué – racier than the family-oriented strategies of other fast-food campaigns.

Convincing the client

This appealed to Bogusky, who knew that BK's customers were spending time scouring the net for entertainment. 'We said let's do something digitally with this campaign. So it was self-selecting, as they had already come up with this chicken character in our first commercials that aired for BK.' This was Cianfrone and Taylor's first work for BK and they didn't have a background or interest in digital: 'The idea was to just come up with good ideas and make digital applicable where it was relevant.' The idea of moving the Chicken campaign online was not an easy sell to their client, however. According to Bogusky, 'We had a great client, but they were a company that had seen eight years of declining sales. We said "your audience is very much the sort that look at mixed content online, so why is your advertising so different?".' According to Bogusky, the clients were not initially enthusiastic about the whole idea. 'When I explained it to them they said, "nah, I don't know – who cares?" I thought we should start to experiment. So we basically scraped $50 out of the TV production.' Yet Bogusky's logic was compelling and right. Online content was different, and the chicken certainly belonged more in digital space.

As Bogusky remembers, Burger King were supportive as the online version was prepared, but 'this whole thing was an after-thought in their minds. We thought it would be really cool, but in their mind we were meant to be doing TV spots. It cost $50k to make, so we said to them if we can scrape this much money together we can do this site. They hadn't thought about digital. When we did it they wanted to make sure that it didn't reflect poorly on them. When it was out and it was a success they were very happy about it.'

Aside from the challenge of producing the work on a tight budget, shifting from broadcast to narrowcast required other significant rethinks.

Styling the Chicken

The team knew that moving the chicken online meant ratcheting up the narratives. As Cianfrone recollected, 'in one of the TV ads the chicken wears a lacy vest, and he's in this basement with a guy who eats this sandwich. In another the chicken does a pole dance. So there are definitely nods to this chicken doing the naughty sort of things that people do, or ask for or want to see done in the privacy of their own walls and not in public.' The team saw opportunities to encourage viewers to participate – 'It was a more personal experience for them. The ability to sit down and have a more personal experience with the chicken rather than a public experience was much better. That's what we liked about it. On your own you can really ask the chicken anything without looking over your shoulder.'

The creative team designed in clues to cue up the site's visitors: 'There were little hints when you look at the chicken. You see things like the garters. On its leg it has a little metal clip on it that you see on farms, that shows possession and ownership. We also had things that indicate ownership and subservience.'

At the time, the most pioneering online interactivity came from the US pornographic industry. Sending typed commands for a performer to act out on webcam was a popular pornographic format from the start of the world wide web. The level of voyeurism on the net had been topical at the time, ever since Jennifer Rigley's JenniCAM in 1996 courted controversy. The porn industry introduced a more structured and commercialized experience. However, for Cianfrone imitation was not the main objective: 'I don't know if we were going for the porn industry, but we were going for awkward and unusual.'

Embracing challenges of technology

At the time, the technological challenge was huge, and they were fortunate to have expertise up to the job. According to Bogusky, the agency's expert in interactive technologies, Jeff Benjamin, really helped: 'he always believed the *impossible's possible*: with the technologies he used things just *became* possible. Back then you could pair new advances with ideas; put up new combinations of technologies and imagine what it would it make, and it would blow up in your face in a really good way.'

Production also posed a challenge for the creative team as the online idea was off-brief. The team had just six weeks from concept to launch, including getting the costume made (two weeks), which according to Cianfrone was the most expensive part of the whole thing. 'We picked a director, casting, we shot the spots then we gave the team just one day to get it online. We showed the company references and the rest of it was straightforward – just very quick.'

Even the list of actions for the chicken was written in record time. According to Cianfrone: 'We put it to the whole agency, "if there was a chicken in your living room and you could ask it to do anything you wanted, what would you ask it to do?", and so we got a lot of interesting responses from people at the time.'

These included Moon walk, walk like an Egyptian, shake your booty, be an aeroplane, hide behind the sofa. As copywriter, Cianfrone captured the best of them and read them out fresh to the chicken as he stood in front of camera. Bogusky was amazed that the list, though 500, proved to be comprehensive: 'As a viral, the key was *what are people going to ask you to do?* That's what was most fascinating for me. Everyone thought they'd say unique things (yet) everyone asked for the same 500 things. That freaked people out – they thought they were being unique by typing in "play baseball", and it was in the first 500 things that *anyone* would want him to do.'

The shoot: 'going for awkward'

'We had an actor, "Bendy Wendy" (that's how she introduced herself), who we got because she could do all of these different things. It turned out she got claustrophobic in the suit and couldn't do it, so we were screwed. We were on shoot day and we didn't have anyone who could go into the suit. So one of the guys who built it from Stan Western Studios, who make costumes for movies, said he'd try it. So he got into the costume and he did awesome. So we told him we were getting ready to shoot this thing for digital – would he be willing to do it? He was. It turned out that he could do anything – any move, every dance... he could do the "Cabbage Patch", he could roll on his belly, so we got really lucky that he could do all the acts that we wanted performing.'

Even the set was low-budget. Cianfrone and Taylor faced challenges in making the space credible: 'We were in this dingy Hollywood apartment. He (the chicken) was exhausted. We constantly came up with new things for him to try and we made full use of that environment. We had to make sure that any possible interaction he could have – pictures on the wall, the lights, furniture – we had to cover that up.' For anything outside the list of coded actions the chicken had a recorded default – 'because of the nature of the internet, people were going to ask (for extreme things) so we had to have a default that told them, "I'm not going to do that – at some point the service runs out!"'

The team recorded nearly all 500 options for the chicken in two days. 'It was a big challenge at the time. We were able to find a way of making it (seem) real time. We could ask a question and it was like it was talking to it (the chicken) live.' They did manage to record the content on professional standard equipment but the creative team degraded the video to make it look more like a consumer-filmed thing. Low tech masked the fact that it wasn't live. It looked like it was tagged, and it was jumpy. And the chicken always had to go back to that same starting position anyway. But the fact that it was low tech helped 'because, one, it helped cover some of the production challenges, and two, it just made it seem a bit more real, because it looked like one of those sites that you pay $9.99 a month for. There are those sites where you have a one-on-one. We even degraded it to make it look more seedy and porn.'

Cianfrone remains happy that 'we were really scrappy with it. We had no money and no location until the night before we shot it. It was just a bunch of us carrying a bunch of lights and cameras up a stairway in a dingy Hollywood apartment. It's so great that sometimes some of the best things happen really fast and you have to be really scrappy, when you just have to think on your feet.'

The Chicken was nearly choked: the consequences of being different

According to Bogusky, the site was nearly pulled down on the first day, because the porn connotation 'hit really hot. That's part of the phenomenon. You can't separate the fact that people tried to make problems for us and that it was mega successful. Trade pubs were trying to embarrass us. People tried to say it was porn and fast food: it did hurt. We didn't want to push the thing too much, but we said "hang on – the ultimate story arc this is going to have (will be worth it)".'

Cianfrone remembers being careful '... in making sure that it didn't get us all fired. It was released a bit earlier than it should have been (before the default "finger wagging" section was inserted), it got leaked out and, before we knew it, it was everywhere. Our IT guy was scrambling, they had to get tons more servers to handle all the demands that were being placed on the site.'

Bogusky recollected the initial anxiety after the wave of hostile press: 'The first few days were crucial – and the client had to hold their nerve to ride the initial storm: This was pretty much the first big swing... it was pretty horrible. It launched, and you'd start seeing the numbers on the site. It was a phenomenon – over a million hits in the first few days. Then the trade and national press were really on it in a way that was uncomfortable for the client – we're more used to it. We had endless calls – they wanted to take it down; it wasn't fun but neat things were happening. It didn't turn good for about a month, when it was not a bad thing in people's minds. Now everyone thinks it's a success...'

In hindsight...

> *The chicken was meant to be a one off. I wish I could say there was a plan but it was just 'let's do this campaign and see what happens... some things happen organically like that'.*
>
> (Bob Cianfrone)

While Teresa Iezzi in *Advertising Age* considered Subservient Chicken to be a 'watershed, in a new era of interactive creativity', Bogusky remains modest on its achievements: 'I think it did a nice job of reminding people that it didn't take a lot of budget to have a lot of impact. In some ways for marketers and clients, it drove the idea that the internet was for real, because it had a lot of free impressions there.' At $50,000 – a tenth of the cost of BK's three commercials at the time – the site illustrated how there was scope to make a big impact using the minimum of means online.

Part of the phenomenon has to do with its 'home-made' aesthetic, far cruder than the polished productions of commercials. According to Bogusky, 'it was scrappy because there was no money! We thought of doing it in lots of different ways – animating the chicken, an interactive animation you could stretch and play with. There just wasn't much money.' Cianfrone preferred its scrappiness because the rough-and-ready idea punched out above everything else. It looked like anyone could have produced it – which was the point.

What also made it so effective was that people could play with it for long periods of time to discover how well thought out the site was. It encouraged play – not sexy or sexual, but more banter to share with friends. Many simply enjoyed the idea of spoofing porn. As one blogger noted, 'Low-budget video, low-budget living room, low-budget chicken costume – if you just typed in a word in the bar below the chicken, you could make the chicken do all sorts of (low-budget) things.' As Cianfrone remarked, 'I guess that's always the way – low-budget behaviour!'

In hindsight, members of the team took different things from the project's success. For Cianfrone 'it was a great experience learning as I was going. I take from it that it's not the budget, but the idea.' Bogusky got to understand the dichotomy of a media maelstrom that became bigger than anticipated: 'You can create successes, but not phenomena; that involves a lot of luck. It was definitely of the moment. Most marketers don't like this type of promotion because it's a hot place to be. It's only when culture tries to make sense of what you've done that it's "successful" or whatever. It wasn't like that at the time.'

The low-down: Chicken's significance for digital advertising

The campaign's success was in realizing what it took to work as an online 'commercial' – detail in art direction, layered narratives and a depth of thought behind the coding. It also created scope for interactivity and playfulness in an environment where consumers felt most comfortable – at home, online, surfing the net for fun.

Media critics often argue that although Subservient Chicken rekindled the brand's relevance, it was not a long-term strategy. As Bill Bernbach, the legendary 1960s advertiser, put it, 'A great ad campaign will make a bad product fail faster.' In BK's case it wasn't a bad product, but what advertisers call 'stickability' – not making the central message inextricably stick to the brand. Many confused the site as an advert for Kentucky Fried Chicken. Yet Subservient Chicken is pioneering because it captured the imagination globally. It inspired enough word-of-mouth activity to spread the link worldwide – even though the message, customers having chicken tailored to their taste, was meant to be an offer limited to the United States. The chicken increased the brand perception of Burger King and, as Cianfrone noted, 'It sold a lot of chicken sandwiches, which is a good thing.'

The campaign is certainly a benchmark in capturing the imagination by using technology in a challenging way. So what sparked Alex Bogusky's passion for new interactivity? Bogusky took his cue from pre-digital motivational advertising: 'For me it was Howard Gossage, who did interactive advertising before there was any capability digitally to interact – he did it through newspaper coupons. Early in my career it was fun, not knowing what the audience was thinking. When the web came along it was easy for us, because finally there was a better way without foam balls and odd forms!' For the best ideas, it's worth looking outside digital to find a spark of inspiration.

Advice from the creator: 'start with a great idea'

So, what would the chicken's co-creator Bob advise anyone wishing to follow in his footsteps? 'Remember – idea first. I think it's really important that you start with a great idea, then you start thinking about execution. That's what "Subservient" was to me. It started with a funny idea – telling a chicken what to do, and then it just grew from there. Starting with a great idea – that's half the battle.'

So how will Cianfrone tell the story of Subservient Chicken to grandchildren in years to come? 'I did creepy things – things that kept people up at night.'

Sound bytes

- If you're making an online viral, don't over-style a strong idea. Keep it simple, 'keep it messy'.
- Develop the idea with enough scope for people to explore and play with the format.
- If you keep the idea simple you design out production difficulties – and unforeseen expenditure.

Further reading

Bogusky, A with Winsor, J (2009) *Baked In: Creating products and businesses that market themselves*, Agate/CP+B, Colorado

Avinash Kaushik

Digital marketing evangelist, Google

Digital discipline

Energetic and passionate evangelist for web analytics and results-oriented digital marketing. Bestselling author and must-see keynote speaker, who has distilled the art of navigating web metrics into an entertaining, engaging and valuable business essential.

Blowing your mind

On a voyage of discovery that took him from a small town outside Mumbai to a brainwashing in Bahrain, the wrong end of a machine gun in Saudi Arabia, the snowdrifts of Ohio, the generosity of General Motors and the glinting gleam of Google, Avinash Kaushik, now the Mountain View behemoth's evangelist for all things digital marketing, has quite a story to tell.

As his bestselling books, *Web Analytics: An hour a day* and *Web Analytics 2.0*, and his hugely popular blog, Occam's Razor, demonstrate, the Indian holder of a forklift truck driver's licence is not bereft of theories and advice on how to help businesses demonstrate the value of their online marketing forays.

Anyone fortunate enough to catch a glimpse of one of his highly acclaimed presentations at any number of marketing conferences around the world will find it impossible not to be struck between the eyes by the symphony of common sense and insight that Kaushik delivers with such passion; on the way back to their place of work, one of Kaushik's favourite phrases, 'It blew my mind', will still be resonating as they sit down and begin to implement his guidance across their business.

Bordering B minus

Born in India, Kaushik lived with his family on top of his father's factory in Vapi, about 200km from Mumbai, and went to a private school where everything was taught in English. His parents put a very high value on his education, and even though he was never an A student, he was very keen to learn and absorb everything around him. A voracious reader, he'd devour anything he could get his hands on, from newspapers to novels and even copies of *Reader's Digest*, which made him good at recalling facts during quizzes.

A given that he'd follow in his father's footsteps and become a mechanical engineer, Kaushik worked in the factory when he had spare time, helping him become business-savvy from an early age. Embarrassed that he wasn't smart enough to make it into one of the more elite public universities in India, he spent his first year studying his heart out at the private one his parents had been saving to send him to. But after the first year learning about conductive electricity and lathe machines, his enthusiasm for engineering waned and he longed for the bright lights and opportunities to be experienced in the United States.

A 'classic village boy', Kaushik had been so wide-eyed during a school alumni talk about living in the United States that he decided the 'land of the free' was where he wanted to be. Getting there, however, was proving a problem. His parents couldn't afford to pay, so he had two choices: join the merchant navy or get lucrative work in the Middle East as a 'glorious indentured slave'.

He chose the Middle East.

His first job after graduating from university, working for the Indian Market Research Bureau, proved the stepping stone he needed and the first real indication of which direction his career would be steered towards. He recalls:

> At the time my job was to interview people and do market research, and that was a very valuable experience to me in terms of understanding how people think and feel about brands, products and services and the motivations that drive them to buy... I learnt a lot about understanding people's perceptions and sentiment and how you collect that data by going house to house or bank to bank and interviewing people.

That experience helped Kaushik get a job with the logistics company DHL, although he was four years below the age limit they were hiring against. He'd ranked number one out of three hundred in their tests and so found himself on a flight to Bahrain for training ('brainwashing' in his words), en route to Riyadh in Saudi Arabia.

Although the Bahrain experience was repetitive in terms of the helpline classes he had to take, he remembers: 'It was a second formative experience for me, and I think to this day, a lot of my work is deeply rooted in this personal passion around customer service and a deep and profound empathy for the consumer.'

One of Kaushik's strengths is the ability to ask tough questions and not to be overawed by some of the authority he encounters within the businesses he helps. In a more extreme example of defiance, he got into a spot of bother with a machine-gun-toting guard outside the Saudi Ministry of Interior while carrying out the ill-advised task of photographing the building. With a gun at his head and the order to say he was a Muslim ricocheting off his ear drums, he stuck to his principles and refused to comply. Let go in the end because they thought he must be some 'bumbling idiot', Kaushik thankfully admits that 'in hindsight it was the dumbest, stupidest thing to do', but nevertheless cites it as an illustration of his confidence in his own philosophy.

Coming to the United States

In 1995 he took a 'leap of faith' and travelled to the United States to do an MBA at Ohio State University. He'd got three college acceptances in all, but fancied Ohio as he was 'sick of the desert' and was intrigued by the prospect of seeing lots of snow. He had saved enough money for 5 months' tuition, but, buoyed by the opportunity to work legally for 20 hours a week as a student, he took a job in the university archives driving a forklift truck.

Job aside, he still had little money to make ends meet so would only allow himself to eat breakfast and dinner. Throwing himself into his studies, he took as many different classes as he could in finance, logistics, international law, marketing and sales. Loving the exposure to all this new information, he joined all sorts of related clubs as well. His favourite was an alumni CEO initiative, because he not only got a free lunch but was able to rub shoulders with the types of senior executives he wouldn't have a hope of meeting in the professional world for some time. Of those precious moments Kaushik says: 'It turned out to be the single greatest thing I did in MBA School because having access to these CEOs, hearing them talk about their companies and asking them questions about their real challenges was such an incredible learning experience for me.'

His first dalliance with the web had come while in Saudi Arabia, when being introduced to e-mail and the notion that someone on the other side of the world could reply to a message the same day had him reeling in amazement. A class in management information systems (MIS) at Ohio State presented the notion of database design, and this learning, coupled with the burgeoning world wide web, started to really sow the seeds of what was to come for Kaushik.

By his second year, the disciplines of symmetry and logic gleaned from his degree in engineering, coupled with choosing MBA classes in finance (a safe option for getting a job when he graduated), MIS and marketing, started to set the tone and light a fire underneath him:

> I got deeper into this world because at the time there was this thought in my mind that I now have access to this information on the internet, and the fact the data could be organized in such a clean way. There was something mind-blowing that would come of this and the fact that I could get the answers so fast fascinated me.

After an internship in finance at General Motors (where he was paid a staggering $175 a day), Kaushik returned knowing that working directly with money was not going to be his finest hour, so he interviewed for a job at the university careers service where he was guaranteed some subsistence towards his tuition fees and started to use his new-found technical skills to make data more freely available:

> One of the projects I proactively took was to create a database for the career services office because all information about which students were going on internships to which company, and which kind of student applied for what jobs, was there. I created a simple front end so that anybody could enter information into it, and I would run a report that the senior leaders in the office could read. That to them was a transformative experience because in the past if the director had to answer a simple question, it would take him weeks of some intern slogging through paper records to find any information. And now the fact that he could press a button and find the things he was looking for, to him was mind-blowing! That got me on this track of realizing that structured information, and the ability to make it accessible to people in a business context, was very useful.

Data-driven business

On graduating from Ohio State with his MBA, Kaushik landed his first job with a company called Silicon Graphics Inc, who asked him to come out to interview to their Californian base in Mountain View. The interview took place in the same building that years later he'd be asked back to lecture in for a company now residing at those offices. A company called Google.

Kaushik got the job and started telling them his thoughts about the web:

> The reason I got invited to come to California is because I was bubbling with enthusiasm about my learnings of the early internet and database design, and the fact that my background was in engineering and I was an MBA. I told them about this idea that I had that we could make data more accessible, and the fact that you could do some things with databases, and the web. So my first job was to work in marketing, and help marketers make better decisions using data.

What Kaushik and his team were able to do was build a reporting interface on the web that synchronized with the company database in an intuitive fashion, creating a simple, low-cost way of accessing data at the click of a mouse. Up until that point, the company had been shelling out money on the larger third-party workhorse, Business Objects. Kaushik claims that, within two weeks of his new application going live, 90 per cent of people at Silicon Graphics stopped using the paid service. It taught him the important lesson that powerful programs are not always the answer. What was important, he felt, was that companies need to figure out what the key bits of information they need are and make accessibility as simple as possible to help organizations be more data driven.

Like so many at that time, Kaushik was a victim of the tech bubble bursting. He was laid off in 2001 and got a new role at DirectTV in their broadband division. It was here that he got his first glimpse of web analytics software and, one more redundancy later, he found himself at Intuit Inc as director of research and analytics for the web. He was no pro back then, but he got the role because he was good at strategy, reporting and business. One of his first actions was to build a new data warehouse and hook it up to Microsoft Excel. When the then CEO saw a report output that showed exactly how much the company was making on the internet, he authorized the hiring of a VP for the web then and there. Kaushik was already making positive waves.

It was while at Intuit that Kaushik started attending conferences where he could learn more about the industry, pick up tips and mingle with suppliers. One of the first events he attended was the eMetrics Marketing Optimization Summit in 2003, produced by Jim Sterne, who has written about meeting Kaushik during lunch at that conference:

> After 30 minutes of conversation, I asked him if he would impart his wisdom, vision and passion via PowerPoint at the next eMetrics Summit. He appeared shocked. He was nervous. He was doubtful. He suggested that he was too new at this subject and too novice an employee to share the stage with the experienced, knowledgeable speakers he had been learning from for the previous three days. I assured him he was wrong. He has presented at almost every eMetrics Marketing Optimization Summit since, and always to rave reviews.

By 2006, he had started speaking at more conferences and making even more of an impact, as Andy Beal, co-author of *Radically Transparent: Monitoring and managing reputations online*, remembers after one such speech:

> The clichés 'on the edge of my seat' and 'jaw-dropping' could not have applied more, the first time I heard Avinash give a presentation on the power of web analytics. He was informative, engaging, entertaining, and just raw enough to keep you hanging on his every word.
>
> I met with him afterwards and practically begged him to start blogging. He was genuinely humble and almost bashful towards my suggestion, insisting no one would want to read anything he wrote. I was not deterred! Here was a man that single-handedly made the world of web analytics interesting, understandable, and fun. Analytics, fun?! I kept pushing him and I'm glad I did, because not long after, he dipped his toe in the world of blogging and that world has never been the same again!

Encouraged by Beal and web strategist Jeremiah Owyang, Kaushik started reading other people's blogs for a period of three months, analysing what resonated with him, who added value, and how language could be used to effect change in the reader's approach:

> I decided I'm not going to write multiple posts a day, I'm not even going to write every day. My purpose in life would be to write a blog post that would meet three requirements that I formed for myself. It would be something incredible, relevant and of value. I formed this mantra, and then I practised blogging for a month and a half where only my wife and my Intuit employees read the blog, because I wanted to see that I could actually produce content that was incredible, relevant and of value. And it turns out I did, and I started a blog, and I was amazed that I got my first two comments.

Those two comments were from Owyang and Beal. But that was in 2006. Six years and over 250 posts later, the number of comments from his army of fans has risen to over 11,000. That's the sort of engagement that tech bloggers and mainstream journalists can only dream of. Kaushik's mind-boggling blog statistics amaze even further when he reveals he's written half a million words in those two 250+ posts, and comments have accounted for over a million words in response.

An hour a day

Six months after his blog-writing debut, Kaushik was approached by the business publisher Wiley who suggested he turn the blog into a book. His first reaction was, 'Oh my god, are you kidding me? Why would people pay for something that was free?'

After some persistence by Wiley, Kaushik finally agreed to write the best-seller: *Web Analytics: An hour a day*. But it wasn't an easy ride:

> It was a very painful process. It took almost five, six months to write the book while I was blogging. And I started speaking a little bit more, and I had a full-time job. It was crazy. I used to come to work every Saturday in the morning at 7, and I would write flat out until 7 at night; Saturday and Sunday. About 70 per cent of the content of the book was new, just because I had never had time to write it. And the book ended up being an astonishing success; far more than I had imagined.

Kaushik would have had to have had a pretty vivid imagination if he guessed his first book would sell over 50,000 copies in English alone, but it did. He'd have to be bordering on certifiable if he ever thought the follow-up, *Web Analytics 2.0* published in 2009, would sell over 40,000 copies, but it did. (Both books were translated into six languages, but there are no sales data on them at the time of writing.)

At around the time of the first book, Kaushik was speaking on stage at a conference in Arizona and he said something 'snarky' about Google. He remembers one man in particular challenging him on the Google comments with probing questions after he'd finished his talk, but Kaushik stood his ground and defended his position. The man turned out to be Brett Crosby whose company, Urchin Software, had been acquired by Google in 2005 and turned into Google Analytics.

Stupid passion thing

A couple of months later, Kaushik was invited to speak to an assembled throng of coders and product managers at Google's Mountain View offices – the same offices in which Kaushik had sat 10 years earlier for his first post-MBA job at Silicon Graphics.

The talk obviously went well because Kaushik recalls:

> At the end of the keynote, two people from Google's management team came and said to me, 'We want you to work here.' And I thought, 'What? Like how? Where is this coming from?' And my first question to them was, 'What would I do here?' And they said, 'We don't know.' They said, 'You just come and work here, and we'll figure it out.' And I said, 'Oh you're kidding me.'

They weren't, so Crosby persisted and Kaushik was offered a consulting role with as many hours as he could spare devoted to Google. He'd be able to carry on writing, speaking and helping add value to other companies, but Google always let him know they had plenty of work for him if he wanted it. Having just been offered a permanent job at Yahoo!, he was caught between the stability of a role with health insurance and benefits, and the uncertain life of the contractor. Kaushik's wife knew what she'd prefer, but knew her husband had a hankering to at least try the professional balancing act and follow his instincts. He told her, 'I want to go and do my stupid passion thing. I don't know what it is, I don't know where it's going, but I'm passionate about this stuff.' She told him, 'Okay, I'll give you a year to go and do your stupid passion thing!'

Needing no more invitation, Kaushik dived in just before Google Analytics was released in its second iteration. With a raft of experience in business intelligence and a user of many tools himself, he was tasked with using that knowledge to help make the tool better. He was able in the first year alone to be responsible for adding features like Advanced Segmentation, Custom Reports and Internal Site Search analysis, which helped the product become more well rounded and competitive. Having had such impact and influence in such a short space of time meant he got pulled into more teams working on other analytics products, helping define strategies and roadmaps.

Able to keep writing and wowing audiences on the speaker circuit, Kaushik's considered showmanship started to come to the attention of senior Google executives and he was asked to start spending time with some of their top clients and help them think differently. He explains:

> For every presentation I would spend time immersing myself in the company, their competitors, and the industry ecosystem and form my own point of view about the savviness of the company's current digital efforts, places where they left opportunity (and money) on the table and the imminent challenges and disruptions they face. I would merge all that with my own digital experience to create a presentation that would lay out the bare truth, challenge the company leadership, present specific solutions and the amazing glory that awaited them – should they choose to take it. Always a tough message, but my hope was to always inspire and drive fundamental change.

As he's spent more time with these big brands and companies, he's come to realize that it's not a lack of data analysis that's the biggest problem they face within the new opportunities the internet provides. It's much more that senior leaders simply have not grasped just how big the opportunities are. As Kaushik puts it, 'there is a lack of imagination when it comes to doing glorious things. We need to truly embrace digital in creative ways and embrace digital's new rules.'

Now five years into his role at Google, Kaushik's remit spans online advertising, social media and mobile marketing and his mission is to 'drive magnificent change'.

Anyone who reads one of Avinash Kaushik's books and blog posts, or sees him present in person, will not help but feel some magnificent change within themselves. His passionate, infectious and inspirational delivery of good, clean, common sense and valuable insight has helped thousands of marketers around the world be much better at what they do.

The fact that he's also donated every cent from the proceeds of his books – $240,000 so far – to charity is testimony to where his interests are genuinely centred.

Sound bytes

- A lack of data-driven marketing understanding and expertise is leaving businesses in the 20th century when it comes to realizing the opportunities the web provides.
- Be passionate about what you do. Leave no rock unturned when looking for the numbers that could turn your business positively. Recruit other like minds to your cause and encourage culture change.
- Try to give a little back. If you're doing well from your 'passion thing', then there's room for some mini-philanthropy.

Further reading

http://www.Kaushik.net

Kaushik, A (2007) *Web Analytics: An hour a day*, Wiley, Hoboken, NJ

Kaushik, A (2009) *Web Analytics 2.0: The art of online accountability and science of customer centricity*, Wiley, Hoboken, NJ

Carolyn Everson

MTV Networks and Facebook

Digital discipline

Inspirational multifaceted builder and leader of digital businesses since 1996. Now head of Global Marketing Solutions at Facebook (a company she suggested MTV Networks buy in 2005), she's urging advertisers and agencies to put 'social' at the heart of more integrated marketing plans.

12

Ninety-nine per cent to go

When the CEO of a company that's asked you to join their ranks tells you at the interview that they're only 1 per cent finished with what they've set out to achieve, many a prospective employee might have balked at the challenge. But when Facebook co-founder Mark Zuckerberg uttered those words to Carolyn Everson, she immediately felt at home. This was not just with Zuckerberg's vision of a legacy of connections that aims to span generations, but with the notion that she had an opportunity to build; build on her experience, build great products, build a great team and help nurture and build individuals in the company's collective mission to 'Give people the power to share and make the world more open and connected.'

As vice president of Global Marketing Solutions at Facebook, Everson's role is to build relationships with all the top companies around the world, helping them understand how to use Facebook to help build their businesses, and evangelize the notion that, with the ubiquitous nature of social media and the increasing consumer footfall across social platforms and enabled devices, brands have to rethink how they approach their marketing efforts by making their campaigns 'social by design'.

A liberal arts life

Turn the clock back 20 years, while Zuckerberg was about to enter first grade at elementary school, Everson was dead set on a degree in the arts from Villanova University which she hoped would propel her into a career as a TV news anchorwoman. Growing up in Long Island, New York, Everson was raised by her mother who was a public school teacher and her father who worked in the aerospace industry. The importance of education and continuous learning had been evident throughout her childhood, as had been the occasional reality check. After an internship at the American Broadcasting Company (ABC) in Philadelphia, one such reality check kicked in and she realized the precariousness of her career choice, deciding instead to look towards banking or law.

When companies came to the university scouting for talent, it was her elder brother who suggested she meet some of the business consulting firms when they arrived on campus. Taking his advice, she found herself on a gruelling round of 14 interviews for a role on the strategy division of Andersen Consulting. She got the job alongside 14 others. The only woman, she was also the only successful applicant not from their target schools of Yale or the University of Pennsylvania.

A baptism of fire: the 23-year-old didn't really know anything about business strategy but doesn't regret that leap of faith because it gave her invaluable experience:

> I spent two and a half years there really actually just immersing myself, and understanding how businesses approach problems, and more importantly,

how you can distil your recommendations. I think consulting gives people really great training and background to assess any difficult situation in a company. I was also allowed to do things at the age of 23 years old that I don't think I would have been ever able to do had I joined a regular company at that time, because in consulting you just get put into client situations and you need to adapt.

One of her clients at Andersen was the pharmaceutical joint venture Astra Merck. To educate herself on strategic alliances, Everson picked out a book from the library by Robert Porter Lynch, whom she then called up in Rhode Island and brazenly asked him to be her mentor for two years while she navigated the vagaries of getting two companies to work together towards a common set of goals and processes. With the willing author helping with her many questions, she set out to further expand her understanding of the field by attending a five-day course at The Wharton School, part of the University of Pennsylvania.

Celebration

It was during those five days that the inquisitive, engaging and responsive Everson was spotted by Charles Adams, a vice president from the Walt Disney Company, who'd been impressed by her energy and enthusiasm while he'd been attending the class. Adams had been so enthralled by Everson's potential that he asked if she'd be interested in moving to Orlando to work for them. She remembers 'I said, "Absolutely!" And that really was the turning point because from that point forward, I never deviated from being with big brands, and really being on the marketing and business development side of the professional world.'

Everson's first role at her first real big brand was to help Adams with the establishment of the master-planned Florida community that was soon to be named '*Celebration*'. Her team was tasked with building the 'cornerstones of Celebration' around five main pillars: health, education, architecture, community/non-profit and technology. Not surprisingly, given where she is now, it was the technology aspect of the project, way back in 1996, that Everson found the most intriguing. The world wide web was in its infancy and she had the opportunity to build, from the ground up, the first-ever town that was completely wired and connection-enabled for the new communication age. Always ahead of the curve, her team also worked on the development of a plan to use Disney characters digitally to help engage and communicate with children about healthy eating. Childhood obesity was starting to become a real problem in the 1990s, and the idea was to use the power of Disney to remind kids to be healthier by using the internet in a new and interactive way. But alas, the Disney brand stewards got cold feet about playing in the health space and scuppered the idea, not least because, as Everson says, 'I don't think that technology in terms of actually really using the web as a key driver was on everyone's mind back in 1996; I think it was just really early.'

It was also too early for Everson to think she had all the necessary education to achieve her career aspirations, so, remembering the emphasis on learning she was brought up with, she took herself off to Harvard Business School in August 1997.

Darkest days

This was happening at a time when would-be entrepreneurs were salivating at the thought of what they could do with the web and were constantly devising new business ideas and models. Everson describes Harvard as a 'frenzy' of activity and says all she wanted to do was start her own business. Taking every class she could to help her on her entrepreneurial dream, she remembered research she'd done at Disney on the pet industry and worked on a business plan around people and their animals. Buoyed by a positive reception to her ideas from her professors, she got on a plane, flew over to California and started to network with venture capitalists in Silicon Valley. Tracking down Greg McLemore, the owner of the domain name Pets.com, she discovered that he was unwilling to sell it outright but suggested they partner. Although the pair managed to raise $5m in funding from Hummer Winblad by the time Everson was in her second year, a clash of personalities with the CEO brought in to run the company meant that her role in the business was short-lived. Disagreements over the vision for the venture and just how engaged you could be with customers on the web made Everson's position untenable. They parted ways two weeks before she graduated from business school.

Devastated by what Everson describes as 'some of the darkest days of my career', she left Harvard without a job and, having turned down roles with Goldman Sachs and Bain because she'd thought she'd be in California helping run Pets.com, she took on consulting and investment work for start-ups before she was offered a role at Zagat Survey, the restaurant guide, while she was working for angel investor Chris Burch:

> It was to help them build their digital and mobile business. At first I turned it down and then I had this moment that I'll never forget where I was literally walking in the city and I saw the little vignette guide stickers on a number of different restaurants, and I said to myself 'What am I doing?' I am on the investment side, and I have never had the opportunity to go build something.

So she asked if they'd reconsider and take her on.

They did, and she spent two years building a team and a robust business plan around the company's digital future so that they could use it to raise money, which they successfully managed to do to the tune of $31m from General Atlantic and Kleiner Perkins.

With her career having crept into the 21st century, Everson was now hungry to build more businesses. After cutting her teeth with Zagat and creating an impressive track record, she set off for Primedia and set about reinvigorating the Modern Bride stable of titles. With people in New York and Denver, she saw this as an opportunity to build on her business development and team-building experience by actually running a business. Inheriting a portfolio that was burning a million dollars a month, she restructured the outfit and by the end of her first year was breaking even enough to attract an offer to buy from Condé Nast.

Everson describes the internet landscape back then as a 'wild, wild west where agencies were making big money building websites'. Large media companies knew they had to get into the digital space and were 'spending crazy amounts of money on technology'. She was persuaded not to go to Condé Nast but help Primedia reign in their digital costs and start building ad revenue. Given *Seventeen.com*, *Gurl* and *TeenMag* to look after, her team, re-badged Primedia Team Digital Group, helped those assets worth $4m in digital revenue become profitable and they were in turn sold to Hurst Magazines.

Turning to TV

Everson soon harnessed a reputation for having a Midas touch, and was persuaded to lead all the classified and direct response advertising at the company, along with the digital side of 130 of their consumer titles. But after three years as a 'fixer upper' getting businesses healthy, she had a hankering to go even bigger and work for a brand she was passionate about.

TV was one area of media Everson knew nothing about. So when she decided to look outside Primedia, a business school classmate, Matt Spielman, suggested she look at MTV Networks. When she got the call from MTV to help run their college channel, MTVU.com, the chance to expand her repertoire of knowledge was just far too compelling an offer and she remembers it wasn't just about the medium:

> It was much more than just selling TV. It was really selling a college audience, and a whole experience which included MTVU.com, the actual TV channel, and then a lot of 'on the ground' events. MTVU was meant to be the incubator for how the business could work differently at overall MTV networks. It was a great experience and we tripled revenue in the first year after building the team.

Everson also recommended that MTV owners Viacom buy Facebook in 2005, after her stepson, who was attending Wake Forest at the time, suggested she take a look at the social networking site because it was 'taking off in the college scene', as she was so firmly ensconced in the college crowd. It's an ironic twist not lost on Everson that, although the deal fell through, she would ultimately end up working at the Menlo Park-based company: 'It's just fascinating how these things come full circle.'

MTV Network's CEO, Judy McGrath, had been impressed with her charge:

> Carolyn made an immediate positive impact at MTV Networks, with passion and fearless drive, always with an eye towards the future. She is restless in the best possible way, truly built for this era in media. MTVU was an emerging brand, one that flourished on her watch, tripling revenue and as importantly,

> relevance. As Carolyn stepped into the COO role across one of the leading sales teams in the industry, she brought that unique spirit and forward strategy to all the brands.

After six and a half years at MTV Networks, Everson had taken on more and more responsibility. Although she had no intention of leaving, because she loved the brands so much, her last role would be COO for their domestic advertising business across all their brands, including Nickelodeon, SPIKE, Comedy Central and MTV. Even though this included digital responsibility, Everson felt that the pace of her learning was slowing down; she knew that, ultimately, a pure-play digital company was where she wanted to be:

> It's hard for any big TV content company to think digital is at its centre, and yet I knew in my heart of hearts, based on talking to clients and based on seeing consumer trends, that it was great for me to learn all these other mediums, but I probably belonged back in a company with digital at the core. So what tipped me in terms of leaving MTV Networks, when Microsoft approached me, was going back to digital and having a global role, because I also knew the trends were really moving in the direction of every client wanting to have a global conversation. It wasn't satisfactory for me to sit with the CMO and only be able to talk about the US business.

From Microsoft to Facebook

Everson's time as CVP of Global Ads Sales and Strategy at Microsoft Advertising was short. It was an 'amazing' opportunity and allowed her to put her feet 'squarely back into the digital arena' and she had no intention to leave. She was bullish about Microsoft's assets across multiple platforms and screens like MSN, Bing, Xbox and Windows Phone and felt that her new company was in 'a really great position to be much more of a solutions provider to advertising clients than a lot of other competitors'. She travelled the world meeting the sales teams and laying out her vision of how they would compete, she gave knock-out performances on stage at events like Advertising Week in New York and Spikes Asia Advertising Festival in Singapore, and she helped inspire and invigorate the business through her infectious confidence and optimism.

But a few months after she joined Microsoft in June 2010, she got a call from someone representing Facebook COO, Sheryl Sandberg. The caller said that Sandberg wanted to talk to her about running their Global Sales and Marketing Solutions organization as the incumbent chief, Mike Murphy, was leaving to take some time off. Everson was torn. She loved the Facebook brand, she loved what they were doing, she'd been a fan since practically the beginning, but, in her words:

> It was horrible timing because how could I possibly leave Microsoft? But I sat with Sheryl and I sat with Mark Zuckerberg, and I realized that this is where I belonged. It was a really difficult decision to come to because I knew I was going to hurt a lot of people in the process, and disappoint my Microsoft team

members. That was really crushing. And yet, I also knew that at the end of the day, people would want to me to be happy and support me in the long run. It was probably the most difficult decision of my career, and yet it also was the easiest decision because I knew it was the right thing for me to do. And once I made it, I have not looked back on that decision. I've certainly looked back on how I could have done things differently in terms of who and when I communicated what was going on to. But I feel like it was the right decision for me because I really believe in Facebook's mission. I fit culturally and I have an opportunity to build. I don't consider it a job; I consider it a passion and an opportunity to change the world.

And build she needs to do. With Facebook hurtling towards a $100 billion IPO (Initial Public Offering) at the time of writing, the advertising industry's eyes are keenly focusing in on Everson and her team's work, as they court advertisers around the world who are keen to harness the power of the network effect and capitalize on the social site's massive, multi-cultural reach.

Everson's different attitude and approach to partnering with advertisers has helped throughout her career, and it's helping her now:

I've built up enough credibility that clients know that I'm not there to just go sell them something. I joke around and say, 'Look, I've been in this business for 18, 19 years and I don't believe I ever really sold anything.' And yet people say, 'Well how is that possible? You lead sales organizations.' It was never about selling an impression or selling another ad unit, or getting another 100,000 or another 10 million whatever. It has always been what I can do to make my client's business better, and what can I do to make my client more successful in their own organization. That was the way I was taught when I got out of Villanova to be a business consultant. I didn't come out and start selling at age 23. I came out trying to solve business problems, and that's how I approach my job.

Creativity and new games

Her experience at Disney and with TV has certainly lent a hand, helping influence the creative community as they grapple with digital. Publishers need good content. If there's nothing to keep consumers engaged and coming back, it doesn't matter what you have from a distribution or advertising platform perspective; if you don't have good content, you don't have a product. She's always made a point to be as close to the creative process as possible and has sage advice for the future of the discipline:

On the creative side, their whole world has changed, and gone upside down, because their briefs used to start and end with a great 30-second spot or a great print ad. And now the job of the creative is actually to completely do two things. One, understand that they're probably going to relinquish a lot of control around the direction of the brand. They can certainly know what the brand essence is, and they can absolutely give guidance on how the brand should manifest themselves. But consumers believe they own the brand just as much as the company believes they own the brand; and so that's

> a dramatic change. And the second is regarding social, which is instead of thinking about a 30-second spot or a print ad as the start and end to a creative campaign, it's got to be an idea centred around people, what they care about and what they will share.

As a successful leader and builder of teams, Everson claims her mantra is all about empowerment and encouraging people to be their own brand. She looks for people that want to lead themselves, who are self-starters and to whom positive results are incredibly important. She tries to inspire others to inspire their teams, and to have an infectious confidence and passion invested in what they do. She looks for 'fire in the belly' and likes to ask if they're 'ready to play a new game'. Watching people 'soar' is most thrilling to her as she feels it incumbent on her as a leader to create the right environment for that to happen. And when it does, that's where she feels the most pride.

According to Facebook's COO, Sheryl Sandberg:

> Mark and I hired Carolyn to build our global business with the top marketers in the world. Her mission was to make Facebook's platform a critical part of our partners' businesses. Within a year, she had made great strides with Madison Avenue and our global marketing partners. Her team has helped brands realize that social advertising is not just an 'add on' – it is core to their business. She has a rare combination of strategic vision, execution abilities and most importantly, true leadership skills.

Reflecting on her career so far, Everson is not sure what she wants to be remembered for just yet because the Facebook journey is just 1 per cent finished. With mobile being the obvious and most pressing opportunity, coupled with the knowledge that the surface of the internet's possibilities has barely been scratched, the intellectual curiosity runs riot in the mind of the married working mother of twins from Long Island who says of what she's achieved in digital over the last two decades: 'I still feel the best is yet to come. I certainly hope that I've not yet had my proudest moment.'

Sound bytes

- Always look to extend your knowledge, absorb new challenges as an educational opportunity, look for gaps in your experience and be prepared to put yourself out to fill them.
- As a leader, empower your teams to inspire others, encourage self-critical thinking, be entrepreneurial and be ready 'to play a new game'.
- Build up your own 'brand' and take on mentors who'll be your brand's 'board of directors'.

Further reading

http://www.Facebook.com/Carolyn.Everson
http://Facebook-Studio.com

Malcolm Poynton

Dove Campaign for Real Beauty

Digital discipline

Executive creative director who produced the first full web-serviced advertising campaign. Dove's *Campaign for Real Beauty* was more of a manifesto than a typical advertising campaign. It was the first multimedia campaign to drive participants to its own fully fledged online community. The campaign featured real women rather than models and reached over 200 million people worldwide, with over 26 million people engaging with the campaign online.

Proving Real Beauty

> *Have you told your wife, daughter, mother, sister that she's beautiful? If not, do it! Do it now! Send her this story and use it as an opportunity to tell her she is beautiful. Pass it on. Our next generation needs to hear it too, along with that old phrase my mother has always used, 'It's on the inside that counts!'*
>
> (Jennifer King in *Ruggedexcellentliving.com*, 2004)

The project's underlying idea was that real beauty resides in each person. To support this, a community was developed to make women feel better about their own beauty. Dove's campaign voiced a different interpretation of beauty worldwide, in a way that became a digital advertising phenomenon. The campaign took cosmetics advertising to the next level and introduced new technologies to advertising as the campaign was rolled out around the world.

A driving force behind the original campaign was Malcolm Poynton, then executive creative director at Ogilvy & Mather London. Poynton – a New Zealander resident in the UK, had been a creative advertiser at the agency Saatchi and Saatchi, but after moving to O&M, Poynton's experiences of digital and his empathy for Dove's mission helped the campaign fulfil its ambition.

The low-down

Poynton's approach was ideal for Dove in 2004. At that time, sales of the cosmetics and toiletries brand were in decline, largely due to having an unclear brand positioning. Their identity was lost in an already saturated market. Dove's parent company, Unilever, commissioned a study called 'The Real Truth About Beauty' to explore what beauty meant to women. It revealed that only 2 per cent of women considered themselves to be beautiful, while 50 per cent thought their weight was 'too high'. Unilever charged its PR firm Edelman and Dove's advertising agency O&M with moving the spotlight off the product and onto women – the majority of consumers, to redress the issue of beauty. The aim was to make all women feel beautiful, regardless of their age, size or features.

Thinking in the new digital way

The *Campaign for Real Beauty* was the culmination of eight months' work by Edelman and O&M in 2004, and was very much a team effort. As the campaign's creative director, Poynton remembers: 'There are many people, client and agency side involved, there is certainly no one creator of it.' When the campaign first launched it targeted a broad demographic of women spanning all ages in the UK. The initial objective was to provoke women to check out the 'campaign' online, then join the crusade to reclaim 'beauty' from the popular stereotypes. Once online, women could interact with and participate in a span of digital activity, from blogs to questionnaires, which served two purposes: IT helped women feel better about their own beauty by reading reassuring content, then participating with like-minded people in what became an issue-centred community. For Dove, it created an environment where the brand could be seen to 'house' the cause – much in the way that product placement works. By becoming synonymous with the issue, the brand could occupy the moral high ground of being a champion of women. The plan was so successful in the UK that it extended to the United States within a year, before being rolled out globally between 2005 and 2007.

The initial UK campaign incorporated what were then new ways of digital thinking. Poynton remembers that 'it was probably the first advertising campaign we'd ever seen where the URL was an end line – it was *campaignforrealbeauty.com*. That was intentional, to drive the conversation online, which was where everyone was going.' So the project's *Campaign for Real Beauty* line was not just a call to action; it was the 'advertising strapline, the URL... and it was the Big Ideal'.

Poynton had a particular personal empathy with the issue at the time. He had a 5-year-old daughter who was factored into the thinking of Dove's target audience: 'she didn't know the world pre-internet or pre-Google – or even pre-smartphone. I realized there's such a huge new opportunity out there.'

According to Poynton, the spirit of the Dove campaign centred on an understanding that, with the internet, advertising was never going to be the same again. Dove's female audience – and young girls in particular – were spending more time online, which Poynton saw as an opportunity for the brand to forge a connection in a different way: 'As clichéd as it sounds, a paradigm shift was going on. Consumers were just not in the broadcast space any more. So that really drove me towards understanding that digital's got to be at the heart of everything that's going on.'

Voicing the issue

To make the campaign relevant amid the burning issues of the day (which in 2004 included the Indian Ocean earthquake and tsunami), the agency needed to publicize its cause, then stir a debate – similar to the way political campaigns operate. A billboard campaign initially agitated discussion. It featured women who had auditioned specifically for the project, who were all comfortable in making a virtue of what others may have considered a stigma – large or flat-chested, wrinkled or freckled. One poster featured a curvy woman alongside the headline '*fat? fit?*'. The copy beneath ran, '*Does true beauty only squeeze into a size 8? Join the beauty debate*'. The campaign's URL was prominently displayed in the ad, alongside Dove's brand mark.

Poynton thinks that the provocative positioning drew on issues that were prevalent in the public's consciousness at the time. 'You had all sorts of issues around anorexia going on, issues around responsibility that the major fashion brands had and, of course, the glossy magazines. Dove were a brand that had a very small budget compared to the genuinely big beauty brands. They weren't actually defined as a beauty brand in the first place, so with a very meagre budget there had to be some kind of sense of what could be achieved. The ideal was to actually help especially younger women, at that stage, understand that beauty was about themselves more than about the images which are an artifice in the first place.'

The campaign's strategy was to challenge the archetypal images put out by the fashion and cosmetics industries, and make new ideals of beauty attainable by women, based on their own inherent qualities rather than an unachievable ideal. To give weight to the campaign, expert support was drafted in. A psychologist was enlisted by Dove and spoke on their behalf at forums to explain why women were uneasy about fashion models in beauty advertising, while trained online advisers advised and blogged on issues related to 'inner beauty' through the *campaignforrealbeauty.com* site. As Poynton remembers, 'Blogs were exploding left, right and centre, so it was just at the right time and the right moment.'

Dove's site soon became a popular forum for women to debate issues such as over-thin models in fashion, and so created discussion around the brand's main cause. This helped to reinforce the campaign's emotive commercial pull – that buying the product is effectively casting a vote 'for real beauty'. 'The ideal if you like was one of understanding that beauty is from within, not this artificial image on the outside.'

Making beauty relevant

According to Poynton, 'We really wanted to resonate more deeply with people and prick that kind of conscience in society over what good size zero has done. Our objective was to broaden the stereotype of beauty and we figured even if we only managed to broaden it by 1 or 2 per cent, you've still broadened it enough to make a difference. In making a difference you would need to fuel a conversation around this.'

To drive awareness, *The Times* in the UK was given an exclusive of Dove's approach and interviewed women that had featured in the campaign. Behind-the-scenes footage of the auditions and photo shoots was made available to television networks. The London-based newspaper *The Evening Standard* covered the story by questioning the idea of female celebrity role models and ideal body forms, while Dove's cause was also articulated through press editorials and daytime television.

Most significantly, the campaign debate took place in real time online, with people who decided to become active participants: 'you're not going to drive that debate or that conversation by obviously just running some 30-second spots – hence the URL to actually create the debate online. Remember this was also at a time where we just seeing the very, very beginnings of social networking coming to the fray.'

When the campaign was launched in North America – through magazine and print ads, billboards and television spots in 2005, it featured six women who became the spokespeople for the campaign on news channel *CNN* and chat shows including *The Today Show* and *Oprah*. Similar to the UK campaign's call-to-action, the women in Dove's campaign stimulated debate and encouraged viewers to participate online. This became the format for the campaign's 'glocal' roll-out: the strategy was global, but the content was local – from the selection of everyday women as models to the website discussions, which were local to each region. Online activities responded more to national nuances of beauty, such as self-esteem in North America and body shape in central Europe.

By 2007 Unilever's PR firm, Edelman, were able to claim that Dove had become the most talked about campaign in the world. It certainly succeeded in pushing viewers of the advertising online, and as the take-up grew so too did the range of online content.

O&M in Toronto added to the campaign with a 75-second film called *Evolution*, which showed the transformation of one ordinary-looking woman into an idealized model, captured through time-lapse video. The film made its point by exposing the processes behind constructions of beauty while focusing on the image of beauty. Twenty seconds of the film illustrated how lighting, hair treatment and a full make-over could radically alter an appearance, after which the face was digitally manipulated – neck extended and thinner, lips and eyes made larger, face size reduced – to re-create the rather familiar press image of beauty. The film's final frame reads, *No wonder our perception of beauty is distorted.* With over 14.5 million video views on YouTube alone, the film certainly had a wider reach than the commercials would have achieved in most countries. Poynton thought the video took the project to the next level: 'Our office in Toronto understood clearly what's meant by "the ideal" and picked up the baton. They carried it further and we got something that was hugely viral. It fuelled its own PR recognition in that space and I think what the industry – and I – took from it was that people are willing to engage (online), with a brand around a conversation. That helps to make sense of a (cause-related) brand online.'

Unlike a typical campaign, the nature of engaging customers online was very different. For instance, the length of time people spent on the *campaignforrealbeauty.com* site ranged from 2 to 30 minutes – far longer than a conventional advertisement.

Another significant difference was in the style of engagement. Rather than rolling out staged information through a pre-prepared campaign timeline, visitors to the site read the information in their own way, in their own order and with their own habits of engagement.

Digital campaigns rarely have linear narratives

Traditional advertising and marketing campaigns have a very linear narrative, but the Dove campaign worked differently. The campaign really came to life once it was up and running. O&M were able to keep adding content to it online, in light of visitors' comments and their tracked activity on the campaign's site.

Those who clicked into the campaign online were able to navigate content in a myriad of ways – through video content, through online forums or through the more scientific evidence posted by the specialists hired in to inform the discussions as they unfolded. There was constant feedback and constant input, so the project was replenished in two directions: firstly by O&M's agencies around the world adding to their own *campaignforrealbeauty* sites, and by participants who chose to be advocates on the issue of real beauty, whether inspired by the cause or simply to feel beautiful within themselves (Springer, 2006). Whatever their motivation, having online participants populating the site and sharing information reinforced Dove's standing, because it could associate with the issue in some depth.

The strategy certainly worked for this type of cause-related campaign. Creating channels for user-generated content can backfire when used in brand advertising because there is less scope to control the nature of new content. In 2010, for instance, Amazon was criticized for not pulling book reviews posted by participants who clearly hadn't read the book in question. A negative review of a book by Michael Lewis appeared even before the book was made available. It transpired that the negative reviews were retaliation aimed at the book's publisher because the book wasn't going to be available in digital format. The nature of Dove's cause, the sensitive issue of real beauty, seemed well positioned to avoid negative user-generated content. Only those likely to favour the campaign's supposition were likely to actively engage.

Film as multimedia content, not commercials

The content in film shot for online use operates in a different way from television commercials. As Poynton notes, 'One of the biggest pitfalls is that an advertising agency will write a 30-second spot, with a period or a full point at the end. Well, the job is done because it was that hermetically sealed 30-second story that had to be told: but that isn't the way of the world. As we are involved in that space we always write spots that have a comma at the end. This is a subtle but profound difference, because it continues online or in the social space someplace else. This is a fundamental change, but it's a very hard one for partners to appreciate because, traditionally, many are of the mentality that you write the story and tell the story in 30 seconds. It's as much a challenge for some clients as it is for other agencies.'

A second key difference is that content designed for multimedia use can engage in spaces where people can be more active in their responses. As Poynton observed, 'When people are passionate about something you can engage them. [Unlike a commercial] you don't need to *tell* that that you are passionate about it: you can be passionate about it if you *show* them. Then they will come and participate. The return on investment is way more significant than it can ever be in terms of a traditional advertising model. It's far more sustainable, so it carries on for a longer time.'

What was new?

From the creative director's perspective, what was groundbreaking in the campaign's approach? 'Things obviously have changed since the inception of that campaign – probably in no small part because of the campaign. I don't think we (previously) used to *involve* people. We just had outward communication *at* people. Now you have the means to involve people and I think that's what the call of the internet or, broadly speaking, the digital revolution has brought, when you look at understanding how even things like Twitter are used now.'

Poynton is impressed that, years later, the Dove project is still a point of reference when it comes to showing how campaign strategies can become an ideological cause. For advertisers, the campaign has come to illustrate how online spaces can give campaigns depth, by using digital formats in a joined-up way. 'It still resonates and it is still referenced. To have that still reverberating and, I guess, kinda impacting people's psyche [as to] what makes beauty. That's a pretty decent thing, I would say. But it wouldn't come from the [traditional] veneer of advertising. It had to be deeper, hence the reason that we referenced it as having an *ideal* behind it.'

Advertising layers

The Campaign for Real Beauty has often been a topic of scholarly analysis, though rarely have its key innovators such as Poynton been part of the debate. The campaign's agenda has often been misrepresented as a form of corporate social responsibility – this was not Unilever's intention. Its strategy has also been derided for still making women buy into the need to improve themselves because it's ultimately about promoting Dove skin cream: as the logic goes, you can be curvaceous as long as your skin is firm. However, while the campaign advertised beauty products, it moved into territory where it brought a community of people together for whom the issue was important. Now reincarnated as the *Dove Self-Esteem Fund*, Dove continues to de-stigmatize fashion ideals and champion more accessible notions of beauty. Dove's mission has proved to be very long term.

A new type of agency

For Poynton, being involved in an unravelling project over time online gave him insights into how to service campaigns. At Sapient Nitro, where he is European chief creative officer, Poynton has assembled the necessary expertise to work on real-time brand accounts. For him, a campaign '... is not the purview of a small group of geniuses that lock themselves up in an ivory tower and come out with a proclamation about the next big thing. Every single person at our desks comes from a different orientation. You have ethnographers, business strategists, enterprise technologists, people who build big bank trade systems and people who are creative technologists. My job is to harness that capability to drive our creative potential. Having a creative officer across the brand and interactive platforms allows us to create an environment where the tech teams are as much a part of the creative as writers, art directors and designers.'

Flexibility is crucial in allowing a campaign to grow organically, as Poynton explains:

> We have director-level leads who have an ongoing relationship with clients. But they [can] burst out in a different direction because the campaign may go down a social path, a mobile path, a broadcast path, or all of those at once. Teams shape-shift accordingly but they always come back to the fact that you need director-level focus with the 'idea engineering' team alongside the business folks throughout a brand's lifecycle.

Nuggets of advice: the long view

Where most of the pioneers have had one big moment, Poynton has remained at the forefront of creative digital advertising for over 15 years. His advice is therefore informed by an ever-changing 'long view': 'Every time I talk about this sort of thing, the point of view moves on further and further, and that's kinda what fuels the dynamism. It's kind of like "how far dare you go?" We just seem to have this insatiable curiosity for "what next?"' So, in 50 years' time, how will we see this era of advertising? 'We're definitely going to look back and say we were scratching the surface. I mean the fact that kids don't recognize a screen unless you "gesture navigate" tells you there's a whole other world around the corner.'

'So, from our point of view, there has never been a more exciting time. I certainly haven't seen one. At the end of the day it's about people and that's the thing, the excitement is you can connect brands to people in much better and more interesting ways.'

Sound bytes

- Digital content gives advertising campaigns opportunities to engage with real depth.
- Digital film content won't be viewed in the same controlled linear way as commercials.
- To run a campaign in real time requires a wider range of expertise working collaboratively and flexibly.

Further reading and viewing

http://www.dove.co.uk/campaign-for-real-beauty.html
Dove Evolution video on YouTube: **http://www.youtube.com/watch?v=iYhCn0jf46U**

Qi Lu

Yahoo!, Microsoft and Bing

Digital discipline

Software engineer and internet visionary whose illustrious career has spanned time at IBM Research and Yahoo! before he joined Microsoft to build out their online services and take on Google with the 'decision engine' Bing.

14

Humble beginnings

For many young men growing up in the 1970s United States, becoming an astronaut might have been the dream profession. Not so in China.

The Cultural Revolution had meant jobs were assigned to post-education workers. What Qi Lu, the former Yahoo! leader of 3,000 software engineers, originally dreamt of doing was landing a prestigious role in shipbuilding. Being part of a company that built vessels that sailed the world was, in China, seen as a glorified occupation. But for the man now regarded as the inspiration behind the search engine Bing, the path to career fulfilment did not lie on the ocean waves.

Qi Lu (pronounced Chee Loo) weighed only 50 kg when he left school and to get into one of the two universities that trained China's engineers there was an entrance exam. Students had to be a certain height and weight even to qualify. After this he sought to study chemistry or physics, only to suffer another setback because his eyesight wasn't up to par, as he was near-sighted and colour blind. Lu's childhood hadn't exactly been easy: he was sent to live in a village with his grandfather because his parents couldn't afford to take care of him, although he chooses to remember his difficult upbringing as a character-forming lesson in perseverance.

All that was left for Lu to pursue with any appetite was mathematics or computer science. His parents asked around to find out what jobs the government might assign for those disciplines, and learnt that studying maths meant their son would probably end up teaching in a middle school. They felt, however, that computer science was the preferable option as it could lead to a placement at a radio factory. Not quite the kudos-grabbing destiny shipbuilding would have provided, but a progressive choice nonetheless.

Thankfully Lu never actually set foot in a radio factory. He gained a Master's degree from Fundan University in Shanghai and, after a chance meeting with visiting Carnegie Mellon Professor Edmund Clarke, was asked to apply to study for a PhD in the United States. Clarke had the $45 application fee waived when he learnt it would take more than four months of Lu's entire teaching salary to come up with the money, and watched his protégé easily earn his doctorate and slip into a role at IBM's Almaden Research Center in 1996.

While at Carnegie Mellon, Lu's dissertation concentrated on the task of building an international framework on top of mock computer operating systems, but like many like minds in the early 1990s, he was distracted by the groundswell of excitement in the software community about the huge potential that the early world wide web was demonstrating. Fascinated by James Gosling's work inventing the programming language Java, which was designed to seamlessly run programs across different computers and browsers, Lu knew that, although his studies concentrated on realizing the potential of computer hardware, his future lay in realizing the potential of the web.

Reaping results

Lu's introduction to search engines came at IBM when he worked with Udi Manber, who was consulting from the University of Arizona, on reimplementing a system called Harvester. Originally a project from the University of Colorado, the research was essentially about building a computational infrastructure to systematically crawl web content, do semantic analysis, index the data – broadly to really understand it. Although the search algorithm work was simply research, many of the players Lu worked with went on to roles at companies that have played a major role in making sense of the web, including Udi Manber who went on to be a vice president at Google in 2006.

Google first came to Lu's attention in 1998 when he presented a paper at the same session as Google founders Larry Page and Sergey Brin at the WWW7 conference in Brisbane, Australia. The company wouldn't be incorporated until later that year, so the project was simply known as 'BackRub'.

He remembers that the audience was amazed at how accurate the result was for one particular search query. Larry and Sergey used 'Bill Clinton' as an example as most other search engines just returned results with references to his alleged dalliance with Whitehouse intern Monica Lewinsky, but 'BackRub' returned the more accurate page on Whitehouse.gov. Lu says, 'It turns out that the technique is actually simple, and you just index more on the anchor text. But it was an important step forward.'

Not particularly astounded by what would become Google the following year, 'there was a lot going on in Silicon Valley at the time', Lu's next role would take him to the heart of one of the internet's biggest properties, Yahoo!

Advised by Chinese digital veteran Ki-Fu Lee to stick to the west coast of the United States, Lu had bagged a role building Yahoo!'s shopping channel. At the time, Yahoo! saw themselves as the 'welcome doormat of the world'. It was their mission to usher in their millions of users and show them 'how beautiful' the web was. Armed with all-important digital data from the hundreds of thousands of searches conducted each day, founders Jerry Yang and David Filo used consumer trends to start building out different services, and their 'guide to the world wide web', as it was originally called, started evolving into more of a portal which really needed a shopping engine, as e-commerce was really starting to take off.

Lu started on 17 August 1998 and, with the help of two part-time engineers, built the Yahoo! Shopping site in just four months. He remembers it as 'real intense work' which left him having to use a support cast on his wrist as the day and night programming sessions took their toll. Over a period of four years, invigorated by the challenge of building yet more products, Lu then addressed other areas like maps, real estate, Yellow Pages and several more projects all revolving around commerce. He says that consumer data was becoming more valuable in informing companies what direction to take next. Likening them to Google or Facebook today, where many users' online journeys begin, the luxury of being able to track massive usage patterns meant that the team had a fantastic opportunity to innovate: 'at the time we were moving very, very fast on building those experiences'.

In early 2002, Lu was asked to spearhead a project dedicated to search that would utilize his research from six years earlier at IBM and lay the groundwork for the launch of Bing seven years later.

Manual indexing

Lu gives credit to the founders of Google for taking the notion of crawling the web programmatically, indexing billions of web pages more relevantly and creating a very powerful company out of it. Although the idea wasn't exactly new – he claims he'd been working on a similar technology at IBM with Jon Kleinberg who'd just finished his PhD at MIT – Page and Brin foresaw the web getting vast quicker than other companies like Yahoo! who were employing human editors to hand-pick websites, write reviews and add them to search directories. Before Google started sending out their 'Googlebot' to comb through websites and rank different pages for different search queries, Yahoo! and start-ups like San Francisco-based Looksmart would employ hundreds of human internet surfers to go onto the web and categorize websites ontologically in a directory which would then be hooked onto other commerce websites. They would then seek to monetize them through banner advertising.

By the time Lu got involved back in the search engine business at Yahoo! in 2002, it had become apparent that having people manually creating indexes of websites was totally unscalable. The tech bubble had burst two years earlier and investors wanted to see more of a return on investment. The days of 'build it and they will come' were over. Yahoo! had started to make a 'tremendous profit' from search through a deal with pay per click (PPC) and search provider GoTo (re-branded as Overture in 2001). They were keen to expand the kind of service where advertisers paid to have their site appear at the top of search engine results for a relevant query, in return for a fee if the searcher clicked on it – and keep pace with Google who had launched their own advertising service, AdWords, and were growing very quickly.

Lu was selected along with Udi Menbar and David Comb to build their own search product. But a huge internal debate ensued towards the end of the six-month pilot with Overture as the new team tried to persuade Yahoo! CEO Terry Semel that they could build a better product. As Overture had already bought search engines Alta Vista and AlltheWeb, it was decided that acquisition, rather than internal development, should be the strategy. So in 2002 Yahoo! bought 'organic search' engine (one that provides search results that are not paid for) Inktomi and then Overture's PPC platform and other properties in 2003. Lu's role morphed into consolidating three consumer search engines and one monetization tool into what became known as Yahoo! Search.

Years later, Lu wonders if buying Overture was the best move. He holds the belief that internet companies who acquire others should be crystal clear on what and why they want to possess a particular technology. He admires Google's strategy of using the internal talent they had and getting the help of an outside consultant in the form of Hal Varian, now their chief economist. Although Overture had invented the advertising model based on an auction where advertisers outbid each other for the top spot in the search results, Google were able to build a system which created a more efficient marketplace for advertisers, generating more relevant search results for users and more revenue for Google. Lu says: 'In retrospect, when Yahoo! owned Overture, it took us a long term to realize our marketplace was designed very ineffectively. And by the time we got there, it was many years too late.'

Leading and making a difference

Over the course of 10 years, having risen through the ranks to manage over 3,000 engineers as executive vice president of the company's search and advertising division, Lu had built up an impressive, almost mythical, reputation for leading and inspiring the company. Colleagues note that his incredible work ethic and motivation to do bigger and better things on the web are significant. He finds this kind of talk humbling but remembers:

> At Yahoo! in its early days, I think there was one very good part about its culture, which was to do what's right, and take care of good people. So leading a large organization was never a goal of mine or something I set out to accomplish or explicitly pursue. The spirit was always to do what it takes to make the company more successful. And we always felt that we were designed for greatness and were producing something fundamental to society. Along the way, one way or another, that's kind of how I ended up doing it. But I always just made sure that I was doing my very best to help the company succeed. And if that means to lead the organization, I would do it. But my main goal is always work on things that can make a difference.

In 2008, however, Lu told Yahoo!'s then CEO, Jerry Yang, that 10 years was a long time and that he wanted to try something different. Focused on going back to China and working there, a chance meeting with Microsoft CEO Steve Ballmer ended with a job offer to run Microsoft's entire online services division which would include consumer channels like MSN and Live Search plus the entire advertising and publisher solutions arm of the company.

Seeing that the digital industry was really only just beginning, Lu felt that the Microsoft role was an opportunity he simply couldn't dismiss: 'The products, the business that we're building is, in my view, of profound importance to our society. And if you get to participate and be a part of building something truly enduring and thriving... I just couldn't pass it up.'

In July 2008, the online measurement company ComScore had global search engine usage at 80bn queries a month. Google accounted for an overwhelming 57 per cent of those searches, while Microsoft and its Live Search product languished with just 3 per cent share. The story was slightly different in the United States, however, with Microsoft at about 9 per cent but Google again dominating at 61 per cent. So why was search so important to Microsoft? With Google seemingly having an unassailable lead, and their company name entering the global vernacular as a verb, why not quit the battle, invest in a new emerging area and dominate that?

The reason is simple. Search is the most powerful mechanism there is for meeting consumers' needs, connecting them with the products, services or information they seek, and providing the all-important data on consumer trends and desires that help inform decisions on where to invest in online services next. Almost every purchase online starts with some kind of search, many offline purchases of cars or white goods start with research conducted online, and with Google revenues topping $5bn for the second quarter of 2008, there was obviously money to be made.

So, with the understanding that search was his number one priority, Lu and his leadership team set about defining their 'Mission Strategy Fundamentals', a document that set out a number of key pillars. Firstly, that their mission in life was to empower every human being on the planet towards knowledge, not just information. Secondly, that they would work towards understanding and anticipating user intent and be able to service their needs, their interests and their aspirations. Thirdly, he wanted his team to fully understand the digital world. With so many experiences becoming more and more digitized, Lu's goal was for his division to be governed by the knowledge that if they understood their consumer's world, they could help serve them by defining the future.

In short, the vision was to come up with a way to: 'Empower people with knowledge by computationally understanding user intent.'

Birth of Bing

Microsoft had already kicked off the planning of a radically new search experience a few months before Lu joined the company. But as Bing's search director and spokesperson Stefan Weitz remembers, the effect of Lu's entrance was instantly palpable:

> We were going to do something big. We were going to attempt to redefine search. We wanted to be *of* search and not just search. With Qi Lu coming on board, the immediate effect was apparent. He has a radical transparency in being very deliberate and precise in his language and thinking. There are not a lot of superfluous words when it comes to Qi. The clarity of thought, even back then when we were figuring this thing out, was pretty prophetic. There's a certain ability for him to set a bold, audacious goal without yelling about it and you feel as though he's thought it all through and has answers for any objections. It's been great to have someone at the helm that has a vision that has been durable and allowed us to pivot the product to maintain that core focus of reorganizing the web to accomplish tasks. It's an enormously complex job. What you see three years later is shockingly similar to what he initially put forth when he arrived.

Microsoft's new search engine Bing was launched officially on 28 May 2009 by Steve Ballmer at All Things Digital in California. On choosing the name, he told Walt Mossberg that they wanted something short, that could be used as a verb and 'that unambiguously said search'. There were many 'unmet needs' in the category and the name was an important step, but it was 'no substitute for innovation'.

Much thought had gone into how to define the Bing search experience and differentiate it from its main competitor. It was badged a 'decision engine'. The idea was to persuade the public that search was broken, that after 10 years or so of Google, users were still staring at 'ten blue links'. The PR claimed that 40 per cent of searches go unanswered, meaning that consumers were not finding what they wanted first time. Bing was going to help them make the decisions they'd come to a search engine to help address, not just throw back results that needed further filtering to actually accomplish a task.

In that first unveiling, Yusuf Mehdi, a senior vice president in Lu's division, showed the audience some of the features, which included category navigation that might include lyrics, videos and music results if you'd searched for a pop star, integrated expert and user product reviews if you were shopping for a particular product, and an in-built travel engine – Farecast – that provided flight and hotel prices, even indicating whether prices were likely to go up or down in the near future.

Mossberg asked Ballmer what made him think Bing would do the trick. The Microsoft CEO replied he didn't expect things to change overnight and that his timeframe was 'lots of years'.

Microsoft was in it for the long haul.

First three years

For a truly global perspective, search marketing veteran Jonathan Beeston, global marketing director at Efficient Frontier, distils the landscape and the impact of Bing's launch on the marketing community three years after Bing's launch:

> In the decade since 2000, Google had grown to enormous levels of popularity in the United States and Europe, exceeding 95 per cent market share in some countries. In that time, Microsoft had flipped between MSN Search, Windows Live Search and then just Live Search, but with little success. Brands were desperate to see some competition, as Google ate up a bigger and bigger portion of their online advertising budgets. So when Bing launched there was at last hope that the fight could be taken to Google. Microsoft had rightly identified that Google had built a great brand over the years, and that Bing would need to do something different, but also look different too. Expensive television ads coupled with a visually appealing homepage that at least announced this was a proposition that Microsoft was taking seriously.

The search advertising technology, Microsoft adCenter, which powered ads on Bing's results pages, had already been around for a few years and had a good reputation. The traffic was good quality and converted into business well on advertisers' websites. When Microsoft teamed up with Yahoo! in 2010 to power their ads too, it seemed like a logical move. Yahoo! had struggled to compete with Google and their own search advertising platform, codenamed Panama, was showing its age. Since the search alliance with Yahoo!, Bing's US market share has increased considerably (to around 30 per cent at the time of writing), but on the whole that's come from Yahoo!, not Google.

There's been considerable 'feature wars' between Google and Bing, which has been great for consumers and advertisers alike. Previews, for example, where a searcher can see a snapshot of a search result page without visiting the site, appeared on Bing long before Google.

That increase in market share hasn't been replicated outside the United States. This is partly because Bing struggles to internationalize features, whereas new Google features are released globally within a few weeks. Also, the search alliance with Yahoo! has been slow to roll out, with the transition in Europe and the rest of the world taking some time. But this is a long war, and as non-search players such as Facebook increase their appeal to consumers and advertisers, there will be plenty of battles yet to come.

Weitz defends the time it's taken to bring some features to market by cautioning: 'given what we set out to achieve and the amount of data we're dealing with to actualize the vision, we're still in the early days. It's an extremely complex software problem.' The essence of that problem is the question of whether Lu and team could take advantage of a computer's inherent ability to process lots of data and to add some value on top of those results. When they realized that they could, the mission was to allow searchers to take action rather than just find information. Weitz summarizes, 'there's more to search than blue links and search can actually expand to encompass the real world and help humans navigate all that data that we couldn't necessarily do without some kind of synthesis or understanding on top of them'.

In May 2012, Bing announced the biggest update to their search experience which includes more social signals in a side bar adjacent to core search results and a snapshot that claims to help the user 'get it done faster'. True to the plan of going beyond blue links, the new user interface uses social recommendation as a factor in helping decisions get made as the team points to research that '90 per cent of people consult with a friend or expert before making a decision' and that 'people are often the most trusted sources of information'.

Lu is in no hurry. There is a sense of urgency surrounding the opportunity his team has in this space, but he's under no illusions that their mission will take time. Investment is being made in the overall infrastructure at Microsoft to keep the pace of innovation on a par with the pace of change in the industry. And it's that investment work, coupled with the opportunity to have an enduring impact on the digital society, that keeps Lu motivated on his gruelling schedule. For him, it's not just about using information to build products and services, but using information and knowledge to enable human beings and help them overcome obstacles.

When asked to pick out his achievements, Lu says he has no answer other than: 'Can you work on things that have a greater impact to make life greater for other people? Are you able to work with people so you become a better person every day? If you can answer yes, that's a good day.'

Sound bytes

- Be grateful every day for your opportunities. Understanding how lucky you are compared with others around the world will drive you on to greater accomplishments.
- Have a vision, create a plan around it and tread that path. Check you're on track, don't rush and be focused.
- When contemplating an acquisition, think carefully about whether you have the talent internally to create what you want to buy. It might take longer, but it might be more cost-effective when integrating into your current business.

Further reading

http://www.Bing.com/Community

Ajaz Ahmed

AKQA

Digital discipline

From the very beginning Ajaz Ahmed has been a pioneer of digital media advertising. He helped drive the internet as an advertising channel, introduced new interactive technologies to communications, and then pioneered the first mobile platform specialist agency specifically for advertising and marketing.

Growing with digital media

We look at our campaign work as delivering a product or an innovation.

Ajaz Ahmed was founder of the digital agency AKQA, with global brands such as Nike, Virgin and Audi calling on their innovation and *ideation* services. In 2012 AKQA became the largest privately held digital agency to join a global holding group (WPP network). The company has been *Digital Agency of the Year* more times than any other company. AKQA was originally founded in London with creative partner James Hilton in 1995 (now in San Francisco), and the company operates out of offices in New York, Paris, Amsterdam, Berlin, Singapore and Shanghai to fulfil the world's main leading consumer markets.

Although he is still a young pioneer, it seems that Ahmed has been prominent since the first wave of digital. He launched AKQA when he was just 21, at the same time as more lauded companies such as lastminute.com were coming to prominence. However, Ahmed did not welcome the role of being a media star of digital: 'When the dotcom hype was going crazy, there was a time when I was regularly appearing in articles alongside people like Kate Moss and David Beckham... I made a conscious decision to switch it all off and not worry about it anymore. To take the focus off me, I stopped doing interviews so that the work would do the talking.'

Instead of following the boom and bust pattern of other digital starlets between the years 1996 and 2001, Ahmed simply developed a company which, in digital terms, has been the model of consistency and steady growth over many years. According to Ahmed:

> We take a long-term view and nurture a culture where our team is motivated to create the best work of their careers. It means a meritocracy that encourages ideas and contribution from every area of the company. It rewards determination, innovation and the discipline to deliver...

Ahmed's story is, therefore, one driven by teamwork and ideas, and in doing so he became a communications leader from scratch. His was a talent spotted at an early stage.

A face to watch

The Sunday Times identified Ahmed when he was just 17 years old as a *face to watch*. He was profiled as a future star of business with a keen interest in marketing. This prediction was astute but didn't envisage the oncoming digital age. Ahmed's business skills were honed during the 1990s, and the early world wide web years, for which he was amongst the first flush of digital. Ahmed himself remembers that, 'I was very lucky to grow up with this digital revolution and the industry taking shape. As a kid, I was interested in computers or operating systems, software and technology, so I had all types of machines running different software. This meant learning how they all worked and how they did things differently.'

Ahmed's interest in marketing fitted with his passion for technology, so his first post-school jobs were with technology firms:

> As a teenager I got to work with three of the world's most influential technology companies. The global business software company Ashton-Tate, that pretty much created the database software market; the computer games maker Ocean software, which was the market leader in digital entertainment; and I worked with the innovation leader, Apple. Apple has continued to thrive and lead the world but the other two companies got bought by competitors. So I learnt a huge amount from leaders in an industry I love.

At Apple, Ahmed learnt how to build the type of company that fitted with his outlook. This included assembling a team that shared his vision and kept you driven:

> I learnt a lot from Apple. The first rule over there is to build great products. The kind of people who build great products are passionate about excellence. So our primary goal at AKQA is to create great work and that means working with people who want to make the best things in the world, who love what they do. For us it's not about being the biggest company. The work is all that matters and keeping it innovative so that we're always trying new things is the most important thing.

Developing AKQA's DNA

AKQA – Ahmed's initials (Ajaz Khowaj Quoram Ahmed) – was Ahmed's first full venture as a commercial company and he has stuck with it through recessions and mergers. Ahmed needed design and creative panache to complement his business acumen. In early 1995 he placed an advertisement in the design journal *Creative Review* for interactive programmers and designers, and interviewed a young design graduate from Southampton Institute, James Hilton. Hilton had won several competitions while a student, and had spent more time developing his ideas with clients than on the rest of his coursework. So when they met they clearly had a lot in common – both 21, both commercially minded and both fascinated by the potential of digital. Plus Hilton was a visionary looking for an entrepreneurial adventure to create great work, which made him exactly the right match for Ahmed:

> When James showed me his portfolio I had never seen anything like it. I immediately connected with his work and fell in love with it. It excited me so much I can still remember the day I met him and I was just buzzing the whole day. Seventeen years on we are still working together. We both made the right decision to go on this adventure together.

From the outset the newly formed AKQA targeted clients whose approach they admired, and sought to win them over by pushing their innovative credentials. The first client to take them on was Virgin, which shared a vision and adventurous spirit similar to those of Ahmed and Hilton. 'Virgin is a company that's famous for its energy, creativity and innovation,' says Ahmed, 'so in a way it was a very natural fit for them to hire a youthful start-up rather than a bureaucratic conglomerate.'

In their first project they went for the radically new. 'We have always viewed the web as software, not as brochureware, and this is what distinguished AKQA from other agencies that were founded at the same time we were.' The goal of their output has been to make it what Ahmed calls 'a defining moment' in the way it uses design and technology in an innovative, ground-breaking and influential way. 'For Virgin we were the first agency to build a site which broadcast live radio on the web for Virgin Radio.'

Problems selling digital when it was new

The idea of using digital formats originally every time became an objective and challenge for the fledgling team. It won many admirers in the trade press and created a CV that boasted an innovation per project. The live digicast for Virgin inspired brands such as BMW, Microsoft and McDonalds to follow suit.

However, the biggest problem they faced at the time was the reluctance of clients to move away from traditional marketing. 'It sounds crazy now, but the biggest problem was telling people how important digital media and e-commerce was going to be. Everyone today can see that it's important, but when we started it was difficult to convince people that it was going to be flavour of the month.'

In practice, AKQA found that their solutions needed to be double-pronged – effective for clients and a demonstration of digital media's potential. Creativity did half the job, as AKQA were winning industry awards and attracting the attention of brands' marketing directors. Being able to show a good return on investment made the case for new media in their clients' procurement departments.

While Virgin were the agency's first client, AKQA's work for automotive brands became highly significant. The AKQA team came up with the idea of searching for pre-owned vehicles online first for BMW, based on specific criteria typed in by web users, in a project they called the *Approved Used Car Directory*. AKQA had smartly spotted that, in the early days of the web, many first-time PC owners went online to check out car prices and hunt for good deals and dealerships.

Automotives early adopters

Their work for BMW was fortuitous. The automotive industry were early digital adopters. Pre-web in 1993 brands such as Land Rover moved budget towards activities through their database of clients and prospects. Ford were one of the first to use microsites, which viewers could get to by pressing the red button on TV remotes during an ad. Such ventures into digital generated direct dialogue and correspondence data. By the late 1990s AKQA realized that they didn't need television – prospective car-buyers were already online looking for deals. In providing BMW with their own branded directory, they knew it would attract footfall because there was already a huge volume of car searches taking place. Early utilities such as this soon drew other automotive brands to seek AKQA's know-how. Ahmed remembers:

> When Fiat saw our work and hired AKQA to create a digital presence, we looked at their competitor sites and found there was plenty of room for innovation. So we developed five world firsts including the first car configuration system that worked on a single screen, rather than have to go through lots of different linear stages. We also included full-screen video walk-throughs of every car to take advantage of the broadband in people's homes. We created a completely new and accessible way to get finance information. We created a real-time customer services engine so people could ask questions and get answers in real time. And we also launched *Fiat eco:Drive* software into the car itself to promote Fiat's ranking as Europe's most environmentally friendly car company.

Fiat eco:Drive analyses drivers' techniques to help them reduce their emissions, and in realizing this part of the project AKQA were looking to flex the potential of digital. This innovation was estimated to save drivers around £400 per year in fuel costs. The capacity to explore Fiat's proposition online gave prospective clients more to go on – and enabled more of Fiat's design ethos and customer care to shine through the online campaign.

Innovation means being the first to do things

AKQA's innovation-per-campaign goal stretches beyond the automotive industry. In 2001, Nike employed AKQA to nudge their slogan 'Just Do It' into online and offline engagement. *Run London*, an online platform and live running event, gave people a chance to participate in a Nike-organized 10 km run. A training timetable, online coach and plan of action to race-day unravelled as runners mixed offline preparation with Nike's online guidance – including advice from Nike's elite sponsored athletes. 'With Nike's Run London every year we created one of Europe's busiest e-commerce sites as tens of thousands of people would rush to sign up for Nike 10K. This site beautifully blended commerce with branding.' Again, Ahmed and Nike were able to make the most of the technology available. According to Ahmed, 'Without the digital and social revolution of the last decade, an idea like this would never have been possible. This campaign was seen by millions, influenced tens of thousands to participate and be their best.'

This set the mark for numerous other 'firsts': with Xbox 360, AKQA's designers developed some of the actual product with its communications. When augmented reality was freely available, AKQA in the United States created the 'Priority Mail Virtual Box' – a program that virtually simulates the packaging needed for US Postal Service parcels, using a webcam.

Such projects fuelled AKQA's keenness to push for business globally, which brought new challenges.

Nurturing AKQA's global outreach

AKQA had expansion plans but were able to remain independent for 16 years. Their principles helped: by giving clients dedicated teams and striving to retain business, AKQA were able to grow steadily owing to client loyalty. As Ahmed explained, 'We found clients who work with a partner for a number of years, rather than churn and re-pitch, get the best results.' Since their first office in Farringdon, London, they have opened offices alongside clients in New York, San Francisco, Washington DC, Shanghai, San Salvador, Berlin and Amsterdam, with over 1,100 employees by 2012. They retained all clients and won business in the UK during the tough 2011 financial year (AKQA's annual global revenue is around $250m). Growth remains part of Ahmed's goal: 'It means taking care of business at home while starting adventures in new markets. It was important for us to be in the heart of Silicon Valley.'

When they targeted the United States, AKQA needed partners with local knowledge of markets who also shared their business vision and their approach to digital. So, in 2001, they teamed with a San Francisco-based agency founded by Tom Bedecarre to get into the US market.

'I met with Tom Bedecarre in San Francisco. He loved AKQA's founding values and we saw eye-to-eye.' Bedecarre became AKQA's CEO while Ahmed took on the role of chairman so that he could focus more on the work. A private equity firm, General Atlantic, also invested. Ahmed welcomed a wider spread of expertise: 'There's now a team of people who are removed from the day-to-day operations of the business, and can look at its performance in an objective way.' Having specialists concerned with their own areas of expertise has been crucial in AKQA's expansion, as the teams are driven to achieve within their own areas. The sale of a majority state in 2012 gave AKQA access to a wider global resource and, crucially, was organized to allow AKQA to continue operating as an independant company within the WPP network.

Be consistent, passionate and prepared to change

Crucially, the agency retained its 'creative edge' tag by being consistent during their expansion. Ahmed and Hilton attribute this to staying relevant – meaning relevant staff, relevant technologies and relevant content, against what Ahmed calls '*Multimediocrity*': 'most advertising makes me feel trapped... But our belief is that great work stops you feeling trapped – it inspires you. I find the word "consumers" sort of depressing because surely there's more to life than just feeding a vast global economic system.'

AKQA's 'ideas led' approach has seen them produce work that capitalizes on digital but is by no means constrained by needing to be online. This strategy helped AKQA's pioneering work for Nike. With the opening of AKQA's mobile app division in 2011, the Nike Training Club app enabled smartphone users to do a daily training regime with a pre-recorded Nike coach. The app was Apple's App of the week in Europe and the United States and then topped apps charts in 21 countries. By 2012 it had been downloaded millions of times, with over 60 million minutes of training recorded through the app.

Ahmed reflects

In hindsight, what are the main first-hand lessons AKQA's founder has learnt from his company's evolution into a global communication business? He sees it very much about not losing the central point of the communications message itself:

> It's about preserving the core values and stimulating progress. That's the Ying and the Yang working in harmony. Great brands have always been about smart and artful storytelling. Great agencies have always given brands a vision of what they could be and helped clients to inspire audiences. It's the agency's responsibility to harness and focus talent to unlock opportunity with momentum and enthusiasm. An agency is ultimately judged on the body of its work, the quality of its ideas, the excellence of its product and the contribution it makes. It must also work at creating and sustaining a culture of invention and seeking out what's next.

Ahmed is happy to challenge the parts of Adland that still resist the advantages digital brings:

> Gone are the days of the couch potato. So there's huge competition for audience attention and if a media is not connected and interactive, it usually isn't important. For example, is there anyone who actually just watches the TV without doing some other task at the same time? Given the myriad of options available, it is somewhat ridiculous to expect audiences to automatically pay attention to advertising as it's never been easier for someone to scan past work created for the lowest common denominator. Also, why are they still called 'Newspapers' when the announcements they deliver are so dated by the time they hit the press?
>
> While there will always be new ideas, services and devices, one lasting truth is that people only have short attention spans when they're bored. We have audiences raised with so much media and technology in their lives that they know how to filter and manage it all pretty well. At the same time the media itself is becoming more intelligent at curating content and services of interest. The result is audiences are far more discretionary because they can dramatically edit what media they choose to spend time with.

Secret of what really works

> *Great agencies and creative companies have always found the best way to tell a client or brand story with the best medium of a particular age. So 100 years ago that was print, then radio, then it was the TV age. Now it's the digital age. And what great brands are doing in the digital age is telling their stories through the technology and really bringing the brand to life.*
>
> (Ajaz Ahmed, AdWeekdotcom, 2011)

According to Ahmed:

> In the art of persuasion, nothing is more powerful than an understanding of what instincts dominate a person's actions and what compulsions drive them. To open the eyes, ears and hearts, nothing stirs people more than love or courage or excitement and that which is fresh and new. Audiences ultimately decide how they feel about a brand by evaluating all its messages, its stories – whether through product, service, conversations, internet, mobile, shops or new devices.

Technology pushes things forward. It has created a level playing field where good agencies have permission to orchestrate a brand's messages in all media.

For agencies to stay relevant, they must broaden their scope, especially in the people hired. Talent that is passionate, curious, inventive, that cares about ideas and making a difference for clients. A constant flow of people with ideas that are rich with elegance, artful, rewarding and enjoyable will keep good agencies ahead. Agencies need also to expand their frames of reference to include what is of influence today and important tomorrow so that work is culture-creating and genre-defining.

To create the ideal conditions for the imagination to thrive, prosper and reach the new frontier, problems should be approached without preconceived ideas and sentiments. There should be more focus on what ingredients will successfully produce a climate where fresh ideas can be conceived, nurtured and grown.

The challenge for agency teams is to ensure that their philosophical approach is about the audience wanting to applaud the work. The best ideas have more respect for what the audience gets out of it – how it will inspire, satisfy or motivate them – rather than bombarding people with messages, functionality and clutter.

Advice to readers emulating AKQA

Ahmed offers three bits of advice: work with strong people; keep continually inspired; and give something back to the next digital generation when you have the opportunity:

> You can see that we're a team that's obsessed with the work. So we look to hire the best people we can find who also share that passion. You need a very innovation- and product-oriented culture. Motives, the reasons for getting into business in the first place, also matter a great deal. Our primary goal is to make the best work in the world for the brands and audiences we serve. We try to do things where we feel we can make a significant contribution. We also have a set of hero companies including Nike, Virgin, Apple, Pixar which have core beliefs, values, processes and people that inspire us.

AKQA's commitment to spotting new talent for new challenges is more than skin-deep:

> Our company's founding motto is: The Future Inspires Us. We Work To Inspire. This evidences itself through our work but also our behaviour. So we also created opportunities for young people to celebrate their ideas and find meaningful careers in the industry. There's a lot of young people around the world who have huge amounts of potential but it gets wasted either because it wasn't encouraged or there were obstacles in the way. AKQA supports charities that promote equal opportunity and economic independence.

For Ahmed, looking to the future stretches further than their work. AKQA makes a point of investing in youth: 'For us youth and energy combined with maturity and experience is the ultimate combination', says Ahmed. AKQA also created the world's largest student advertising competition with Future Lions. Future Lions (**www.futurelions.com**) gives young creative teams (who are the same age as Ajaz and James were when they founded AKQA) from all over the world the opportunity to showcase their work in front of the world's best agencies at the Cannes annual advertising festival.

Today, AKQA are as entrepreneurial as ever but are more specific in their positioning. They still attract accolades – between 2005 and 2012 AKQA won more awards than any other digital agency and at least one *Digital Agency of the Year* award every year. They have carved a position as the leading mobile agency specialists and creative *ingénues* in leveraging social channels. They have maintained their position as a top creative digital firm because they have never moved their focus from being innovative, which they've nurtured over the years into a creative habit.

Sound bytes

- Stay innovative – treat each client as an opportunity.
- Remember what motivates you – keep that spark at the forefront of decisions.
- Embrace change as a challenge. Don't look to defend positions – be creative.

Further information

http://www.Akqa.com
http://www.Facebook.com/AKQA
http://Twitter.com/AKQA

Martha Lane Fox

Lastminute.com and the UK government's digital champion

Digital discipline

One of the original dotcom entrepreneurs from England. Co-founded travel and e-commerce company Lastminute.com, which floated on the UK stock market to a huge fanfare in early 2000. Now the government's digital champion, she's set the challenge of getting 10 million people online by the end of 2012.

Brave new world

When Martha Lane Fox left Oxford University aged 21 in 1994 with a degree in ancient and modern history, at her own admission she knew nothing about business, branding or building teams and companies. But a chance meeting with the founder of a small strategy consulting company, Spectrum, triggered her off on the road towards digital business and, in particular, the potential of converging offline practices with the internet. Spectrum is also where she met Brent Hoberman, the man with whom she'd later found Lastminute.com. And thrown into a world which was rapidly changing, she describes that career decision as an 'incredibly important' pivotal moment in her life.

When Lane Fox got the call from Hoberman to consider a new venture in 1998, the start-up environment in the UK was not the feeding frenzy that was occurring in the United States. The 'brave new world' was just opening up and Lane Fox remembers that only a few e-commerce companies were around when the duo were producing their business plan. Networking events for entrepreneurs like First Tuesday existed in London, but as Lane Fox and Hoberman 'set off on their merry way' at the beginning of that year, they became true pioneers of a model and brand that continued to endure.

Gut instinct

The idea for Lastminute.com came from Hoberman (Lane Fox says she'd be 'mortified' if she'd ever given any other impression). Its premise centred on Hoberman's dislike of the hassle surrounding booking weekends away. Realizing that the internet was presenting a powerful combination of scale and connection, he soon saw the potential for linking suppliers and products to customers, and helping to shift inventory that is often, quite literally, at the last minute.

While Hoberman concentrated on the technology, Lane Fox's interest revolved around the brand and how it could be built; what culture could be formed around it; and how it could be distinguished from the 'real world' brands in the travel and leisure sectors offline at that time.

As they sought funding, Lane Fox reflects that her decision to join Hoberman came from a 'gut instinct' that they could make a success of it and the desire to work hard. Her parents had been instrumental in furnishing her with self-assurance, suggesting that they might even have been 'appalled' had she gone into banking, law or accounting, 'They liked the idea that I would be doing something different, and challenging, and more where I could be in control.'

The importance of building a reliable team was a lesson that Lane Fox learnt early on: 'To me, I think entrepreneurs are people that have confidence in their decisions, have a clear vision, but at the same time can also realize that it's incredibly important to have a team around you, and that you can't do everything alone.'

By 2000 the company had secured several million dollars in funding from the UK airports operator BAA, Sony Music Entertainment, Starwood Hotels, Mitsubishi Corporation Finance and others. A stock market flotation was on the cards, and such was the pair's media profile at this point that a report in the UK newspaper *The Guardian* suggested that the potential value of the company could well exceed a billion dollars. The hype surrounding the business, with many describing Hoberman and Lane Fox as the internet's first celebrities and as symbols of a resurgence in UK entrepreneurship, certainly created a buzz around the flotation, which was clearly affected by the hype. With broadsheet and tabloid interest, the launch of Lastminute.com on the stock market had impetus, gaining wall-to-wall media coverage that many who were in the UK at the time will remember.

On Tuesday 14 March 2000, shares in Lastminute.com launched at 380p, surging to 510p within the first hour of trading. At its height on that day, the company was valued at £768m and the co-founders notionally had a combined fortune on paper of over $200m.

Asked at the time how long they might stay with the company post IPO, Lane Fox told the press that 'Six months is the initial lock-up period, but obviously we are both here for the long term. It's far too early to comment on what we might do in the future.'

Dot bomb

As it turned out, those six months were an important period as the team fused together to battle through the bursting of the dotcom bubble. As internet companies all over the world suffered the consequences of over-valuation and the failure to live up to expectations, Lastminute.com saw their share price slip to less than £1 in November 2000. The company survived through losses of £54m in 2001 and even returned its first pre-tax profit in 2003, the moment Lane Fox saw as the perfect time to step out of her role. Lastminute.com is still operating successfully today, having been acquired by the US company Sabre Holdings in 2005.

Looking back, she feels that it was a tremendously rewarding time in more ways than one:

> I feel extraordinarily lucky actually, more than proud perhaps, that I was able, at such a young age, to have this extraordinary experience, and to be part of a small piece of internet history, if you like, in terms of how the internet hit the UK, and how e-commerce grew. I personally really loved the period of time just before the IPO because we were just beginning to get traction, customers were buying, and we had a hint that this could be a big business and not just a UK business. We were recruiting some really interesting senior people. It was still a size of company where I could stand on a desk on a

> Friday afternoon, and we could just talk about what happened during the week, and people could share their stories, and we could have a doughnut. It became harder as the company got bigger to do that.

If Lane Fox is walking down a London street and sees a billboard or climbs into a Lastminute.com branded taxi cab, she feels 'strange' as she had so much to do with the bright pink logo, tone, look and feel of the product, and not just the customer-centricity. But she also senses pride 'at the longevity of some of the essence of the brand that I contributed to'.

With substantial personal wealth and business experience few had ever had, the world was Lane Fox's oyster. Shortly after leaving Lastminute.com it was announced that she'd be heading to London's Oxford Street to join the department store Selfridges as the 'right-hand woman' to (then) new owner Galen Weston. While relishing the chance to build out the retailer's internet business and apply some of her online savvy to their offline operation, Lane Fox's world came to an abrupt and shattering halt while on holiday with her boyfriend in Morocco.

Involved in a terrible car accident that injured her limbs and pelvis so badly that she needed dozens of operations in the following months, she describes the calamity as 'a funny twist' that took her the best part of six or seven years to really emerge from. It was, in Lane Fox's words, a 'very deep pain and distressful funk', being 'high on morphine and slightly shell-shocked' for a number of years.

Lucky voice

As the long road to recovery grew shorter, the opportunities to get back to some kind of work and normality began to arise.

Trips to Japan to visit friends were punctuated with nights out at local karaoke bars, where patrons spend money for a private room to drink, sing and party the night away. A unique idea in Lane Fox's mind, she ploughed her own money into a joint venture with Nick Thistleton to bring the concept to London's Soho area and launched the karaoke bar Lucky Voice in 2005 to 'spread happiness through unforgettable singing experiences'.

Seven years later the project has blossomed, with another couple of bars around the UK and a number of franchises. It's also seeing a growing online presence as technology has allowed the team to help users create a karaoke machine from their computers with over 8,000 songs to choose from. For Lane Fox, the Lucky Voice adventure started off as a bit of fun that she knew would work, but its success has surprised her, as she reveals: 'We didn't think it was going to grow to be quite such a beast.'

Over the years, other non-executive director roles at media company Channel 4, UK retailer Marks & Spencer and digital decorating company mydeco.com have kept her busy, as has the launch of Antigone in 2007. A charitable organization, Antigone helps charities with grants so they can use the web and mobile technologies more effectively in areas of health, education and criminal justice. It's this philanthropic work coupled with her place in web heritage that almost certainly led to the UK government knocking on her door in 2009.

UK digital champion

Asked by then-prime minister of Britain Gordon Brown to help define how to get the nation's most disadvantaged communities to use technology, Lane Fox set the UK a challenge to help get 10 million people online in an initiative that she never really thought she'd 'feel so personally' and 'take quite so to heart'.

In July 2010, she launched a 'rallying cry' in the form of a Manifesto for a Networked Nation which stated:

> The 10 million people in the UK who have never been online are already missing out on big consumer savings, access to information and education. They will be even more isolated and disadvantaged as government and industry expand ever faster into digital-only services. We must change our mindset from one that shields people from using the internet to one that helps empower them to get online and enjoy all the benefits.
>
> We need to recycle and join up our existing infrastructure and exploit the assets and the skills that we already have.
>
> We need to be ambitious, 'think internet first' when we design services, and put the needs of the hardest to reach at the heart of industry, charity and government. There is a social and moral case to make sure more people are online but there is a clear economic case too. We will all be better off when everyone is online.

With that charter, Lane Fox fired the starting pistol for Race Online 2012, an initiative that hopes to have helped 10 million people in the UK get experience in using the internet to help educate and enrich their daily lives.

Reflecting on how the internet had changed her life and spurred her on to give something back, Lane Fox was deeply moved by the stories from the people she talked to when she was gauging just how deep the problem was. One troubled young man from Leeds had been found in a bus shelter high on crack: given some respite after a spell in hospital, the man visited a centre where he was taught to use a computer and learnt that as a DJ he could sell his music online. Lane Fox describes meeting him on the other side of life's crisis as 'humbling'. He'd looked her 'straight in the eye' and said, 'The internet saved my life. There's no question.'

That inspiring story and countless others keep Lane Fox resolutely on her quest despite so many detractors:

> I think a lot of people think I'm bananas. I think a lot of people think I have a vision that's never going to be achievable. But I still believe it's absolutely right to aim for what we're calling the Network Nation where we get 98/99 per cent of the country on the internet. Race Online 2012 is a campaign to get stuff done.

And get stuff done she has. Gov.UK is a beta site that aims to bring all government internet outreach under one umbrella and comes from the UK's Government Digital Service which was set up as a direct result of her reporting back on the state of the nation's digital capabilities. She feels the British government is taking the idea of technology and the urgency for online services for all seriously. It's not all down to her, she's keen to add, but the work she has done has contributed to a focus and commitment around new broadband networks and how information technology should be taught in schools:

> It moved up the agenda, but I would always argue it could be further up. I think it's just very important that we keep championing the start-ups, championing the small digital leaders, championing the kind of wider ecosystem. I believe it is going in the right direction, not the wrong direction. I don't think I could do it with such gusto if I didn't think that because it would just be too disheartening.

Building connections

As someone who has been at the very top of her game at such a young age and with so little experience, Martha Lane Fox embodies some of the essence of entrepreneurship. She has a 'can do/will do' attitude that takes natural intelligence and common sense and combines it with eloquence and a dogged work ethic. The early days of Lastminute.com were a training ground for later ventures but also an inspiration for many other women around the world looking to succeed in business. The key, she says, is to be able to convince others as well as yourself:

> I think anybody starting anything, whether it's a social enterprise, whether it's small business, or whether it's a little charity, or even when starting a new job, I think that to do a good job in anything, you have to be in a slightly competent sales mode. You have to be convincing that you can do the job, and you have to be convincing that you can build customers. You have to be in a sales job whether it's investors, whether it's suppliers, or whether it's to the people that you're working with. To me, one of the key skills is to build a connection with what you're trying to do; otherwise you will go nutty because you have to spend so much time thinking about it.
>
> Being in love with what you are doing and 'really feeling it' will help you succeed. 'Living' the product, being in constant sales mode and having a resounding faith in your mission helps your state of mind as you plough on persuading customers and suppliers alike that you're worth investing time and money in.

When it comes to potential over-enthusiasm in business, a 'small bugbear' of hers does surround the word 'passionate' which she thinks has become 'the most overused word in the English language'. She explains that she sees it a little differently: 'I think it's just really important that you take a real pride in what you are trying to do and that you really enjoy it. I've seen people on stage saying they are really "passionate" about supply chain management, and I often think, really? Or is it that you think it's a really great idea and you love what you're doing.'

Maybe it's the English sensibilities in her, but Lane Fox insists on injecting some balanced realism to building a business too as there will be times when:

> It will get hard, you'll get pissed off, there will be horrible challenges, and you'll wish you'd never done it. So you have to stand back and go, my god, look, I'm doing my own thing, I'm creating this great idea where I'm helping people do something they couldn't do before, and those are the things that you do need to hang onto because it's really difficult at many points.

Her advice to start-ups looking for funding is sage. With more investors around than when she and Hoberman were knocking on doors, she urges would-be entrepreneurs to 'look in every direction and under every stone' and that you look at their track record as it's vital that they've had success and that you actually like the people involved. The investors you choose will be part of 'your story and adventure' and it's necessary to build long-term relationships. Think laterally too. They might not have invested in your exact sector, but they may have experience in others that you intend to involve in your business plan further down the road.

Lane Fox believes that those who don't put the new media landscape at the top of their agenda fail to do so at their peril. During the 14 years since Brent Hoberman asked her to start Lastminute.com, technology and the internet are now at the heart of many companies. This positive evolution has given Lane Fox the opportunity to help businesses look at customer behaviour, help structure organizations and influence culture change without her impact necessarily coming from a box labelled technology. Yes, she's tapped constantly for her knowledge and experience in the tech arena, but she's glad it's no longer a sideline issue which has handed her a 'fantastic opportunity' to learn, grow and contribute in other areas.

While still young for a digital ambassador, Martha Lane Fox hopes to continue championing the use of technology to help alleviate social problems. Since she kicked off *Race Online* in 2012 she says she's been 'a real advocate for technology, not for technology's sake, but to really help disadvantaged groups in deprived communities and places with tricky problems'. She's deeply conscious of the opportunities she's had in her life and, as a woman, wants to show that there is an opportunity afforded to people by the use of the internet that means they can start a business. She's adamant that that they don't have to fit the mould of what they think an entrepreneur should look like.

A true dotcom pioneer and business inspiration, she was a 25-year-old Oxford history graduate who knew nothing about starting a business but believed that she could learn, gather good individuals around her, work hard and be good to people. If she can inspire other women to be confident and 'go it alone', she thinks 'that would be pretty cool'.

Sound bytes

- When seeking out investors, check their track record in areas you might want to expand to. Get to know them as people. You have to like them as they're going to stick to you like glue.
- Realize that you can't do everything. Surround yourself with good people who are as geared up for the mission as you are and have skills you don't necessarily possess.
- If you're successful, reflect on how lucky you are, because many businesses fail. Consider giving a little back by mentoring or helping other like minds to edge ahead.

PHOTO: Bill Wadman

Kyle MacDonald

One Red Paperclip

Digital discipline

Trading up the innovative way. Kyle MacDonald is the man who used the internet to trade up from a paperclip to a house through trading sites – then carved a career on the back of it.

Story behind the paperclip trade-up

The story of Kyle MacDonald's one red paperclip is, by any measure, extraordinary. MacDonald attracted global press attention for trading up from a paperclip to a house within a year, in what became seen as a lesson in modern exchange values, but also what can be achieved online. MacDonald's story didn't stop with the last trade: his digital journey has subsequently taken him worldwide and has opened other avenues as a speaker, writer and serial project-maker, originally because he harnessed the potential of the world wide web. It is MacDonald's pioneering spirit that makes him a phenomenon of the digital age.

Kyle MacDonald wasn't a conventional student at university in Vancouver. 'Most people seemed to know what they'd be doing at the end, and they'd be trying to get a job. I was learning things I was interested in – looking at maps, geography, urban studies... In my entire time at school I didn't imagine working in an actual field.

'In summers I'd travel and work, but it was social – something to do. It wasn't a means to an end. I ended working on projects at the last minute, but when I went travelling I started writing about those things and I began to find writing much easier. I would write stories and send e-mail stories back, newsletters. And as things progressed I set up a blog.'

As a keen surfer with a love of travelling, MacDonald felt inspired by the journeys of several other writers who had taken challenges and embraced them with a tangential view of the world:

> I started to read a lot of travelogues that were similar – especially books from the UK. I read Tony Hawks' *Round Ireland with a Fridge*, and realized that all he really did was go on a cool adventure and write about it. It was like a self-replicating idea where you'd go on a trip and it fuelled other adventures. So I thought 'I wouldn't mind trying to do something like that'. So I started doing little web projects and blogs, and writing about specific adventures I was doing.
>
> One of these adventures involved delivering different postcards from the Galápagos Islands, then he then I came up with the Red Paperclip idea, which was essentially a version of the game 'Bigger and Better'.
>
> I pretty much stole the idea from a childhood game we played around the neighbourhood, where you started with something small and traded up gradually to something bigger and better. So in my trials and writings I just, very casually, started trading things. I had no intention of it being a huge thing, but as soon as the first couple of trades started happening and people started to understand what was going on, I got a lot of encouragement to start taking it right to the limit.

Searching for a journey

At the same time you had Danny Wallace and Dave Gorman, who, like British-based comedian and author Tony Hawks, undertook unusual projects and recorded the journey afterwards.

Hawks' book was first published in 1998 – just as the first internet boom was taking place. It was the first of a genre to chronicle a journey based on an unusual starting point – in this case it was a bar bet that the author couldn't transport a full-sized refrigerator around the country of Ireland. As MacDonald points out, this was pre-blog and before quirky travelogues became more mainstream: 'I think the cool thing there was that it was obviously deemed a full project, where today lots of things start somewhere like Facebook and they don't really happen. So I liked the conceptual side.' In Hawks' book his journey was as intriguing as the simple quirky supposition, and sparked others to take on imaginative journeys of their own.

As MacDonald recollected:

> There was a whole genre of travel writing I was attracted to – Bill Bryson, Pete McCarthy... that I really enjoyed reading. Dave Gorman (an author and stand-up comedian) and Danny Wallace (writer and friend of Gorman's) fitted into that. Then I realized that I liked the conceptual side more than the writing. The concept of interaction – these guys had storylines and they used the internet to make it happen. That was the key for me – not just sitting on the internet and doing an internet-only project. It was a two-way mechanism as if you're using a telephone or the post or actually being there in person, and storytelling. That was the key for me – I was always trying to tell an interesting story. It was more fun to do and hopefully people would enjoy it more.

Gorman's first adventure was in 2000 with *Are You Dave Gorman?* – a documentary-style journey that researched and interviewed other people called Dave Gorman. This was followed by *Dave Gorman's Googlewhack Adventure* (2003), which involved researching '*googlewhacks*' – a Google search query of only two words, without quotations, that returned just one search result (these were slightly more common then than today). Danny Wallace went on his own bizarre journey, travelling across the United States on a mission where he could only say 'yes' to people. Gorman and Wallace, like Hawks, incorporated specialist-interest social networks in their work.

MacDonald's idea was in a similar vein, using available internet trading platforms (not so much Craigslist as eBay). Such sites offered a realm of possibilities for MacDonald who sought his own adventure.

The format was deliberately simple:

> By putting it on the web and going, 'alright, we've got this... who wants to make a trade?' The reaction was immense. But the actual underlying, underpinning key of the entire project was going and meeting people for real and visiting them by travelling around – not just sitting on a computer all day. It was pretty outlandish in some ways: trading a paperclip for a house seems impossible, but as you make each of the individual trades it made quite a bit of sense. Each trade was legitimate and each person opted into the whole trading system. It was weirdly logical and at the same time, an illogical thing to do!

Why a paperclip

Why start with a ubiquitous paperclip? Paperclips have a rich symbolic history – they were even worn as a sign of resistance by Norwegians against Nazi rule in the 1940s. MacDonald's reason was more practical and immediate:

> It was literally the thing on my desk. I knew I didn't want to start with money – attention would have been on its evaluation. I remember looking down and thinking, 'this paperclip is simply the smallest thing you can get. There are smaller things but it was the smallest recognizable object. Perfect. I don't really like them – I had 200 of the red ones. It was simply a recognizable object – like a famous brand, the same level of semiology. I love the simplicity of it.
>
> It's interesting that a paperclip is literally worth less than one penny. But if it's famous, then it's like art work. That publicity was the key factor in raising the value to groups of people. A lot of people would take Banksy's work and say it's worth millions, but there will be an old lady down the street who would walk by it every day and would say 'I literally wouldn't give a penny for it'. So it's that relative value that was the absolute total fascination for me – how people value things.

MacDonald's journey

The text used in the first ads was consistent – 'When I started the copy I asked "do you have something more valuable than a red paperclip? I'm going to trade it for something bigger until I get a house or an island." I tried to illustrate the idea. The goal of the house wasn't specific at the beginning... after a few trades it became more of a hard-line thing – I said "yes, I'm going to trade all the way to a house" and I even changed the copy on the website. And that's when it emerged as a headline: "My name's Kyle and I'm trying to trade a red paperclip for a house." Although that wasn't specifically true, it outlined in one sentence what was going on. And most of all if you say something like that it got people's attention.'

The big claim proved not to be the most productive way for commercial exchanges because it created over-demand – MacDonald was inundated with offers from people who wanted to join in:

> I would get three or four hundred different trade item offers, which I was trying to value in my head (not just monetarily, but if they would be good to re-trade). It was not just the items but the people: I made more of an effort if the people were interesting because working with good people was more important than the monetary value of the items. It was more important than simply making swaps to get ahead, ultimately it made the story so much better.

As the project grew in scale it became hard work – 'I was working 14 hours a day, 365 days a year during and after the event to pull this off. It was obsessive. You don't need this level of very hard work but it helps. Painters make things look easy but it takes a lot of work to get there.'

TABLE 17.1 The 14 trades in 356 days

	On...	Kyle traded...	up to...	via...
1	14 July 2005	1 red paperclip	fish-shaped pen (in Vancouver)	Craigslist
2	14 July 2005	pen	hand-carved door knob (Seattle)	Craigslist
3	25 July 2005	door knob	Colman camp stove (Massachusetts)	Craigslist
4	24 September 2005	camp stove	Honda generator (California)	Craigslist
5	16 November 2005	generator	'instant party': empty beer keg + IOU note to refill + neon 'Bud' sign (NYC) **First press articles appear (Canada)*	Craigslist
6	8 December 2005	'instant party'	one Ski-doo snowmobile (Quebec) traded with radio DJ	Craigslist
7	14 December 2005	snowmobile	2× trip to Yahk, British Columbia for February 2006 (British Columbia)	Oneredpaperclip.com
8	7 January 2006	1× trip to Yahk	motorized cube van (Montreal to Vancouver via Yahk; then to Toronto for trade)	Oneredpaperclip.com
9	22 February 2006	cube van	recording contract, with Metal Works (Toronto)	Oneredpaperclip.com
10	11 April 2006	recording contract	1 year's room rent in Phoenix (Arizona)	Oneredpaperclip.com
11	26 April 2006	room, Arizona	1 afternoon with pop star Alice Cooper	Oneredpaperclip.com
12	25 May 2006	meet Alice Cooper	motorized snow globe	Oneredpaperclip.com
13	2 June 2006	snow globe	movie role, in *Donna on Demand*. Traded with film producer Corbin Bernsen	Oneredpaperclip.com
14	5 July 2006	movie role	two-storey farmhouse in Kipling, Saskatchewan	Oneredpaperclip.com

As the trades got higher the project developed into a news story. MacDonald and his trades attracted media interest which grew with each trade. This in turn made the trades themselves relevant to news outlets and the blogosphere. It even had an impact on the trades, which were not as obviously bigger but certainly more intriguing.

Media snowball: managing an unravelling story

'When the media first got involved I was surprised. I said I'd love to talk about it but why are you calling me? Once the news agencies, newspapers and radio stations started calling in and trying to get updates, deep down inside I was thinking "these people must have something more important to talk about". But even deeper down I was "ok – let's make it interesting for them, and use this to the advantage of making this a cool happening for everyone, and see how far I can go with this – the storytelling, the marketing..." – it was being opportunistic and making the most of the situation for everyone involved.'

For MacDonald this involved ensuring that his trading decisions fitted with the integrity of the project and maximized the potential to keep the story alive and interesting for followers.

'Storytelling helped a bit, but I have a love–hate relationship with storytelling...: I've written short stories and presented them at fringe festivals in Canada. They are a huge underlying passion of mine but it was strange doing a story that was so well known in advance.' The press attention made MacDonald aware that people were following the story as it happened, and it became a unique challenge – a one-time event:

> It wasn't like I could go back and write different versions of it. It was trying to tell a story while marketing the idea that it might happen, while trying to make it all work at the same time! It wasn't all a pre-planned itinerary months in advance – it was all very open source and in real time, the entire time. In fact the only aspect that was not in real time and was openly uncontrolled was all of the trade offers coming in. I couldn't think of a mechanism of how to make them public immediately on the website – it might be easier with some of the tools available now.

Retaining the integrity of the project

'There was a lot of media, hype and strange values that didn't exist at the beginning. One thing that I didn't want to do was to cannibalize the integrity of the project for fame. I was getting a lot of offers just to do trades that made no sense whatsoever – "If you go on TV we'll just give you a house. Just wear our company's t-shirt." I said "ok, how are you going to use the current item I have?" and they said "we don't want anything – we just want the publicity". I'd be happy to do that, but not in the trade!'

As a consequence MacDonald was picky about his trades. Integrity involved reflecting on the issues of value it provoked:

> At one point I wound up with an afternoon with Alice Cooper. It's like a priceless thing – you just can't go out and purchase this. But to many people it was worth nothing – 'I've don't know who that is – I wouldn't give anything for that' – while others would say they thought it was worth the current car they were driving... I'll work for 6 months for this opportunity. That was it, right there – the publicity fell into that realm.

To a small town in rural Canada that was looking to attract residents, the publicity was worth the ultimate currency. According to MacDonald, it was something they didn't have a budget for but it was an instant opportunity to re-brand their town and attract interest by attaching to the story. 'So when I ended up trading a role in a film for the place in Kipling, it was exactly what they wanted. Acknowledging the publicity helped other people realize their aims.'

The housewarming party became an end-of-project celebration. 'We had 12 of the 14 people there. That speaks volumes for the people that became involved in the project.' However, soon he traded it on:

> Great town and the people were wonderful. But our experience of being there was a bit like being in The Truman Show. People had their pictures in front of it, but as time went on I realized that it wasn't really about the house but the idea. The town is now known as the One Red Paperclip town, the house is now a café and one of Kipling's main tourist attractions – and I'm really proud to have helped one small Canadian town.

Throughout the project, the fascination for MacDonald lay in the story; it was in the different perspectives of relative value that captured the imagination.

Collaboration, open source and digital storytelling

Kyle MacDonald's story incorporates a number of digital qualities – notably the significance of storytelling, especially in real time, the power of collaboration and keeping conversations open source.

There are many careers made online applying the skills that MacDonald used. There are wordsmiths paid to be 'brand guardians' – people who are the mouthpiece for brands online, managing blogs and being the voice of online branded characters.

> *Working real time makes for an agile creative storyline. You have to be able to react to news and weave the brand message into audience responses. If you get it right, the excitement in communicating with the brand directly and perhaps seemingly influencing the campaign spreads the message.*
>
> (Robert Urquhart, the copywriter and voice for several brand characters)

Then there are many thousands who make their careers trading online in various forms: at one point there were gamers who traded in-game and developed offline real currency through platforms such as Second Life. Today there are many thousands who make their living by trading – on eBay, Craigslist or through other online trading platforms. Online trading is a multimillion-dollar global industry and MacDonald's genius wasn't just in the idea but how it was managed during and after trading.

MacDonald now has a number of activities that collectively make a dynamic career: speaker and consultant to brands globally, a storyteller and project-maker. In the spirit of One Red Paperclip he only takes on projects that he is passionate about. He makes a living following his own curiosity:

> There's an underlying theme in places especially like America [where] independence and self-reliance are ideals. There's a great video on the internet about self-reliance where a man makes this thing that looks like a toaster [see Thomas Thwaites, 'Making a toaster – from scratch'] and it takes him six months and $10,000. There's interdependency that's in all of us – in capitalist or socialist environments... [and] I'm fascinated in how this happens. There's one school of thought that says 'don't tell people about your idea': I'm the opposite. Tell everyone about your idea and you'll get leads. People will help you.

Making sense of MacDonald

MacDonald describes himself as a curator of content – 'an art gallery has someone who picks out specific pieces. If they leave them it's kept in a store room. With all these crazy offers and potential outcomes I pulled out the ones that told a good story potentially.'

MacDonald sees that he was positioned as being Of The Moment: in 2006, *Time Magazine*'s Person of the Year was '*You*' – meaning the internet users. Blogs and YouTube were becoming very popular, and his story worked with this view. 'I'm sure I got pinned up as the person that shows you how you can use all these tools and think outside the box to make the internet work for you. That was, sort of, my specific goal – it wasn't about the house.'

The press latched on to the tale, highlighting the value of the house and making it an eBay or gap-year story (neither was true 'but that didn't actually matter. They fixed it to their own narrative'). 'Someone said it wouldn't work in France... someone else said "only in America". Nonsense! Then when the markets crashed in 2008, some said "bartering's the new thing because people don't have much money".' Ultimately MacDonald wanted to share his experimental journey with a global open-source community; all lessons should be shared, he argues:

> Whether you know how to tie a knot in your shoelace, if you teach a child this they will know this, they're going to know it for life, and they might go on to teach another million people. Sharing that knowledge – you don't necessarily need to barter it or win some game, simply sharing it – and keeping things in circulation is my passion and usually a collaborative effort. I wanted to inspire people to do their own stuff.

As MacDonald is now synonymous with paperclips, this will be one journey that he will never be able to leave. 'Of course, now people constantly hand me paperclips... I don't even like them! I like the idea of them more than the actual thing. I traded it away because I didn't want it anymore.'

Advice for those emulating the One Red Paperclip

From MacDonald's perspective:

> The initial step is easy... actually starting. Any sort of collaboration involves a function of telling people about it, following up on a lead and doing something. Start small and think big... it's harder to stand out now. It's easier to create and post content but the level of competition is harder now with more readers and far more content creators. It's harder to self-restrain in putting things out that aren't that good. Take the time to make it right, rather than just putting it out there.
>
> Also, do something that you believe in and want to do. Then start small and think big. Go as far as you can in total immersion in the project, and do it as if it's real life. Use the internet as a mechanism – as a two-way device. Don't just sit on it and do everything there.
>
> You usually find that people are willing to trade. Making it exciting for them to trade is good – I found that some people were attracted just because it was an interesting project or because they wanted the associated publicity. For the vast majority that wanted to join in, to trade, they wanted the actual item. Anything you own, or have, or can do or any sort of knowledge you have – there are people out there would put a very serious amount of value on that.

Is One Red Paperclip repeatable? 'Absolutely. It would take the right concept and the right person, but if anyone really wanted to do it, it could still be done. But there would have to be a different element to get that scale of media coverage. Perhaps if someone was more extreme with the trades...'

Sound bytes

- Consider how you'd manage the 'story' of your project in real time, as open source.
- Don't over-anticipate how your project would unravel in the public eye; you'll have to judge constantly which values are most important to your project.
- MacDonald: 'An idea is rarely a reality without collaboration. Open out your network and remember everything you have – knowledge, goods, whatever can be valuable to someone online.'

Further reading

Gorman, D (2004) *Dave Gorman's Googlewhack Adventure*, Random House, London

Hawks, T (1998) *Round Ireland with a Fridge*, Random House, London

MacDonald, K (2007) *One Red Paperclip: How one piece of small stationery turned into a great big adventure*, Ebury Press, London

Jess Greenwood

Contagious Magazine and R/GA

Digital discipline

Cultural planner and trend de-constructor who writes and speaks, inspiring advertising creatives and brand marketers to understand the future of digital and tell more meaningful and engaging stories.

Infectious appreciation

For many creatives in the advertising industry, receiving an accolade at the Cannes Lions Festival or an IAB MIXX award might be the pinnacle of their career, as such recognition is as highly noted as an Oscar is in the movie world. For some, though, getting their work recognized in *Contagious Magazine* is just the ticket to roll out the red carpet and crack open the champagne.

For many commentators in the advertising industry, just keeping the lights on in the office and the presses rolling is an achievement, let alone finding yourself being asked to speak at a marketing event sandwiched on the billing between international fashion designer Donna Karan and former US President George Bush.

As a career highlight, Jess Greenwood remembers her time sharing thoughts with the US fashion and political elite as fondly as the time she was told by a Brazilian executive that his team had partied hard after being featured in the magazine she wrote for because they felt 'like that was the metric by which their creativity should be judged'.

Founded in 2004 by Paul Kemp-Robertson and Gee Thomson, *Contagious Magazine* was, as Greenwood remembers, a considered reaction to the ever-changing media landscape of the time. With backgrounds at Leo Burnett Worldwide, and in publishing as founders of *Shots* magazine, the pair saw a gap to fill in the knowledge and understanding of the new wave of digital channels beating down the doors of creative departments in London where they initially set up shop.

Providing a platform to help brands and agencies cut through the clutter was a shrewd move given that US online advertising spend was up 33 per cent on 2003 to $9.6bn, according to a report by the Interactive Advertising Bureau (IAB) and PricewaterhouseCoopers, and the UK industry was set to blossom by another 65 per cent in 2005.

Greenwood, who was working for TV and video magazine *The Reel* at the time, remembers vividly: 'I was in the meeting when Paul came in to pitch what *Contagious* was about, and I remember it just looked stunning. They put a lot of thought into how it was going to look, and how it was going to be laid out, and I thought it was really fascinating the way that they had approached the content of the magazine in a completely different way, more like an intelligence briefing than a news update.'

Doing something different that offered value was important. They were already pushing boundaries by proposing a publication about advertising that didn't sell advertising on its pages. Looking back, Greenwood muses on some of *Contagious*'s less fortunate competitors: 'There are a lot of magazines gone because they weren't allowed to differentiate their editorial focus into various other areas. They were published by big publishing companies that only know how to print magazines, and they weren't able to diversify in any way.'

It was this agile potential, coupled with Paul and Gee's passion, that drew Jess to join the team the following year.

An Italian job

Like many of our pioneers, Greenwood fell into advertising and digital through a lust for language and the written word. A graduate of Birmingham University in the UK, her degree in English and Italian was precursored by a role assisting the 'head of spin' at The Vatican in Rome, and then took her to Verona where she studied semiotics with Umberto Eco (who 'never turned up') and learnt to 'swear like a true Italian', while working in a bar to pay the rent.

Wanting to chase down a job that incorporated her love of language, Greenwood felt that she was 'pretty typical of a generation that doesn't know what it wants to do when it grows up'. She had a positive outlook but had no career trajectory: 'I just kept saying yes to things when they came up which I think is quite important.'

Two things really set the scene for the hop, skip and jump into the thick of *Contagious Magazine* and six years at the cutting edge of the advertising industry. Firstly she moved to London and then discovered the power of the web.

Chock full of creative agencies, advertising thought-leaders and innovative publishers, London held much for the budding media careerist, including the British Broadcasting Corporation.

In 2000, the BBC tapped into the dotcom era with a series called Attachments, a fictional series about an internet start-up at the time of the dotcom boom. It ran for 26 episodes and, in an early precursor of the ways in which TV and the web now work together, included a website and online forum to mirror the operations of the company in the series.

On the forum, a group of people were gathering to understand the connecting power of the web. Greenwood says:

> There was a really, really healthy, interesting crew of people from all over the place writing and engaging on this web forum, a very early iteration of the idea that eventually everyone who had something to say would be doing it online. There were lots of exceptional writers and lots of people working in media who really felt like they were part of something special. That was my introduction to the internet – basically the crazy things that people do in internet forums and the sort of intrigues that you can kind of re-create by communicating with people on a daily basis that you've never met. Now, internet dating has completely busted the idea that online connections are less powerful than offline ones. In 2001, we were just figuring that out.

Lucky break

Greenwood's role with *Contagious* came at a time, she feels, of enormous luck, as 'it was a strange time for the advertising industry – nobody was really sure how things were going to pan out. The production side of things was changing an awful lot as more and more focus went towards digital – it was an interesting time to join, just as everything was turning over.'

Back in 2005/2006, fragmentation was a word used regularly in advertising press. As Google was making strides with their search business, accumulating hundreds of millions of dollars in revenue all around the world, new advertising technologies called *rich media* from companies like Eyeblaster and Tango Zebra were making online marketing experiences more complex for creatives but more engaging for users. Everyone was asking whether this was the year for mobile, and advertising holding companies and big brand CMOs were finally waking up to the fact that this online phenomenon was here to stay and were starting to pour more and more resources into figuring it out.

'Fragmentation' was perhaps the wrong description, as traditional brand marketers were simply realizing that there were more online channels opening up, and when they integrated with the offline world – TV, radio etc – digital could hold some very valuable consumer data, accountability and revenue opportunities. The race towards a more comprehensive digital understanding and tangible return on investment was on.

The *Contagious* crew had spotted this trend and were mobilizing to capitalize on it. They considered they had a good grasp on the industry and what made a good digital campaign more creative.

By taking the initiative to cover all aspects of the industry and write as much as they could about new work, they grew in confidence that, because they had a 360° view, their analysis was fair and accurate. Add trend data to an innate understanding of the players to back it up, and you have a powerful mix of current opinion and future prediction.

Contagious's early years were dominated by production schedules. Greenwood describes it with a wry smile as 'like a beautiful, golden age – when all we did was publish a magazine'.

With offices on Carnaby Street in London (a fearfully expensive place to work as a young woman with a penchant for fashion), the magazine was set to be published quarterly, so the team would spend a month out and about in the industry meeting people and discussing the great and the good over 'a lot of lunches'. Then there'd be a month of planning followed by a month of deadlines.

Looking back on those days, Greenwood wonders how they ever filled a hundred pages given the ubiquity of digital permeating all other aspects of advertising today. She's seen a meteoric rise in the level of understanding, usage of the internet and awareness of the *Contagious* brand since the days of going to the Cannes International Advertising Festival in the south of France where they'd be asked what *Contagious* was and which award they were up for:

> It's been really interesting watching the industry turn itself around and not only get an idea of how to market digitally or how to create digital creativity, but also to get its head around the fact that it's a fundamentally important thing to do from a business perspective. Because in 2005 very few people in advertising thought that. Very few people realized it would be as big as it is.

Evolving from current commentary to future trend prediction was an obvious next step, Greenwood remembers:

> At that point, everyone was trying to figure out how to get TV ads to come on the internet based on the understanding that people were now starting to spend time online. An enormous advertising cottage industry sprang up around the creation of banner ads, but there's not really much you can say about banners. So it was a really interesting time for *Contagious* – trying to peel back what sort of future the industry might have. What happens when you get beyond the banners, and beyond the buttons? What happens when everyone has access to high-speed internet, and what happens when everybody does have a mobile phone? In 2005 they didn't, and we had no idea how it would evolve. And every day it changes again. It's so fascinating to watch.

Technology plus creativity equals success

Back then, there was a 2005 equivalent of *Mad Men*'s Don Draper walking the halls of most agencies calling themselves ECDs (executive creative directors), but who were deaf to the 'you should be doing this' brigade. Greenwood recalls they needed to be influenced differently:

> You couldn't get their attention by saying digital marketing is going to be big. There were plenty of people in the agencies saying that already, and plenty of digital agencies springing up to take advantage of client demand. However, there was – and still is – a school of traditional creative that places more importance on film and TV because that's where they think the real creativity lies.

So *Contagious* showed them with 'an absolute emphasis on HOW technology could be deployed creatively. We spend a lot of time breaking apart why certain things work, and why some campaigns really hit home.'

Greenwood says that one of the most fundamental and fascinating shifts occurred in the move to projects, over campaigns:

> If a campaign is something that's defined and finite before it goes out of the door – if your media is bought and your assets finalized – there's no way for anyone to engage with that creative after the fact. You send it out, and turn your back, and move on. That's a campaign. Projects, on the other hand, require nurturing and monitoring, a more fluid and ongoing approach to production and management. They're more challenging for the agency and client, but more fun for the end user, and arguably a smarter way to steal a march on the competition than simply outspending them on media.

The most interesting evolution *Contagious* has observed in the last couple of years is the increased collaboration between the marketing department and other areas of the company – product development, or customer service, or data systems. Greenwood explains:

> One of the things that the internet's done is turn companies inside out. Bad PR – people complaining about how poorly they were treated online – is par for the course. It's therefore become really important for anyone involved in advertising to have an eye on all these other consumer touch points, managing how the brand presents itself everywhere, not just through marketing. It's a great opportunity for the industry as a whole to expand the way they operate.

Working hard on industry relationships and establishing the brand for a couple of years paid off in 2007 when they were approached for more trend intelligence. Having a breadth and depth of knowledge across a multi-disciplined staff meant that valuable insight in the right hands could have competitive advantages in the marketplace for some agencies. So the Contagious Feed was born, which now enables big brand and agency clients to have paid access to a bespoke stream of data, campaigns and information, from 'what's hot' with popular culture to nuggets on emerging technology and social media.

Contagious never seemed to have a definite plan, other than to do what they did well and with great intelligence coupled with ease of execution. As Greenwood recollects, 'there's a certain degree at the beginning where I think we really didn't know what we were going to do next. But it's been an interesting journey to figure out how – figuring out what people need and the most effective way to give it to them. It's a very challenging time, and it's great that *Contagious* is in a position to be able to help out.'

Inside out

The third and final arm of the Contagious business is Contagious Insider, their consultancy which builds on the magazine's insight and Feed content, to provide bespoke guidance to businesses who, in simple terms, think they've lost their mojo. Greenwood ran Insider since its inception in 2008:

> It's basically the creative consultancy part of it. It can be anything from lighting a fire under the creative department to get them more inspired to get them do better, more experimental and innovative work, to helping clients with their issues and helping them structure themselves and organize themselves in order to be more creative. Contagious partners with a number of third parties to build a solution that solves each problem in a unique way. We're firm believers in strength through collaboration.

Karen Adams, senior director of integrated communications at Kraft Foods, is a fan of this approach:

> Contagious is on the absolute pulse of creativity and helps clients take the leap into new territory. The name is no mistake; their passion for creativity is absolutely contagious. They mesmerize, inspire and leave teams with nothing short of craving for more. There is no 'cookie cutter' here. Contagious tailors information to meet the audience background and

objectives, and you can count on Jess Greenwood to elevate marketers' expectation of great.

What Greenwood and team were doing was stimulating creativity and ways of thinking that capitalize on the huge amount of information now available to us through Twitter, and other social networks and news sites, by encouraging brands and agencies to do some things differently to the way that they've always done them. A hard thing to do when you're in the belly of the beast. Greenwood confesses:

> Contagious is a filter to help the amazing talents within the advertising industry make sense of how their world is changing. There's a ton of information out there, and very few filters. It can be overwhelming. But it's also true that a current knowledge of the technology and media landscapes is now fundamental for the creation of exciting and effective advertising. So I think that's what Contagious does – it basically encourages people to be active and engaged with stuff that would otherwise just pass them by.

What should success look like?

To many, this might seem a little obvious. Of course we need to be active and aware when technology and internet platforms are evolving so rapidly. So we work up a real-time stream of consciousness and have some great ideas, ideas we think will have legs in connecting our message with the right consumer with whom we'll build a beautiful relationship. But how do we know if that idea is any good? How do we measure the success?

Greenwood loves this conundrum. 'The measurement question is always hilarious to me because a lot of the people who are complaining that digital marketing is too difficult to measure are the people who used to throw a print ad into the ether every six months and then claim to be able to measure that. The metrics question is not an excuse to do nothing.'

She recommends three ways that in their totality give advertisers a very good handle on how well their campaign has performed:

- Business metrics – Did my sales go up? Did it have a tangible effect on my bottom line? Did I attract more consumers to my brand?
- Brand metrics – Did more people talk about this? Talking about your brand is very, very important. Were people drawn to it? Is awareness and brand recall all on a positive trajectory?
- Engagement metrics – Did people share the content? Did they comment on it? Did they sign up for more or when did they stop engaging?

For Greenwood the engagement metrics are the most fascinating in this age of social media opportunities. Understanding what it is about a particular video or game that keeps consumers coming back and telling their friends, coupled with brand and sales numbers, helps close the loop and drive a virtual cycle of digital success for those companies who put weight behind the importance of measuring the idea's impact and not just marvelling in the idea.

Don't define yourself too early

Shortly after our interview, Greenwood announced a career move from Contagious to R/GA, an interactive digital advertising agency based in New York, to take up a hybrid role in business development and strategic planning. It's an evolution that makes sense for someone who has helped pioneer deep thought and analysis of where the digital marketing industry is headed, and been able to present it in an approachable and engaging way, either through the written word, on stage at any number of events around the world, and though her Insider workshops. Of her new role she says:

> R/GA's an extraordinary company, capable of the kind of game-changing ideas and systems that reinvent businesses. It's amazing to be part of the conversations that lead to that kind of change, whilst exercising my hyperactive tendencies to be working on everything at once.
>
> The part of the job that I find most exciting is taking all of that strategic thinking and knowledge of the marketing landscape that I learnt at Contagious, and bringing it to bear on real brand and business problems. I think there's a tendency in marketing to err either towards the over-theoretical, or the over-practical. Having an eye on the bigger picture is important, but it's figuring out what to do with the knowledge, and how to make it work for you, that I really enjoy.

On how to get ahead in digital advertising and pave the kind of career path she has, Greenwood says you don't necessarily have to decide early on exactly what you want to do when you grow up. She was inspired by a TED talk by and conversation with Sir Ken Robinson who describes the danger of having a predefined destiny too early on in education, as it kills creativity. She's never had a clear idea of where her career was heading, but she was always open to new things, simply 'being interested in stuff that goes on, and how it fits together'.

Her other advice is to pursue projects outside your job that might feed back into your professional life in a deeply dynamic way. Being creative in your spare time leads to more creative thinking during the work week:

> It is a gift to be living in a time where your own personal interests are every bit as valuable to professional success as the way that you operate in the day-to-day of your working environment. It's an amazing time to be joining the working world. If you are coming into media or advertising and creative professions like that – there's enormous emphasis on being a well-rounded, interested creative person.

So get a hobby. Now!

Sound bytes

- Know your work can be measured. Embrace digital and the metrics by which you can demonstrate success. Numbers can always tell a compelling story.
- When setting out your stall, show how it's going to be different and how it is going to make people feel. Spend time understanding your customers' needs and demonstrate how you'll meet those needs in ways they wouldn't necessarily expect.
- Stay curious and open to inspiration from anywhere. Creativity can be stimulated in the most unlikely of places. Your physical place of work may be stifling it, so get out more.

Further reading

http://www.ContagiousMagazine.com/
http://Twitter.com/JessGreenwood

Zhang Minhui

Sohu.com.cn

Digital discipline

As marketing director of Sohu, the massive Beijing-based digital media corporation, Minhui managed advertising across digital platforms during its key years of growth from 2002 to 2010. Sohu's interests span many online formats and Minhui negotiated how marketing would work through search, social and entertainment platforms, and developed commercial opportunities through Sohu's interactive media. When Sohu created new formats, Minhui made them commercial. Minhui's ability to spot the potential in emerging formats in China has made him a pioneer of new frontier media.

The low-down

Sohu.com.inc (translates as Search Fox, f. 1996) is a digital Chinese language service working across a range of online formats. It is best known as a search engine with sponsored content, although search is just one of its ventures. Sohu engages millions of Chinese subscribers through platforms spanning entertainment, community sites and mobile services. Its biggest platforms have tended to be online multi-player gaming and brand advertising, an operation that services the full spectrum of Sohu's formats.

Sohu's brand advertising business offers commercial advertising services through all of its platforms, to companies driving their businesses online (as of 2010 Sohu had over 1,600 content partners). The most populated sites are *sohu.com*, a portal through which over 40 content channels and social communities can be accessed, such as *ChinaRen*, a site with 90 million registered youths. With over 505 million internet users throughout China in 2011 – more than the entire population of the United States – Sohu houses some of the world's most populated sites (source: The China Internet Network Information Center). Each of Sohu's platforms has niche sub-channels spanning news, television (TV), sports, entertainment, business and finance, women, automobile, and information technology.

Sohu's development was centred on its existing networks and users until, in 2005, the media-owning firm was chosen as the official content service sponsor for the 2008 Beijing Olympic Games' online throughput. Sohu built and hosted the Olympics website, which prompted a rapid expansion to such an extent that, by 2009, even Fortune had identified Sohu's rise as the world's third-fastest-growing company.

Managing the commercial content during this period was Zhang Minhui's role. His route to leading creative marketing for Sohu came 2 years after he graduated from University in Guangzhou, where he had already been identified as a future leader in digital.

Mingui's story: four key eras in China's digital history

Mingui graduated in 2000, at a time when companies in China were starting to set themselves up for the digital boom. 'Even before I graduated I was approached by a company who came to recruit at the campus.' They came to talent-spot because, claims Minhui, '...at that point students were being envisaged as the new force of the internet'. Before he even graduated Minhui had been designing and developing web portals. Minhui subsequently went on to experience first-hand several stages of the digital age in China. At the time he graduated, however, when the internet market was small, Minhui remembers that 'there was no money to win for our work, but there was a lot of investment in anticipation of the coming digital age'.

On graduating, Minhui was first employed in Sohu's social community Chinaren.com, the first online web portal in China which became the group's biggest social network. He was there when Sohu were awarded the Beijing Olympic Games project. For Mingui it was a career-boosting moment because he was set to work on navigating the linkage between ChinaRen and the Olympics online content across the network. Mingui proved himself during the campaign by making the platform commercial for a Chinese audience without slowing access and navigation for those outside China, who were unfamiliar with the text and advertising-rich pages that Chinese web users were accustomed to.

The other key period that Mingui saw as particularly significant was when video channels and gaming sites became, in his words, 'very hot' between 2004 and 2011. Attracting advertisers was no problem given the volume of Sohu's footfall. However, managing commercial content such as banners, branded characters, landscapes and formats, without saturating gamers with advertising, created a challenge that was a balancing act and called for ingenious methods of engagement (which Minhui made his forte). Paid-for advertising was Sohu's primary means of income generation. Therefore, styling the raw and commercial content, devising rules and becoming the guardian of the sites were crucial in retaining the interest of China's growing internet community. It is here that Minhui can lay claim to making a significant difference in shaping online marketing.

However, in 2010 Mingui realized that 'there's a big chance and challenge for mobile marketing. I think that will be the future, to move from desktop to mobile, which is why I moved from a desktop-based search engine company and network company to mobile-based advertising and media.'

So Minhui's journey to date charts the story of China's decisive moments in digital commerce so far: from the start of the commercial internet, via the 2008 Beijing Olympics and China's digital opening up to the world, through video and gaming to mobile marketing. Minhui has pioneered marketing through an era of unprecedented change.

How one innovation became Sohu's digital breakthrough

Early in his Sohu career, Minhui experienced how world events were catalysts for digital innovation. 'In 2003 during the time of the SARS crisis, no one was allowed to go out to big meetings in conference halls. In that special circumstance we took the chance in launching a video conference facility for press meetings on the internet. It was the first of its kind for the brand *Intel*. At that time Intel's keynotes, presentations, video and conference interactions with audiences were directly through the internet, and were in real time. Remember this was absolutely new then. Users shared comments no matter where they were (geographically). It became successful because there were more than 2,000 people engaged in that meeting. It became seen as the first conference press meeting through the internet.'

This was a coup for Sohu, who demonstrated their ability to champion new solutions in times of crises. Sohu's ability to rise to the challenge boosted their reputation as China's digital platform pioneers, which in turn helped to fill their advertising space. Minhui's marketing role during this time shifted: it was more to do with keeping advertising content interesting, as the huge volume of banners, pop-ups and sponsored links could easily have cluttered sites and driven users away. Minhui was required to create original ways of keeping users engaged with content – and with paying advertisers.

Commercializing video, the Sohu way

In 2006 Mingui was developing marketing across Sohu platforms when video-sharing sites started to flood digital spaces in China. Entertainment sites were springing up across the internet and home-produced videos were pulling huge numbers to video sites. Sohu created their own video-sharing platform and, in 2006, *Youku* (similar to *YouTube*) launched across China and quickly became a market leader. Minhui noticed that user-generated videos had the most creative and interesting content – not that produced by professionals. Minhui thought that 'during the Web 1.0 period, it was the portal editor that was offering content. With Web 2.0 it became the audience itself, web users that were offering content to each other. This makes me think that Web 3.0 is about the interactivity between users, editors and all the internet providers, interaction between all groups, sharing material.'

This scale of sharing was already happening in 2006, and one of Minhui's greatest innovations was to link the most talented keen amateurs from Sohu's site with professional filmmakers. A competition for Nokia called 'Short Short Movies' targeted 19–25-year-olds (although some applicants were nearer 40 – there was no age restriction). The competition was to produce scripts and the best seven would be made into professional-quality movies distributed across Sohu's network. Mingui picked three young star directors from China's film industry and launched the competition for subscribers through mobile internet channels, initially requesting scripts and storyboards. The scripts judged most innovative received a Best Film Award and were produced as 5- to 10-minute films. The aim was then to reach a wider audience by encouraging the films to be shared through word-of-mouth, watched and distributed by millions of subscribers. This aspect of the project could not be controlled – Minhui had to rely on the films themselves and the director's abilities to realize the stories. 'In the event,' remembers Minhui, 'each shortlisted film succeeded in being downloaded millions of times.' The project proved very successful. Some winners turned professional after the competition, while the competition made its hardware sponsors Nokia relevant across China's huge online mobile communities.

Realizing China's first user-generated project on an unprecedented scale brought massive challenges. The difficulty for Mingui was not the 'technical part' of setting up the voting process or handling participants' comments, but 'the user part' – how and why would mobile users share the seven winning films? 'It came down to the content and how good it actually was. This is why we hired hot young directors who would realize it in a far better way than traditional filmmakers. Minhui didn't want to leave the film's success to chance: he released 'behind-the-scenes' clips as tasters before the films were launched, and put out elated content to launch the stories in waves. He also admits to 'trying to see what feedback from the audience would tell us; how they would react and whether we should change the strategy on several occasions. Fortunately it proved to be very successful.'

Commercializing game play, the Sohu way

Sohu also drew up marketing strategies to maintain their massive gaming community by controlling upgrades through their own exclusive channels. Sohu software must first be installed on gaming computers, which gives Sohu scope to install updates and expansion packs to some 200 million public and private computers.

Sohu's most effective gaming community is their gaming news platform *17173.com*, a gaming information portal, with over 111.4 million people engaged in its many types of gaming entertainment. *7173.com* has become a destination for game players seeking news of new launches and player feedback, mostly on the site's populated message boards. The scales on which Sohu's gaming operations run are huge: there are nearly 600 game zones to cater for the varying gaming tastes on the many millions registered with *7173.com* alone. There are even contracted agreements in place with thousands of internet cafés across China, so that the gaming experience can take place in both public and private spaces.

Analysis: commercializing digital space

Sohu's range of digital engagement gave Minhui and his marketing team enough scope to be creative for their paying advertising clients. Beyond posting advertisements in text, rich media and video format, Minhui drew on Sohu's massive audience reach to use tactics from film and other industries and apply them through the company's matrix of web-based platforms. While Sohu's pricing methods for online space were mostly no different from many platforms globally (costed on live-time with click-through rates), they created enough scope for innovation. When this worked with user engagement, such as Nokia's 'Seven Short Movies', it illustrated to advertisers the capacity to try new marketing approaches. The boost in word-of-mouth and user-generated initiatives helped Mingui to persuade clients that creative approaches were more likely to be adopted and deliver better returns on investment.

In addition, Sohu's marketing team could draw on in-house video content that had been produced for specialist platforms across Sohu's network, including an alumni club, blog, e-mail, message boards, web messenger, micro-blog and social networking services. Such circumstances can only arise by being a leading market player, which meant that marketing for Sohu required big ideas and a strategic approach to resolve the logistics of huge audiences.

In some ways Mingui had an advantage in working with a massive brand. Like Apple in the United States or the BBC in the UK, when it comes instilling trust in users it is established media giants like Sohu that rank alongside friends and family in being trustworthy. These are the brands that have served them the longest. Mingui's role was to return that trust in commercializing the space of a communications powerhouse.

Pioneering the territory of mobile technology

Minhui considers that the biggest moment in China's digital history is the mobile market. It only became a fully fledged phenomenon in its own right in China during 2010 but has grown more rapidly in China than anywhere else in the world ever since:

> In my opinion the desktop market for digital will continue as the biggest portal with the most amount of information on it for searching. But the mobile market is more about very specific, defined areas of information needs. The mobile audience is already being defined as smaller clusters (smaller than the desktop or tablet markets have been even). So everything needs to be finer and polished in the design of the mobile port and its content.
>
> The difference between mobile media and traditional internet media is similar to the distinction between newspapers and the internet. The speed of response needs to be very fast – as real-time as possible. This is the era when the whole society will become more digitized and more mobile, because the level of technology is now available.

It was the challenge of mobile marketing that led Minhui to leave Sohu's guaranteed mass markets to take up the challenge of a rapidly changing and emerging mobile market. 'I switched to mobile marketing because it is still at the very beginning – in China and worldwide. *3Gi.cn* is a very large portal and being in charge of the whole of its marketing is a mind-blowing challenge. I have much more experience than when I was a novice at Sohu 10 years ago. It's just the right time to enter this territory. I feel like I am at the beginning of the rise of a new hotspot for digital marketing, which is hugely exciting.'

The evidence certainly backs up Minhui's view. There were 900 million Chinese mobile users in 2011, compared to 15,509,000 internet users with broadband connection. In 2012 the number of smartphone users surpassed the 340 million mark, which represents roughly 65.5 per cent of all internet users (source: *Wall Street Journal*, 2012). China's DCCI data centre predicted that, by 2013, up to 720 million mobile phones will be used to access the internet in China, at which point mobile phone internet use will overtake accessing the net through computers (source: sootoo.com). The economic forecasts for the mobile market are also compelling. According to EMarketer, China's mobile advertising market will double in scale by 2014 (to $1.16bn) (source: EMarketer, 2011).

Beyond the statistics there is also a cultural imperative in pushing mobile platforms in this part of the world. As 3G mobile technology has gained popularity in China since it was first launched there (in May 2009), it is not just youth but their parents, the 40–60-year-olds who were the first generation to adopt Apple and PC technologies during the computer boom of the late 1980s, who are also driving this market. Parents have larger disposable incomes and, particularly in China, family bonds and maintaining parent–child communication channels are important. The mobile era will help families keep more connected, and the commercial industries will see servicing this relationship with facilities and apps as the pioneering terrain of mobile communications. Therefore the prospect of the sheer reach and relevance of mobile technology for the Chinese market is going to fuel the rush of communications firms finding their way into mobile advertising.

So perhaps Minhui is right when he asserts that applying digital marketing to mobile technologies 'will be the next challenge. The move from desktop to mobiles, and the huge opportunities that will provide for marketing is, for me, where it's at and what I want to be pioneering.'

In hindsight

Given the eras of digital advertising Minhui has experienced during his career, it is surprising that he considers that his greatest contribution has been in simply making marketing commercially relevant for different platforms. As Mingui puts it, 'The greatest achievement for me has been to bring marketing to the fore – I use the phrase "industrial-realized" marketing. With each new format it has required a totally different way of reaching audiences compared to traditional internet businesses, which have a totally different way of marketing. I think what I did when working for traditional internet companies was to put different campaigns and strategies together for different types of industries (and different online platforms). Before this it was more chaotic, and you need to handle all kinds of clients. I was trying to categorize different types of industry and to summarize what types of feature need to apply to their marketing. That has been a constant in all of my work till now.'

It is the newness of the challenge, and the scope to be a pioneer over again, that spurs Minhui on – '(mobile's) still at the very beginning. Now we only have simple marketing methods, but over time I will work on it. We will create more strategies and methods for mobile marketing. Within several years it will be as large as desktop.'

So given that Minhui remains focused on the now-and-next of digital marketing, he rarely looks back and reflects on his legacy during digital's early pioneering years in China. However, when pushed, in 50 years' time Minhui would like to be thought of as 'one of the creators of mobile marketing in China. That's my generation in general and my company in particular. Developing this is more important than my earlier achievements in overcoming traditional media.'

So from Minhui's perspective the best is yet to come. He even has a clear perspective of the landmarks he wants to achieve next: 'I will change the mobile market from being a small cluster now into a mass market. Don't forget that, in China, we have well on the way to a billion mobile users. So, if we can get them, it's already a mass media.'

Nuggets of advice

For readers wishing to get into marketing through mobile technologies, what advice would Zhang Minhui give?

'For those who have not entered the industry yet, I would suggest that they dive in as soon as they can because experience is an illusion: we can talk about it all the time but once you get into it the experience you bring to a situation can be the difference between realizing a project and the project remaining a dream. The only way you can get to know any digital industry properly is to become part of it. So start now!

'For those who are already in the digital marketing business, my message is "hold on together", to experience all the difficulties and the hopes. I say this despite all the uncertainties of a new market during a global recession: the market is still massive at its starting point. People are already there but so far the real marketing achievements haven't been realized yet. In China our starting point is over 900 million users – that's the future.'

Sound bytes

- Minhui experienced four phases of China's digital history: the first wave of digital marketing (from 1990); the cultures around online gaming (from 2003) which China has championed; Digital China's growth up to the 2008 Beijing Olympics and the boom in platform formats to support user-generated contents.
- Minhui considers that the biggest moment in China's digital history will be the mobile market. With most of the population owning mobile technology it is ready to become an instant mass market.
- The PC, tablet and laptop markets may continue as portals with the most information available. However, the mobile market requires more specific, niche information presented in a different way.
- Experience counts for a great deal when rising to the challenges of new digital frontiers.

Further reading

Wang, J (2008) *Brand New China: Advertising, media, and commercial culture*, Harvard University Press, MA

Stephen Fry

Digital discipline

Celebrity, early-adopter of technology and all things digital, who is globally revered as a prolific blogger, Twitter power-user and technology industry commentator.

Arse, poo and widdle

On the morning of Wednesday, 4 February 2009, the world woke up to continued headlines of global economic gloom, war and political strife. Nestled in amongst these depressing column inches, however, was a story of triumph over adversity. The previous evening, the British actor, TV presenter, author and comedian Stephen Fry, along with several others, had been descending in an elevator at Centre Point, a high-rise building in London's West End, when it got stuck. During the 45-minute ordeal, Fry had whipped out his phone, taken a photo of the metal box's occupants and shared it with his then 110k followers on the social networking site Twitter.

'Ok. This is now mad. I am stuck in a lift on the 26th floor of Centre Point. Hell's teeth. We could be here for hours. Arse, poo and widdle', he exclaimed in less than 140 characters.

The innocuous story turned out to be adverse: who likes to be suspended 26 floors high for 45 minutes? However, it became an inadvertent triumph not just for Fry, as it cemented him as one of the world's first celebrity pioneers of real-time social media, but also Twitter, the San Francisco-based start-up, whose founders were convinced they'd cracked a simple way to use the internet to share morsels of information to a wide readership by harnessing the power of the network effect.

The *New York Times* later claimed that Fry's moment in the lift had done 'as much to raise Twitter's profile here [in the United States] as the photograph that Ashton Kutcher posted on Twitter of the rear end of his wife, Demi Moore, did two months later'. Twitter was growing as a fun communication tool within the technology and online marketing community, but with one click of 'send' the following morning's reportage reached as far afield as New Zealand. The concept of real-time engagement with celebrity, and the power of sharing news snippets that could spread like wildfire, was clearly illustrated in that moment. In the eyes of the popular press, it was a moment that captured the essence of Twitter, and helped it become the ubiquitous real-time information-sharing platform we see across the media today.

Digital introductions

Twitter was far from being Fry's first foray into online media or technology. Very much an early adopter, he'd bought his first computer at a store in Manchester in the early 1980s. The Acorn BBC Micro B, along with some word-processing software, sparked what Fry describes as a lifelong love affair, one that would continue to blossom after he unboxed his first Apple Macintosh computer in 1984 and beyond as he kept pace with the evolution of an industry chock full of such 'dorky wizardry'.

By the late 1980s he'd begun to experiment with the internet and was a prompt subscriber to Demon Internet who were one of the first internet service providers in the UK:

> I didn't actually know anybody who had an e-mail address except other people around the world who were like a kind of community of radio ham operators who were in their 40s and 50s. So the only reason you'd e-mail someone would be a complete stranger in Spokane Washington to ask him how you might tweak your subnet mask, or write a script just to be able to get online better using the various protocols on, obviously, dial-up modems at the time which were very slow.

Following the launch of the world wide web, Fry's appetite and imagination around this new playground grew. It's not as if he could foresee how vast the web would grow, or indeed what it could do for commerce or business. 'I had no more of a sense of it as having a function than an early motorist would think about commuting when he first tried a car.' But he found it deeply exciting, 'a very primitive latched-up sort of space full of enthusiasm'.

Although he didn't have any interest in making money from the net, it didn't stop the flow of ideas or adjust his desire to evangelize. He claims he had 'exactly' the idea for a crowdsourced online encyclopedia like Wikipedia, and regaled it to Alan Parker (of PR firm Brunswick) in the snooker room at the Groucho Club, explaining, 'I wanted people to lower buckets and draw up information, but also load buckets full of information, and leave it behind.' Although he never followed up on that idea, he did try to persuade John Birt, the then director general of the BBC, that he should get himself an e-mail address and secure the internet domain name BBC.com. Birt was too late, and the American company Boston Business Computing snaffled the address, only to sell it to the broadcasting company in 1999 for a reported $375,000.

Beyond captains of industry, Fry's influence extended to the British government as well. Through the 1980s and 90s, he'd been doing 'a bit of speech writing here and there' for the Labour Party while they 'were in the wilderness', and remembers Peter Mandelson coming to his house in Norfolk in April 1997, prior to Labour's landslide victory in the General Election that Mandelson helped engineer, and showing him a website for the very first time.

New web beginnings

At the turn of the century, Fry had even coded his own site, albeit a simple affair with a few links and titbits that he thought his fans might find of interest, and it was around this time that he got an e-mail out of the blue from one Andrew Sampson.

An Australian former stage manager who'd been transitioning his career towards TV and the online space, Sampson had been thumbing through a copy of Fry's book *Moab Is My Washpot* on Fifth Avenue in New York and decided to look him up online. Fry's website was no longer live, but Sampson, encouraged by their similar backgrounds in theatre and interest in the internet, thought he could help. So he contacted Fry through his agent and offered to redesign the site for free. 'I thought we had a lot in common and said I didn't want any money, kudos or credit. Being the guy he is, he said yes, great idea', Sampson remembers.

Originally just a destination site, StephenFry.com launched in 2002, consisting of the actor's biography and a photo gallery. Although it remained passive for a while, Sampson would add updates if Fry published a book or was in a film, with the help of designer Nicole Stewart: 'My job as a producer has always been to provide a platform for Stephen, so at the point he wants to add a forum, or the point he wants to add a blog, it would be ready for him to do that.'

That point came in 2006 with Fry's TV documentary on depression, an illness from which he himself suffers. Back in 1995 the actor had walked out on his commitments to a West End play (*Cell Mates*), which turned out to be a manic episode he revisited in a candid and poignant two-part broadcast called *Stephen Fry: The secret life of the manic depressive.*

Recounting his experience with bipolar disorder, he interviewed a number of sufferers, including actress Carrie Fisher and UK pop singer Robbie Williams, about the condition. Fry says that the programme aimed to expose what a 'hidden and dark subject this was, and how swept under the carpet it had been for so long and how it was stigmatized by society'.

The UK public's response to the programme was overwhelming. His office received over 5,000 letters per week on the subject, so Sampson added a forum to the website where viewers of the show could connect, swop stories and support each other. Fry reflects on the success of the addition:

> It's marvellous to think there are, one hopes, people whose lives are more settled or more happy simply through the medium of something like a forum of this nature. Especially one which openly discusses things like mental health. It's a terrific side to what is a very complicated issue that's the internet politically, and socially, and culturally. We haven't even really begun to understand what it is going to do for us.

What was beginning for the *SamFry* team (the name of their business partnership) was the understanding that there were other things they could do on the web that were both helpful and engaging. Fry's first response was to start writing a blog.

Enter the blessay

As a prolific author of fiction, comedy and musical libretto, Stephen Fry's vocabulary is naturally more expanded than most. So a thirst to indulge his passion for smartphones and share his thoughts with a clamouring public eager for some intelligent celebrity analysis resulted in his very first 'blessay' (blog essay) called 'Device and Desires'. The piece, published in September 2007, ran to over 10,000 words and began with the caveat that, while filming in rural Norfolk, he was 'in a field fondly fingering a phone. There will be errors here. Forgive me. This is a blog, not an article, and I haven't time to get home in the evening and do much more than check the hyperlinks. You aren't paying for it. I'm human.'

The post was a huge driver of web traffic to the site because readers seemed to appreciate a personal view from someone they felt knew about the subject. Because of his existing media profile, Fry was someone they could feel empathy with as well. Support and feedback on the post came in droves. One commenter remarked at the time, '308 comments so far, wow! Now this really is a shining example of how you can use Web 2.0 to great effect.'

The blessay's success drew the attention of *The Guardian* newspaper in the UK, who offered Fry a column which they called 'Dork Tork'. It ran for a year until October 2008. In it he sought to share his 'passion for the new; to review, rave over and ramble on about the latest arrivals in the field of digiware, and occasionally to stand back and survey the field'. The column was reproduced and published simultaneously on his own blog, an astute move as he'd obviously started to build up quite a following, a following that would explode during a filming trip to Africa, South America, Southeast Asia and New Zealand after Andrew Sampson suggested he use his dormant Twitter account to keep followers entertained on his travels.

Fry signed up to the social networking site on 15 July 2008. He recalls, 'I'd heard about it and thought it just sounded silly, which it does, and so I hadn't thought much more about it. Then I watched a sort of rather sweet pencilled cartoon on YouTube that they had describing how it worked and I thought, that's really not for me. It was people sitting in the café saying, "Hi I'm at the café." And I thought, oh good god help me now. But as I do with almost anything, I signed up because I thought, oh there's no harm.'

Twitter takes off

But later that year, as he was setting off to make a film about disappearing species, inspired by the writer and Fry's friend Douglas Adams, called *Last Chance to See*, he realized that the remoteness of some of the locations in which they'd be shooting meant wi-fi access for a laptop would be limited and quash any whim to update his blog. So he took an early version of the Flip camera, filmed himself packing up his mosquito net and insect repellent, and posted the clip along with a jokey commentary on his site, which was just about to get re-launched by Sampson. At the last minute, it was suggested that they add a widget to the site that had Fry's Twitter feed embedded in it to give it a bit more of a real-time feel.

As he set off from Heathrow Airport, Sampson pushed the new site live. By the time he stepped onto the plane Fry had 2000 followers; by the time he landed in Nairobi his followers had tripled his eager audience to 6000. 'Then I started to tweet while on this journey. And it got bigger and we just watched it grow, we watched it move to 10,000 and then 15,000 as I filmed in Africa; it was absolutely bizarre', he recalls.

Bizarre maybe, but this was just the beginning. The mere mention of Twitter on a UK TV chat show hosted by Jonathan Ross drove more followers to Fry's Twitter account. The programme marked Ross's come-back in January 2009 following a three-month BBC suspension, drawing a viewing audience of over 5.1 million. The show garnered news headlines claiming that the pair had 'set Twitter alight' and British viewers signed up in droves.

Less than two weeks later, Fry and Sampson got stuck in the Centre Point lift and that 'event' sealed a pivotal moment in Twitter's (and social media's) brief history to date.

Reflecting on the language he used in those lift tweets, Fry relishes the opportunity to be himself on Twitter. They are his words, selected in a moment that echoes how he feels right then and not filtered by time or some PR person or journalist. Authenticity within the 140 characters allowed is key, he urges, 'because you can smell a line of bullshit instantly!'

The secret, he says, 'is to be yourself under all circumstances, and don't pretend to be someone else when you're on Twitter, and somebody else when you're on Facebook, and somebody else when you're with your family, and somebody else when you're with your friends. Try not to compartmentalize your life into different identities.'

Being too earnest online is just dull, he feels, but balancing being himself and the enormous power he now wields (with nearly four million followers at the time of writing) has proven a tricky path to navigate, especially with the umpteen requests he gets to promote good causes.

Responsibilities to followers: a thin line

The pressure of the 'painful and difficult' decisions he has to make about which charities or cries for help he supports can be awkward. His team has a system which will filter sometimes 300 appeals in a day down to a few, and he'll attempt throughout his tight schedule to share them himself. 'It's kind of like constant voices. I try and get through these e-mails when I'm in the back of the cab, or between meetings, or rudely in the middle of a lunch with someone just so that they don't build up so massively that I have to stay up until three in morning.'

He takes the responsibility very, very seriously but despairs at how demanding some people can be: 'The public don't pay for me to be on Twitter, they don't own me. Of course they want to get noticed, and they feel that it's a tiny effort on my part for a huge result for them, and that it seems almost childish, and unfair, and selfish, and celeby of me not to accede to their request. But, so it's tricky.'

Not as tricky as having your followers cry suicide, though. With seven-figure numbers of people hanging on your every word, coupled with Fry's much-publicized bipolar disorder, there's a subset of his following that are attracted by a kindred spirit, but obviously need help. If he doesn't tweet for a couple of days or respond in a timely fashion he says:

> There are people so needy, so desperate, so mentally codependent on me that it is a real worry that if I don't pat them on the head at least once a day, they get very hysterical and I then I get direct messages from their friends and they're saying, 'Stephen's hating me, and I'm going to kill myself.' I'm really not kidding you. It's very upsetting and there's nothing I can do about it. I mean, all I can do is be as kind as I can, but briefly just say, 'I'm still here, don't worry. Sorry, I'm just very busy.'

And between writing, presenting and acting, Fry's schedule is very busy. So much so, he entrusts most of SamFry's entrepreneurial work to Andrew

Sampson. They make a great team. Sampson is, as Fry puts it, 'very brilliant at forging links with other people in the area of app development and all kinds of other aspects of the digital world'. He'll bring Fry along to meet 'intelligent and brilliant people who have come up with remarkable ideas', and if he likes the idea he might help promote it as the public face, but he's adamant he's not in it for the money. 'I think if people go into it wanting to make money, they probably won't be too honest. I don't think greed is ever a good way of going into any business.'

Although Fry is not keen on his reputation as an Apple fanatic (he desires and encourages 'bio-diversity' in the technology industry in order to spur continued innovation), he does see Steve Jobs as a mentor to his attitude towards entrepreneurship and thrilling invention:

> Steve Jobs showed that the first response human beings have to anything is emotional, and to some extent artistic. Aesthetic in other words. It's like a dog, you look at it, and you think, 'awww'. And if someone tells me about a new phone, or a new device, I don't ask them to list the functions it can do; I want to play with it. And if I play with it, and I find it doing things that are exciting, and new, and intuitive, and fun, then it's lovely. The same with a dog, you don't say, 'How many tricks can it do?' 'Oh, my dog can do 19 tricks.' It's how much you love it. It might fetch you your bedroom slippers, but it's a companion, it's with you all the time.

Earthquakes, wildfires and political unrest

Somewhat reluctantly, Fry's influence in bringing Twitter to the masses and real-time news and views to the media is with also with him all the time. At the Cannes International Advertising Festival in 2009, Biz Stone, one of the co-founders of Twitter, was interviewed about the uptick in their usage:

> The growth has been astounding and surprising and I wouldn't necessarily attribute it to any one, specific thing. There's always something happening in the world that's helping us raise awareness of Twitter. And that can be anything from significant world, global events to celebrity usage, people who already have a large fan base suddenly deciding that they love Twitter and telling all their fans about it. So we've seen it over and over again, big conferences, big events, earthquakes, wildfires, political unrest, Stephen Fry, you name it. All these things contribute to a general awareness and then there's the natural organic growth of a service like Twitter that is native to the web and mobile phones.

Asked to attend conferences on marketing and give his views on why he's been a contributing factor in Twitter's success, Fry lays down some ground rules:

> If anybody asks me a question about harnessing potential, I'll walk out. If anybody talks about business models, I will walk out. These are things that not only I find insufferably boring, insufferably tedious, but they're greedy, and it's always the greediest person in the room who loses.

Richard Eyre, former chief executive of ITV and chairman of the Interactive Advertising Bureau in the UK, remembers one such conference:

> When we met in November 2009, he was approaching his millionth follower and seemed as bemused by this as by the first 3000. A fortnight earlier he had resigned from Twitter or, as he put it, 'committed Twittercide', because of unkind comments, but had been wooed back by an upsurge of Twitter love.
>
> He said that the bile that had driven him away was the very worst aspect of the internet and though it was far outweighed by genuine stuff from lovely people, it was like being invited to drink a glass that was 'only 1 per cent urine'!

Stephen Fry still actively engages with followers on Twitter. He also continues to blog, author, present and act in films and TV shows and, interwoven with this, he's pushing digital boundaries with Andrew Sampson on projects that excite them.

Although certainly very wealthy as a result of all his talents, money is not his driver, as his advice to would-be web tycoons suggests:

> You have to love it. You absolutely have to love it. Don't think of the internet as this thing that makes you a billionaire; it is complete delusion. Of course some people are billionaires, but that's going to happen in any field. Just enjoy the ride, enjoy the creativity that it gives you, and the fact that all the successful things that have happened on the internet have happened because they're human, and in a sense being human is firstly emotional, and secondly it's trying to fight consciousness. What you've got to be driven by is what fucking fun and how unbelievably exciting it is.

Sound bytes

- Be driven to try new technologies and platforms, understanding where they might fit into your marketing and promotional activities at some point in the future.
- Create experiences that are fun, engaging and stimulate emotional connections. They are what endure and endears you to users. Don't be in it for the money either.
- Love what you do. It's the best motivator for you and people that work with you.

Further reading

http://www.StephenFry.com

Fry, S (2010) *The Fry Chronicles: An autobiography*, Michael Joseph, London

Pioneering places

21

India, China and the Middle East have the strongest-growing economies despite the post-2008 global recession. Because the timing of their growth coincides with much digital innovation and the rapid global uptake of smartphones, it is commonly assumed that these emerging countries will be at the forefront of pioneering digital.

In fact the countries with the highest uptake of digital media are Norway, Sweden and the Netherlands (Bahrain is fourth, followed by Denmark and the UK. The United States is 14th. Source: UM Wave 5). From this it would appear that the northern European countries have been digital technology's early adopters, and to an extent Scandinavian countries drove the first generation of digital: from early mobile technology – for instance, the Opera browser software came from Norway, to Ericsson – mobile phones originated in Sweden, while Nokia hailed from Finland. However, their small populations mean that their impact has been in creation and early adoption rather than usage. If one adds together all the mobile phones in Norway, Sweden and the Netherlands, where an average population of 71 per cent are digitally tuned in, it still accounts for less than one-thirtieth of the total online activity in China (952 million). Of the 1.6 billion people connected to the web in 2009 (Green, 2010), a significant proportion come from the United States and the emerging pioneering territories.

The motivations for going online appear to be slightly different in China, where those on social networking sites Renren, 51.com and Kaizen001.com tend to be looking for fun, compared to France where social networkers are looking to advance their careers, or the United States and the UK where self-promotion and influencing others rank higher in the list of priorities.

At present, the emerging future powerhouses of digital still lag behind the United States in terms of global influence. In order for China, India and Middle-Eastern countries to overtake the United States, central and northern Europe as digital power-states, they must first overcome their own limited digital infrastructures. Internet usage across these emerging countries has been relatively low because the quality of cabling does not stretch far into rural areas from the major cities. It is in villages and outposts across China and India where the majority live. Consequently there is a big disparity between urban and rural engagement with the internet and other digital formats.

In 2010, for instance, only 6 per cent of the Indian population had access to the internet, which still amounts to 63 million (from a population of 1.05 billion). The disparity between rich and poor in India is less significant for the uptake of digital than the gap between urban and rural communities.

In China the rate of internet take-up is higher, at nearly 38 per cent (of 1.3 billion), which fits with China's view of itself as being at the forefront of digital hardware production (source: The China Internet Network Information Center). For a country that had few domestic landlines per head it now has the biggest uptake of mobile phones – China Mobile has over 650 million subscribers in China alone, which makes it the world's largest operator. China has a booming advertising sector that has impacted on how digital reaches the Chinese masses. Jing Wang, in the book *Brand New China: Advertising, Media, and Commercial Culture*, described how Chinese advertising became highly commercial post-Mao, from a standing start. By 2005, towards a million people worked in advertising and total advertising billings exceeded $18bn (Wang, 2008). Since Wang's book the momentum has continued. By 2012 over 1.5 million people were working in China's advertising industries, with revenue totalling $45bn and an annual growth of over 13 per cent (source: IBISworld).

In the Middle East the web has reached roughly 40 per cent of the population – 14.5 million of 363 million people (source: Universal McCann). This in itself seems unremarkable compared to other countries, but as 75 per cent of citizens are under the age of 25 in Saudi Arabia alone, and given the economic might of the Arabic regions, the Middle East is the part of the world that is about to undergo the most rapid transformation in their use of media. In Bahrain and the United Arab Emirates, where internet penetration stands at 85 and 76 per cent respectively (the United States reaches 75 per cent), the sheer volume of youth making use of social networks and scouring the net for content has steered more market advertising spend online.

So the next countries to pioneer digital communications will be determined by their sheer size and reach, and by the proportion of their digitally native population, whose activities will ultimately determine where budgets for commercial communication will be spent.

China, India and the Middle East each have local behaviours and factors that shape their approaches to digital. Given that these will have a wider international impact, it's worth considering each in turn.

China

Pundits outside China usually assume that the country's cautious approach to foreign businesses operating on its mainland prevents global networks being equally dominant in China. The stand-off between Google and the Chinese authorities has been well documented, but the issues are not to do with favouring home brands. In practice it is the cultural difference, the sense of national pride and the sheer size of China that mean that it is capable of maintaining its own digital ecosystem without the force of any legislation. Although global brands such as Amazon and Facebook have tried to adapt to the Chinese market, their Chinese equivalents Jayo and social networks Qzone (for youths), Renren (for twenty-somethings) and Kaixin (for thirty-somethings) have already established the lion's share of the market.

According to Tang Lei, of iMag Interactive in Shanghai, the main reasons why overseas brands – including digital services – have not cracked the Chinese market is that they picked the wrong partners to enter China, underestimated Chinese pride in national brands or underestimated the cultural difference of the Chinese market – often falling short on all three. For instance, when Apple first launched in the United States, Chinese shoppers discovered the product being sold cheaper overseas, which damaged its reputation in China. When the company dropped the price, Chinese brands responded by radically reducing the prices of their handsets so that their overseas rival could not compete on cost. While the Chinese market is willing to try out new technologies, on balance they prefer national brands because they are formatted and designed for the nuances of Chinese communications.

This principle extends to search – the Chinese favour home-grown search formats. Baidu is the top Chinese language search engine and, for the country with the fastest adoption of mobile phones, it was the first search site to set up WAP- and PDA-based mobile search (source: Alexa.com). Although it operates exclusively for the Chinese-speaking world – 93 per cent of users are from mainland China – it still attracts more daily traffic than Wikipedia, Windows Live or Twitter. The fastest-growing search engine in China, Sohu.com.cn, which grew in prominence through its involvement with the 2008 Beijing Olympics, incorporates multi-player gaming, which (rightly) presumes that many young Chinese habitually flit between information searching and gaming in between their highly developed social networking activities.

Sina, the Chinese media company, has become the dominant digital service provider across China. Sina owns its own telecommunication networks, runs the most populated site SINA.net and social platforms such as Sina Weibo (a cross between Facebook and Twitter, with over 70 million users). 'Sina style' suits the Chinese way of reading information – it is visually loaded with many pictures and dense with text-based information. There is a rich history of information presented this way in China – newspapers are also text-rich compared to other nations' printed press. However, issues such as bandwidth to third-tier (emerging) cities and rural communities mean that sites have been developed around file size restrictions. Therefore the scope for being creative with online communications rests with the way basic media is used, rather than in the message content itself. As bandwidth is much bigger in the 'first tier' cities and urban centres (notably in Beijing, Shanghai, Tianjin and Chongqing), there is far greater use of internet services and, ultimately, more is spent on online advertising to urban audiences than elsewhere in China.

TABLE 21.1

Equivalents	
In the West	In China
eBay	Ali Baba
Craigslist	Ganji
Amazon	Jayo
Facebook	QZone, RenRen, Kaixin
MSN	QQ
Twitter	Sina Weibo
Google	Baidu, Sohu
YouTube	YouKu
Apple	China Mobile

SOURCE: Ray, iMag China

Heavy users of the increasingly popular (Sina) Weibo social network are predominantly first-tier city residents and are clearly the aspirant target market for online commercial communications. Weibo doesn't directly sell individual ad space on its site but space packages based on the level of sponsorship. With over 20 social networks having more than 10 million users each, it is worth noting that the majority carry advertising – mostly text-based banners. Advertising is their primary means of generating revenue.

The most popular Chinese instant messaging service QQ (712 million users) has a wide reach but has not made inroads on the high-end white-collar workers in China – those with the largest disposable incomes, who tend to prefer MSN. Therefore its sister company, the social network site Kaixin, has tended to bear more commercial messaging because of its reach.

Given that display advertising is the main source of revenue for social and search in China, the Chinese have become used to visiting sites that carry a high volume of advertising messages. They are also accustomed to trying out a wider range of network sites than most Westerners, given the range of Chinese language networks vying for their attention. However, they are also used to high levels of engagement and expect a high level of capability, where motion capture is the norm in most systems. Children in particular expect high

TABLE 21.2 Top five social networks in China

1.	Qzone	teens	481m regular users with over 637m active accounts
2.	Renren	students, white collars	170m regular users
3.	Pengyou	students, white collars	131m regular users (slightly younger than Renren)
4.	Sina Weibo	white collars	120m regular users and growing; popular microblogging service
=5.	Kaixin001	white collars	popular through social games
=5.	51.com	rural and small cities	178m users but only 40m active

SOURCE: TechRice/Kai Lukoff, 2011

levels of interactivity from their parents' phones – over 100 million are smartphone owners. While many young Chinese and high-end users tend to have iPhones, Android handsets have the bulk of the market.

In terms of the content of digital communications, much of the format-pushing work is being generated by the largest advertising firms. These tend to be the multinational agencies – corporations such as WPP operate throughout China, so agencies such as Ogilvy and JWT have a presence in the main Chinese cities.

What this means for creative content in China

Chinese youth quickly adopted the 'big four' digitals – mobile, PC–laptop–tablet, video content and social networks – so there's plenty of scope for creative agencies to push playful interactive content. In 2012, a campaign by JWT Shanghai for Wrigley's Extra chewing gum featured the Taiwanese film stars Eddie Yu-yen Peng (彭于晏) and Gwei Lun-Mei (桂纶镁) in four storylines – one for each brand flavour. Each had a clear narrative so that the content would work on any size screen and at any resolution. The four slots became 'must see' content and snowballed across all types of media – it played on headrest screens in taxi cabs, on television, it was heavily viewed on youKu, in online pop-ups, on elevator digital billboards, on business buildings and in cinemas simultaneously. By the time you read this book it may have well have been viewed through more media than any other commercial ever, such was the appeal of the two actors.

In terms of sheer engagement, the same agency ran a popularity contest in 2011 through a series of snappy films for Media Markt (technology store chain) featuring shop managers. In each spot a manager addresses the camera to make a pitch, explaining why viewers should vote for them. Winning shop managers and selected viewers won products from Media Markt for participating. The strategy, fast pace and Japanese-style treatment (films were stylized in post-production) made it distinctly different from formulaic commercials and it attracted much unpaid-for publicity on Weibo, Renren and on the brand's blog and social network pages, with viewers keen to vote for their favourite manager. There was content for viewers to review, comment on and share through discussion boards. So the Chinese love of technology and chatting was pivotal in making the strategy work.

Perhaps the most far-reaching contribution to creative content from China so far has been in gaming and novel technology mash-ups. Given the drive by the Chinese government to move more output from manufacturing to the creative industries – from 'made in China' to 'created in China', a rise in the international profile of Chinese communications is hotly anticipated in the near future.

India

While India is set to become a giant in digital communications, it is still just developing its basic digital power lines to rural communities and small towns. As the digital infrastructures are far more developed in cities and less so in rural communities where the majority of the population resides, much of the advertising is city-centric, targeting the top 1 per cent with the largest disposable incomes. Non-luxury brands often start with the aspirational 1 per cent and then introduce diffusion tactics to engage the mainstream. For instance, one shampoo brand ran price promotions exclusively for the highest income earners. To extend their reach, the same brand in 2011 started producing 1 rupee (2 cents) sachets targeting the mass less-well-off market across India. While urban–rural and rich–poor tensions make it difficult to address Indian audiences collectively through digital channels, a bigger problem is the number of dialects – 17 regional languages are spoken across India, which makes advertisers struggle with language and reference points in national campaigns, with the exception of cricket, which has universal appeal.

In Indian cities there is a huge Facebook community – second only to the United States – yet while national brands tend to have a presence on Facebook, few are pushing their involvement with the medium enough to get talked about. According to Santosh Padhi, chief creative officer of Mumbai-based agency Taproot India, 'They just use 8–10 per cent of the money to do something. It's usually the last thing on the table because most is going into TV advertising. So brands, agencies and media planners are treating it as a stepchild, but soon the stepchild will be feeding the whole family.' Facebook use is growing at such a rate that the company is customizing its presence for India in 2012. Brands tend to have a presence on Facebook simply to be noticed in a space where their customers socialize.

According to Padhi, no digital campaign has 'rocked the country' yet, although there is scope for brands to take off through digital space. As cricket has such a following in the country (especially after India's Cricket World Cup win on home soil in 2011), campaigns tied to the sport have massive viewing figures and have the capacity to drive viewers online. During the Indian Premier League in 2010 and 2011 the advertising agency Bates India ran a campaign called Panga League (panga means 'take head on') for the leading cricket team Chennai Super Kings. It featured 180 short 10- and 20-second films on YouTube that profiled everyday people revealing how they cope with the things life throws at them by tackling them head on. The much-awarded work sent a message to other marketing and advertising agencies that online media can reach a wider Indian public if the idea has sufficient appeal.

Markers in India

Brands in India have been less inclined than their advertising agencies to spend on digital channels. From a creative perspective, according to Santosh Padhi, 'The issue is that clients who can get a solid grip on the digital medium tend to come from overseas. Because it's mostly centred on youth the more senior brand managers haven't seen it work from personal experience yet. It will take clients, strategy teams, creative and media planners to make it happen.'

Although India has plenty still to do to fully embrace the digital communications era, it has a rapidly expanding digital network and expanding advertising industry (the industry has grown between 3 and 5 per cent annually since 2010). Advertising agencies, like the Indian economy, are returning large annual profits despite the global downturn. In 2011 JWT India reached a 44 per cent profit – the largest in WPP's global network over the last three years. With more advertisers being encouraged to produce campaigns through television, advertisers are using networked channels as the launch pad for content that soon finds its way onto YouTube, where it can be tagged on social network sites. This is especially true of youth-oriented fast-moving consumer goods and sports brands, which advertise heavily on the youth music channels MTV, VH1 and V Channel.

What this means for creative content in India

Indian youth are heavy users of mobile phones, typically to keep in touch with their networks of friends, and they tend to use PCs and networks such as Facebook, Orkut and Google Plus to keep connected and find content to talk about. There was enough evidence of this for Airtel, the Indian-based telecommunications company (India's third biggest), to reposition their promotion away from professionals and towards 18-year-olds, where they would need to take a new approach to content.

Airtel's advertising agency Taproot India saw that the brand should no longer drive its for-all-the-family credentials or push the services available through mobiles: instead they developed a more youthful positioning and personality with the proposition 'you need all kinds of friends, and for this you need Airtel'. The proposition was based around friendships within groups. In particular it identified Indian youth who characteristically pestered parents into buying them the latest technologies. They were an age where their 'family' were college classmates, so the agency drove a campaign around them as a point of reference. This approach worked for those older than the target audience, who would have formed their own social groups when they were that age.

The commercial that launched the campaign in 2011 featured college friends singing about the friends they have. It was accompanied by a jingle-based track with a strong beat. The narrative featured the typical types of friends that youths had within their social circles, including movie buddies, a 'proxy friend' who covers for you in class and an SMS friend who is constantly sending updates. It closed with the line 'you need all kinds of friends'. The advertisement was immediately popular – within three days the commercial had been watched by over one million on Facebook and YouTube alone, which prompted the brand to fund 21 further spots on the same theme, to run as TV commercials and on YouTube and Airtel's website. The films were recorded in 8 of the 14 common dialects used in India – English, Hindi, Telegu, Tamil, Bengali, Gujrathi, Karnataki and Asami, and introduced 21 other typical types of friend, including a 'vassoli friend' – the henchman who gets debtors to pay back, a 'sub-title friend' who talks too quickly and a constantly hungry ('bhukkad') friend, who reminds the viewer that 'I'm paying and I'm eating – it doesn't affect you!'

The campaign's success across India was matched by the communications industry's enthusiasm for Airtel's approach. In addition to numerous creative awards, it received accolades for effectiveness after recording a 13 per cent rise in awareness in the campaign's first quarter of operation in 2011. The campaign became viral and occupied many inches of blog space, as the character types caught on. It affected repertoire buying, with more than 25 per cent of youth switching brands to Airtel, and by 2012 over 21 per cent of Facebook users in India were accessing the networking site via Airtel mobile (compared to 6 per cent Orkut and 5 per cent Twitter. Source: Telecom24.in).

The success of this campaign (apart from winning India's first top honours at the Cannes Advertising Awards) rippled through the communications industry in 2012, where more campaigns were launched on television and then subsequently unravelled with more content online. It seems that television continues to be the big driver for launching content because there are such massive viewing audiences in India, despite the number of channels (over 1,400 in

2009). Big attractions, such as the Indian Premier League, guarantee huge television audiences and work well for launching new content and stoking interest. However, now that mobile phones are more capable than before – they can use images and film, not just text – brands in India are discovering that there are ways of appealing to consumers through personal devices. It tends to mean that campaigns are recorded in the most accessible languages for Indians – Hindi and English. Given that more Indians can afford mobile technology than PCs or tablets, it is likely that the mobile market will be advertising's most prominent frontier for years to come.

Middle East

The Arab world has undergone seismic shifts that have been motivated by political and demographic changes, and technology has been a significant catalyst in making change possible. The Arab Spring protests started in December 2010 and swept through Tunisia, Egypt, Bahrain and at least seven other countries during 2011, during which the role of personal mobile technology as a tool for government opposition cannot be understated. In Egypt and Tunisia in opposition protesters used social networking sites – primarily Twitter and Facebook – to mobilize their collective voice. Much of this activity appears to have worked with similar levels of orchestration found in political campaigns (see Chapter 1). Messages were posted on sites for targeted action and masses of supporters responded. As the population in Middle Eastern countries is becoming increasingly youthful, most have personal technology at their disposal and are active users on social networks.

The Arab world's advertising markets have grown and the uptake of digital media is still at a higher rate than the rest of the world, although the impact of the Spring Rising unsurprisingly damaged the advertising spend in countries affected. In Egypt, for instance, advertising turnover dropped from $1490m in 2010 to $962m in 2011. Yet the global downturn had less impact on ad spend in the Middle East. When the global media market slumped in 2009, the Middle Eastern market slumped 14 per cent but recovered from 2010, when it went back to 2007 levels of spend (source: Zenith Optimedia, 2012).

Given that the majority of the population are under 25 and active users of media, it is surprising that commercial communications remain conservative, and are still concentrated on traditional media of television, press and outdoor. There is a disconnect between the online activities of the young, who occupy music, celebrity news and chat sites, and the landscape of predominantly offline advertising and marketing in the Middle East. Soccer and MTV Arabia fill the screens of bars across the Middle East. Arab men check out Hip Hop stars such as Saudi-based Quasi online, while Arab pop princesses such as Lebanese performer Nancy Ajram, who continually touches on regional sensitivities, has a massive following and motivates more young women – and some men – to blog on her antics. The media disconnect between online youth and offline elders might have something to do with an underlying conservative advertising business, strongly influenced by the advertising traditions from Dubai, Lebanon and Egypt, which remain the dominant model across Middle Eastern countries.

What this means for creative content in the Middle East

The passion for driving and the heat, which makes outdoor nightlife highly popular, means that outdoor advertising in the form of megacomms (outdoor billboards), mupis (backlit billboards) and guiguntos (footbridges wrapped in advertising hoardings) are still prime eye-catching media. The 183 m Kings Road Tower is a big digital canvas with an advertising facade that faces drivers from over a mile away. In cities such as Times Square in New York, Piccadilly Circus in London or the Shibuya intersection in Tokyo, screens are confined to pedestrian areas, yet in Saudi the roadside landscape is increasingly becoming digital and interactive, with QR readers linking billboards to online content.

While brands and advertising agencies continue with more conventional forms of advertising, therefore, it is the media becoming digital that is bridging the gap between established offline media and what is now possible through digital formats.

According to Mohammad Abudawood, head of Procter & Gamble in Saudi Arabia, the Middle East's advertising culture is undergoing a paradigm shift and, as citizens spend more time online, budgets will follow the trend. However, in practice, advertising content is simply being applied to a more diverse range of media. This makes sense as there are multiple media channels in the Middle East, and it is often the case that national television networks are picked up across the Arabic-speaking world. There are over 658 television channels spanning specialist interests in music, sports, religion, current affairs, light entertainment, sales and children's entertainment. In Saudi Arabia, residents have the highest take-up of smartphones and have access to over 200 magazine titles. This is at a time when the youthful majority are finding their voice through digital webcast and radio sites, with more commercial channels springing up since 2010. Youths spend up to three hours a day on social network sites, while 12–19-year-olds spend nearly two hours a day online (compared to 2.3 hours watching television) – so the content of commercial communication is becoming more of a dialogue online, while the main drivers to online content are pan-Arabic celebrities, mostly from Lebanon, Saudi Arabia and Egypt through music channels and YouTube.

Part of the problem for different countries is that advertising content is not specifically regional; instead it tends towards a pan-Arabic voice, which reflects the cosmopolitan make-up of most advertising agencies in the Middle East. Typical agencies, especially global agency groups with bases in the Middle East, are populated by staff from Lebanon, Dubai, Asia, the United States and the UK, and most of the big brands tend to distribute the same footage to separate countries to localize through over-dubbing and post-production. Across the Middle East, separate advertising centres have gained a reputation for bringing different strengths to pan-Arabic advertising – Lebanon for style, Egypt for humour, Dubai for strategy – all of which export well across Arabic-speaking countries.

However, there is still a common complaint that commercial content tends not to be local enough for discerning viewers. It is for this reason that indigenous advertising agencies such as Full Stop in Saudi Arabia have worked particularly well in running national campaigns for the country's Travel Ministry and Information Technology Commission, as well as an online campaign featuring animated characters for AlBaik's 'Clean Up The World' social cause campaign. According to the agency's founder and creative chairman Kaswara Al-khatib, it's not just the visual language and accents but also the cultural subtleties that can cause offence. He described one Coca-Cola commercial, set in a Saudi restaurant where a Saudi-looking male spotted a girl sitting with her mother. The male approaches the girl and writes his phone number for her in the mist on a coke glass, which in Saudi Arabia would be seen as insulting to mothers and was therefore banned. Such local differences, argues Kaswara, are commonplace and highlight the opportunities for local agencies to thrive in a growing global marketplace, where technology can support local content in addition to Arabic-wide campaigning.

The Middle East remains a sleeping giant in digital because, according to the head of Optimedia in the region, there is 'a lack of understanding – but only at the moment'. There is growing realization in media agencies that marketing campaigns and advertisements can be ably supported by apps, but clients are not yet willing to make the leap with investment.

Sound bytes

- India, China and the Middle East are the emerging giants of digital communication. This is because of population sizes in China and India, and the rising proportion of youth across the Gulf states.
- They tend to have their own digital cultures, which have not yet exported around the world.
- China has its own digital communications ecosystem, characterized by text-rich, advertising-bearing social networks. The population are heavy users of mobile technology and advertisers are capitalizing on the potential this offers.
- India's technology-using population are mostly within large cities, as India's digital infrastructure has not yet reached smaller towns and villages. Advertising content tends to be broadcast first on television, then streamed though video-sharing and social network sites.

- The Middle East saw the potential of social networks driving political change during the Arab Spring uprisings from 2010, but the potential has not yet been harnessed by the region's commercial communications industries. Although more digital billboards are appearing across cities in the Arab states, with so many television networks across the Middle East most advertising budgets are spent on television commercials and traditional forms of outdoor advertising. TV advertising content tends to be pan-Arabic.

Lessons from pioneers

22

Lessons from Pioneers reflects on trends identified by pioneers that have shaped the agenda for digital communications.

Some of these appear contrary to given wisdom. For instance, *not being original* was a recurring theme with many pioneers, as was *not* being a forerunner: being of the moment was deemed better. This section also reflects on the wider significance of pioneering actions identified in the cases. For instance, how will crowdsourcing, convergence and the plethora of new app technologies impact on professional creativity? These and more are discussed from the pioneers' perspectives to identify the bigger scenarios at work.

Not being original

> Many people think you need to start something that is completely innovative, different, completely groundbreaking. You don't. I think you have to have something... that people understand. You can out-execute your competition by being agile, being more nimble. Once you're established, then you can be more innovative.
>
> (Gurbaksh Chahal)

The terms 'new', 'innovative' and 'groundbreaking' preface most nudges forward in digital communications. Many platforms claim to be the first of their kind, and online marketers still plug new 'big ideas' for digital. Yet originators rarely make big bucks from eureka moments. To generate revenue from an original innovation – on or offline – requires up-front capital to protect intellectual property (IP) across separate continents. IP is hugely expensive with up-front costs, which is why a system of angel investors and matchmakers lead the best digital advancements towards the ownership by large corporations.

When Gurbaksh Chahal sold each of his companies, he subsequently identified how to overcome the issues that forced him to sell – in Chahal's case customer reach and owning customer data – to move up the control-chain. Original ideas in digital cost a lot to service, so originality was not deemed the most valuable asset to be a pioneer.

Make sure customers understand your idea

Businessman Chahal and journey-chaser MacDonald, pioneers that are driven in different ways, both suggest that easy-to-understand activities were more significant to their success than being original. Moreover, it was thought to be much easier to take customers with you as a clearly communicated brand through different iterations of your business. This was the case with Feigelson's AWAL and Mingui's work at Sohu.com.cn. For one of the best embodiments of this, look no further than Apple Inc.

Apple is original about being 'original'

Apple has been wily in applying innovation from a variety of sources and making it work for their customers in a way that, to date, no one has bettered. They discovered through earlier ventures like the iMac (1999) that by launching something radically different, other brands 'snuggled up' by copying their interface or the look of their distinctive hardware. Everything from soap bars to jewellery latched on to Apple's aesthetic – semi-opaque 'blueberry' casing, matt finish, curved planes, lower-case lettering – to do what marketers called 'borrowing interest'. After that, before the iPhone was released, features that were synonymous with Apple, such as distinctive radius corners, were protected by patents taken out around the world. Therefore Apple made one significant creative leap with IP at the heart.

Their next big leap was to create an application platform and a commercial opportunity for others to create in Apple's space. As Jon Buckley of Mesh explained: 'What they did was to create a big infrastructure to execute ideas easily. The process of producing apps was as simple as possible, with its intuitive user-interface and simple operating system.' Apple's App Store features infrastructure guides to help creators through the development and approval stages, and they have simplified the user experience in a way that other platforms haven't. Even their 70/30 revenue split is straightforward.

The consequence has been that many creative apps work better on Apple systems because they were created primarily for that environment. A criticism sometimes levelled at Apple is that the app market can be limited by their vision, because many apps have been originally shaped within Apple's operating system. However, if developers do not go through Apple, they are missing out on their most relevant (and largest) market for applications.

Apple has therefore shaped its own creative ecosystem, where it is the gatekeeper to content. Apps are selected from millions of submissions and, if approved, added to the App Store where Apple then take 30 per cent of accrued income. Apps clearly became a massive format for Apple, with the 10 billionth App Store downloaded in January 2011 and an App training licence system in place for colleges in different countries. Apple has even marketed hardware around apps, with press and magazine ads showcasing the best apps exclusive to iPhone. Apps encourage users to explore the potential of new technologies such as quick response (QR) code readers and augmented reality (AR) in a fun, interactive way.

Crucially, Apple's app infrastructure helps to replenish Apple's brand identity and relevance. In Buckley's words, 'Apple created the infrastructure and app developers add creativity on top'. By taking crowdsourcing to the next level they delivered the framework to let others go and create.

Pioneering commercial models

Wrong models

Online innovators have addressed the expectancy for free content online. For pioneers like Kyle MacDonald free content was essential; for others like Feigelson and the music industries he works with, free content has proved problematic. In a climate of free share, it took time for buying non-hardcopy music over the net to catch on. Sharing is what the internet does easily: commercializing is another matter. If there is no up-front notice that content needs to be paid for, the expectation has been established that it should be free.

There is no one way to commercialize digital innovation, and too often the wrong role models are heralded as good practice. The argument – voiced by Chahal – is that the digital trade media tend to get hung up on new and unproven technologies. Consequently catchy ideas are confused with good business prospects. Chahal asserts that many companies trading in digital space forget the simple premise that they are, first and foremost, a business: being online is in many respects irrelevant. There are many cases where being new and dynamic attracted large-scale capital investment before producing an operation model: in technology (for instance, Nortel Networks), market analysis (Groupon and group buying first time round) and music service (unsign.com), there were projects backed before growth plans were evidenced. Not all proved good investments.

Until recently, websites could even be evaluated on their footfall. Spotify, the Swedish music-streaming firm, were able to convert reputation into capital because they retained a popular following and built trust within their nervous music industry.

A more extreme and potentially far-reaching version of confidence-based value was when musician David Bowie leased the future of his recording catalogue. According to the broadcaster and economics pundit Evan Davis in 2009, Bowie applied a method called 'securitization'. According to Davis, Bowie estimated the amount of money that would be accrued over the next 10 years from his back catalogue, and sold it to get cash up-front rather than waiting for the funds to trickle in over a decade. The estimated worth of the shares was projected from a mixture of past earnings and continued optimism over Bowie's future commercial popularity.

Performance-related pay

Evaluations based on trust and footfall like Bowie's projected worth, occur less frequently in a recession. For larger digital communications firms the pendulum has swung the other way, with some considering pay-for-performance contracts to finesse their client relationships. By sharing risk they are expressing confidence in their abilities to deliver.

In 2011 the media agency UM hired consultants McKinsey with a view to rethinking their agency-fee model. Performance-based pay was thought riskier but more profitable in the long run, because it retains bigger clients who have traditionally risked more on advertising and marketing. The argument was that with accurate measurement and planning tools now available before and during campaigns, margins could be accurately forecast. Clients would therefore be able to reduce their margins of risk. According to UM's Mark Middlemas, UM's contract with Chrysler in 2011 included approximately 20 per cent of payment based on pay for performance, with key performance indicators related to sales, share and brand perception.

In their book *Always On*, media specialists Christopher Vollmer and Geoffrey Precourt reckoned that, in an increasingly dynamic environment, outcome-focused metrics had shifted the focal point of advertising from exposure to results – returns on investment, and suggested size of viewership/footfall, length of engagement viewing behaviour and sales as key measurements (Vollmer and Precourt, 2008).

In 2008 the London-based advertising agency Clemmow Hornby Inge tried a creative approach to negotiating metrics. They introduced a Big Ideas Room to their agency where client marketing and procurement teams generated positioning strategies and activation plans. As well as creating interpersonal bonds, they reasoned that sharing the ownership of ideas with clients would key them in to big decisions made, rather than passing the creative rationale along a word-of-mouth chain. It also helped to convince their clients of the ethos of the campaign. They would, of course, also be less likely to disentangle the shared idea and account from their creative agency.

In this sense, channelling budgets into strengthening relationships with clients is a good strategy if it develops strong bonds during an era when the reach and effectiveness of many media formats have still not yet been discovered.

Social's indirect ROI

The role of social media within this debate has become clearer in recent years. According to UM's Wave 6 research on The Business of Social (2012), brands have branched out from their own microsites to the stand-alone social environments of Facebook and Twitter, as customers lost interest in what had become siloed brand websites. As a medium for marketers, treating social space as commercial space has some way to go, and as UM's Wave 6 report noted, 'popular measures of success, such as "likes", pokes and tweets, are no more than proxies for more meaningful brand objectives'. Placing a branded presence within a social network will not produce direct returns on investment. Instead, social spaces nurture and maintain the relevance of relationships in the same space where their customers are communicating. This is not, however, a universal truth and one should not underestimate the effect of a $100bn IPO for Carolyn Everson and colleagues at Facebook, in creating new experiences for brands to engage with consumers and generate a more direct-response return on investment.

Social space is attracting much attention from brands but is not in a position to operate fully as a commercial space for brands. That said, Jon Winsor created a commercial advantage from his network of elite sportswomen. Winsor challenged the payment chain and took on the role of gatekeeper, so that advertisers had to pay a premium for branded access. Winsor is, however, a notable exception.

In summary, as commercial digital media space is still developing a mass-market form, there is a tension between the tightening of payment for media services and the more fluid investment spend on new, unproven technologies. On the one hand, financial arrangements between agency and client have scope to change. New tools to measure effectiveness have made more nuanced payment models possible. However, lessons from the early years of digital, marked by boom and bust, have not been learnt by investors when it comes to funding digital innovation. The terrain of digital – technologies, sites and infrastructures – remains hot for prospecting venture capitalists willing to speculate on where the crowd-swell will bubble up next.

Repositioning creativity

Two themes – harnessing user-generated content and skills convergence – recurred during interviews with the pioneers.

Harnessing participants

Thomas Gensemer spoke of channelling the energy of Obama's supporters through the mybo.com site: 'When you see a video submitted from a field event – that the campaign manager had nothing to do with, how do you re-broadcast and spread it to supporters to keep the momentum going? It's a piece of campaign energy you can then share, so you can have people shaping their behaviours off it. That two-way relationship was something new.' Gensemer's approach was not top-down nor was it simply channelling a groundswell of opinion. But it did rely on users wanting to participate in content and engage by adding their own.

John Winsor founded Victors & Spoils by outsourcing creative briefs and rewarding the best submissions. He structured a system where talent was fairly rewarded, based on delivery. Winsor maintains that there is a large creative online community, often found uploading to YouTube, that is keen to take creative challenges online. There might not be the consistency of content that having staffed agencies would provide, but competition certainly produces dynamic results – as Victors & Spoils' work for Harley Davidson illustrates.

The knock-on effect, of course, is that professional creativity in the communications industries is migrating to a performance-based income model. Full-time work in the Western communications industries is harder to find, and the success of outsourcing creativity, though small now, is attractive to agencies needing to keep overheads down.

Since broadband widened the potential for interactivity, media production and marketing firms have tried bypassing creative agencies and instead harnessed untried talent. In 2008 Doritos set up a competition called 'You make it, we play it' as part of an engagement marketing campaign. They invited budding creatives to devise, create and submit their own commercial, with the winning entry broadcast on prime television during the half-time ad break of an international soccer match. The open brief attracted over 900 entries, mostly from 16–24-year-olds (Doritos' target market), and generated a buzz amongst Doritos' core demographic. The winning entry was purported to have cost £6.50 to make (it cost Doritos a £20,000 winner's prize and an estimated £45,000 for a 30-second broadcast slot).

The approach was not the first of its kind – Pringles Crisps in the UK (Procter & Gamble) ran a 'home-made advertisement' competition culminating in a primetime slot on Christmas Day in 2007. However, Doritos' approach was so successful that they extended the ad challenge to the United States and Asia.

The stakes were higher in the United States, with the winning entry to be broadcast during the peak advertising slot of the year, the legendary Super Bowl (XLIII) half-time break. The US competition received over 1,000 entries and while the winners shared spoils of over $1m, Doritos' return was an audience averaging nearly 99 million, the competition's site received over 2 million hits and, according to Bizreport, reached a billion page impressions. The advertisement and its back-story were so talked about that it was ranked 'The Best Ad of the Year' by *USA Today*'s Super Bowl Ad Meter.

It would seem that with the growth in online creative networks, those commissioning solutions have greater scope to open up calls to all-comers, in a manner akin to talent competitions.

Skills convergence

However, professional creative expertise is an essential part of the mix when it comes to servicing campaigns in real time. The variety of skills required to gel, mash-up and service brand sites needs the nimble imagination that Gensemer described in making big decisions within a limited window of time.

Malcolm Poynton, chief creative officer at SapientNitro, spoke of needing 'a bigger variety of skills in the creative department'. Nigel Vaz, the agency's senior vice-president for northern Europe, points to the staff mix in SapientNitro's large open-plan London office: 'Every single person at every one of these desks comes from a different orientation. So you have ethnographers; you have brand strategists; you have business strategists; enterprise technologists; people who build big bank trade systems like those that built [Sapient's web presence for gambling firm] Ladbrokes; people who are creative technologists who built things like Share Happy – the smile-recognition vending machine. Our chief creative officer harnesses that capability to drive our creative potential.'

In the fields of advertising, marketing, search and social, the same creative skill-sets can be applied to different types of digital work. According to Poynton, 'More typically we find we're competing with Google, Skype, Z-box, with any new product or services in the marketplace, the BBC as well for this kind of talent. I think it's showing appetite in the creative community to actually get into the game, where all of this fantastic progress meets the consumer.'

Lessons from established and new masters of convergence

Of the pioneers not included in this edition of the book, there are two that illustrate how convergence can be harnessed to make communications rich and interactive.

In 1977 Bob Greenberg, founder of communications firm R/GA (Robert Greenberg Associates) Media Group, designed film credits for blockbusters including *Alien*, *Superman* and *Altered States*, in an era before technology became interactive. The company in those days used computers to service motion graphics. Fast-forward to 1986 and the studio became digital, expanding into TV work including commercials for Coca-Cola. Then in 1995 Greenberg made a fuller transition into digital, billed as an 'interactive advertising agency', and serviced IBM's massive volume of web content. After projects for Verizon (*Beatbox Mixer*) and Nike (*Nike+*), which stretched the interactive ability of digital channels, Greenberg plans on moving into what he termed 'functional integration' in 2013. This will be based on creating customer-centred digital services.

In a move similar to Ajaz Ahmed of AKQA (who evolved operational models with technology), Greenberg shifted his creative business through a number of iterations. R/GA went from a boutique agency to an interactive shop, then into 'full-service' before expanding across continents. Staff can even collaborate across continents through the company's digital resources. A changing work model has allowed R/GA to grow with the media of each era. However, the creative impetus has remained consistent. A thread linking all eras of R/GA's work, according to Greenberg, has been storytelling – no matter what format it takes.

A more recent visionary is Olivier Rabenschlag, who is the creative Agency lead at Google and was previously the first-ever group creative director of media arts at TBWA\Chiat Day in Los Angeles. Rabenschlag hails from Dusseldorf and schooled in communications at *Buckinghamshire New University* in the UK before a journey that took him to Dare Digital, Ogilvy and CB+P. Rabenschlag's journey has included playful microsites for Axe Lynx (*Axefeather*), the live interactive *Music Is Life Is Music* experience launched at the Grammys in 2011 and the Nissan Leaf iAd – all using different media interactively.

The convergent world he describes is one of fluid links between communicator and subject and old and new media:

> The best thing that has happened in my career so far is that we can trace user behaviour in real time. We can visualize their response and move the storytelling in real time. TV has turned into an invitation to explore something else, something richer online. The communication path has been extended from broadcast to online, and now that transition can be seamless.

Rabenschlag's fluid world of communications makes advertising and marketing a fluid and transitional activity, with constant reiterations that are informed by real-time feedback. 'When you launch something online you can see what they say about it, then go back and refine the creative in response to the consumer. Then you can launch it again – it's unique to the digital medium. They call it *constant beta* – it's never final and always evolving as the audience and the world evolves.'

As Henry Jenkins observed in his book *Convergence Culture* back in 2006, the reality television genre – particularly *American Idol* (or *The X-Factor* in the UK; *Crystal Romance* 水晶之恋, 果冻 in China) – was 'the first killer application of media convergence' (Jenkins, 2006). By tying programme content to commercial opportunities and a myriad of participation opportunities on and offline, commercial communications has had over a decade to reiterate and refine its fluid-forms-convergent dialogue. So convergence has actually been completed – and is at its very best when no one actually notices that they've moved from watching to engaging and then participating.

All platforms and no content

According to Forrester, by 2016 almost $77bn will be spent on online advertising, 35 per cent of overall ad spend. Most of this will be on search, followed by display advertising, mobile and social – although mobile and social could surpass all targets if their potential is harnessed. Like apps, they are an emerging market with a young creative discipline attached.

In light of this, Poynton's optimistic view of a creative community getting 'into the game' is poignant. For at this moment in time there are many opportunities to produce something radically groundbreaking because the potential of much digital technology has still to be realized. As advertiser Mark Earls observed in his book *HERD*, word of mouth is really powerful and people like finding excuses to talk (Earls, 2007). If the media can handle it there's room for commercial communications to ratchet up several notches. It is in this spirit of discovery that digital creatives have scope to shape digital space. They can become the new pioneers of digital simply by giving platforms their own voice.

The scope for technologies such as AR, QR codes and GPS navigation is beginning to be realized, in terms of taking customer experiences and depth of engagement to another level. For instance, Disneyland added a layer of AR interactivity to Disney Parks for smartphone users in 2010. In November 2011, to mark 83 years of Mickey Mouse, the mega-billboard in Times Square, New York, became a huge interactive AR experience, where people could virtually interact from a hotspot with Disney's leading characters.

In Seoul, Korea, the potential of QR codes was realized with the world's first virtual reality store in 2011. Created by Cheil Worldwide, a poster featuring grocery goods and a QR code enabled subway users waiting for their train to order their shopping online.

In the UK in 2010, a video for the band Arcade Fire's track 'The Wilderness Downtown' re-appropriated Google's Street View technology with user data, in a collaboration between Google's Lab Technology Team and designer Chris Milk. The resulting pop promo was able to personalize each video viewed by incorporating footage from the viewer's location.

In each case the technology's potential, fused with lateral thinking, design and real-world application, made a leap of the imagination. The far-reaching prospect for the creative industries is that it will take content creators – the plethora of specialisms connected to filmmaking, animating, photography and graphic design – for such capability to be realized.

One challenge is to help each digital medium find its own 'voice'. What does it do differently and better than all other media? If creative expertise can crack that, they will have a benchmark on their hands – as Poynton's Dove Campaign for Real Beauty and Bogusky's Subservient Chicken for Burger King achieved.

A second challenge is to create content that works across all media formats, on different scales and streamed in different bandwidths.

A clear distinction is drawn between content that is both interactive and in real time, and pre-recorded content such as videos and film. Interactive requires a team to service the project while it's live (as Nigel Vaz described at SapientNitro). Pre-recorded commercial content requires a distribution plan, an ability to work in many formats and a reason why viewers would want to share it.

Matt Smith, director of strategy at The Viral Factory in London and an expert in content creation, sees this challenge evolving in two ways:

> Multi platform and trans-media content – these are not the same, but share the imperative to work across multiple channels, present new challenges for content makers. These divide roughly into two categories: *creative* and *production*.
>
> The *creative* imperative is to work out how to work across the different contexts and viewing habits and still engage audiences. The solution to this challenge is usually a variation on 'make it really good'.
>
> The *production* imperative was historically harder: how to make content that works across a huge variation of different screen size and resolution. The solution here is to worry less about production quality, and more about ideas, narrative and entertainment value.

To work across a range of resolutions and at different scales, extreme-viewing scenarios are a major consideration. For instance, on a mobile phone the ambience of a film is likely to have less impact than its narrative, subject and message, and smaller screens are certainly in the ascendency, both displacing many of the functions of PCs, and as second screens, used in conjunction with broadcast television for some real-time interaction. Martin Sorrell, CEO of the WPP communications network, identified the 'small and perfectly formed' mobile market as a priority area for his network. Spend on mobile advertising tripled between 2011 and 2012 (from $5bn to $15bn worldwide) and, claimed Sorrell, customers want mobility and targeting – particularly in the fast-growing markets of India and China.

It is in China that good examples of multi-platform content are taking off. JWT Shanghai's big-budget short films for Wrigley's Extra in 2011, featuring two popular Taiwanese film stars, became one of the most watched online clips within a month of being launched. However, it more the case that big ideas on tight budgets, like the Subservient Chicken, determine issues of production quality.

The term bandied about by creative content developers is 'network appeal': this is where content resonates in a way that sticks in the mind, is shared and makes viewers want to participate. Jon Buckley reckons that it is similar to the catchiness of good television, with more opportunity to engage. 'Bear in mind that you want to get copied. Remember television programmes of old – you copied brilliant stuff in the playground the next day. Now you can be part of it.'

The web's short history includes examples of much-emulated content, both non-commercial (check out the Back Dorm Boys, Where the hell is Matt? and The Evolution of Dance) and commercial (check out Diet Coke/Mentos Experiment, Budweiser *Whassup and Nike Keepy Uppy on YouTube*). The thread that runs through them is that they captured the imagination in an accessible way: maximum impact using the minimum means. Perhaps this is the mantra for multi-platform content in an era of reduced budgets.

Running in real time (not being ahead of the game)

> I had this crazy idea that we were going get a skating magazine company, and shoot the tricks and for a 'How To' website – I think it was in 96. So we put an enormous amount of resources in it – digitizing view, editing, links on eBay and around it online – and all the time all we had was dial-up. We were way too early in the idea of creating content. It was fun to play with, but so much of innovation isn't about the ideas. It's being in the right place at the right time. Too early and they fail. Too late and they fail.
>
> (John Winsor, founder, Victors & Spoils)

Being in the right place, at the right time, is a recurring theme through the pioneers' stories. In all cases their histories before digital made them the right people to capitalize on opportunities in their field. Some were held back by the technologies of their day, especially where infrastructures were not ready to realize their projects. This was the case with Denzyl Feigelson and AWAL: 'By 2000 we were desperately trying to sell downloads but it was too early. Technology then was too clunky and it took too long to download – bandwidth wasn't there; people still used dial-up; the idea of paying for music online wasn't understood; people weren't that interested in spending money on artists they didn't know. So we kept physical distribution going on one side, but we desperately wanted to get into digital distribution. We knew it was the future.'

Timing was a key tipping point: Kyle MacDonald's off-the-cuff remark during an interview about trading up to a house was one instance, at a point where online trading was booming; Stephen Fry tweeting from a stuck lift or discussing Twitter on primetime television was another. Both happened when 'their media' was becoming newsworthy in its own right. As blogger and 'brand voice' Robert Urquart explains, 'Working real time makes for an agile creative storyline. You have to be able to react to news and weave the brand message into audience responses.' Where Fry may have done this by accident, MacDonald certainly did this by design.

Running in the present

Gensemer observed that brands found working in social media challenging because it required quick reactive responses rather than following pre-planned agendas: 'So many companies were still applying the lessons of direct mail to digital efforts – in the tone and the copy as well as the cadence of the thing. They were trying to plan it three months out, as if they were going to hit the printing press! We needed to teach them rapid response...'

Alex Bogusky found that he had to manage a difficult scenario in real time, where the popular press became so hot on their project that the client contemplated taking the site down. How they managed the situation in real time ultimately made their work pioneering in the fullness of time. As is the case with most pioneers, rarely were they seen as pioneering at the time.

Create something useful and never assume

Avinash Kaushik actually practised blogging for a few weeks before launching his now hugely popular Occam's Razor because he wanted to make sure his writing was going to be useful and of value.

Martha Lane Fox's businesses have always satisfied a need. Whether it was late breaks and emergency gifts through Lastminute.com or the desire to let off steam at the end of a long work week with a few beers and a couple of karaoke songs, she's always found a gap in the market that addresses a specific craving. Lane Fox has now taken that a step further with her Race Online 2012 helping millions of people in the UK find uses for the internet in their daily lives.

In each situation our pioneers stated the importance of validating assumptions with the rich data afforded to them by the internet. Measurement proved crucial to understanding and explaining success, but it also uncovered different trends that might not have been considered. A prime example of that was June Cohen's web toolkit which was rapidly transformed into Webmonkey when the web logs showed it was Hotwired's most successful initiative.

Understanding the users and their motivations was also how Vanessa Fox managed to drive change at Google. Joining a company once considered less than customer-centric, Fox managed to translate the needs of webmasters into a reciprocal value exchange with the Google product management team, which created wins on both sides. Putting customers at the heart of her decisions and corroborating her ideas through the display of concrete data meant that Fox was able to build a solid product that has been useful for both Google and millions of site owners for many years.

Enjoy what you do!

Every single one of our pioneers had an infectious love for digital, the companies they have worked in and the businesses they have built. It would be too easy to assume that as they've been so successful, they were in it for the money.

But this was not the case.

June Cohen became so disillusioned with Silicon Valley and the start-up scene in the late 1990s because her peers were so motivated by cash. She quit the industry to do something completely different and if she had not been coaxed back by Chris Anderson to re-launch TED.com, millions of people all around the world might have missed being inspired by those talks through online video. She came back because of the challenge – she missed being at the cutting edge and making a difference.

Jaron Lanier may have sold a few companies, but financial reward is nothing to him compared to the thrill of working on some of the most radical technologies ever to be invented. When Lanier sees what he describes as serious talent squandering time with trivial projects in pursuit of a fast buck, he wonders how they'll feel looking back on their careers, having added so little to society when they could have contributed so much and had a blast doing so.

Danny Sullivan surrounds himself with a team at Search Engine Land that oozes passion for search and social media. Their love of those channels shines through their writing and keeps their audience motivated and coming back for more.

And Qi Lu's demanding work ethic means that he wouldn't have time to spend money anyway because he's too busy loving his job contributing easier ways to complete tasks and enabling people in the world.

Our pioneers agreed that having a real thrill working in the internet world based on what you are learning and how you can make a difference was by far the most important reward for them.

Ten steps to becoming a digital pioneer, from the people who got there

So, what lessons can be distilled from the stories of the pioneers? There are (literally) hundreds of clues in this book about what makes great ideas pioneering. Here are just a few:

1. You don't have to be original, but relevant and 'of the moment'.
2. Operate as a business first, and consider your funding model.
3. Rethink the payment chain and how you engage creative services.
4. Some of the best ideas come from stepping outside the sphere of digital. Many of our pioneers had 'other lives' that informed their innovations.
5. Make sure your team is designed for the job, and content is designed *for* its purpose. Don't let technology dictate what you do. Be user-centred.
6. Enjoy what you do – consider early on if you think it's worthwhile.
7. Make decisions in real time: don't expect a campaign to roll out online to a pre-determined agenda.
8. Make something that satisfies needs. Look for ways to fulfil an audience's desire rather than force in digital where it will offer little that's new.

9. Find signposts to success in the rich data digital provides to measure your work. It's all there – you just have to look.
10. Create experiences that are fun, engaging and stimulate an emotional response. Keep it simple.

Many of these might be self-evident. But it's the *way* these perspectives were applied that made the difference.

The 20 pioneers of digital in this book are significant, not just for what they've done, but for what can be learnt from their experience. Apply the lessons from their success stories in advertising, marketing, search and social media, and in 10 years' time someone might just write digital's next chapter about you.

JARGON BUSTER
Specialist terms explained

+1 Google social search experimental feature (see also *Google+*).

advergame An online bespoke game that has incorporated a brand or product within its content. This sometimes takes the form of *in-game* or *pre-game advertising.*

advergaming Usually part of a broader advertising campaign.

advertainment An advertisement packaged as entertainment. Used in content programming.

adware Software downloaded onto computers that displays ads based on the user's computing activities. Some software collects customer data based on computer habits. Also called *spyware*.

affordances The capability of a medium; what it can do and what it allows users to do – for instance, to remain anonymous on blog sites. The term is often used in the fields of linguistics and discourse analysis.

aggregator Term used in the music industry to describe a money-making format, usually a system or programme, designed to accumulate income as it becomes more active over time.

API Application Programming Interface – where companies open up their technology for third-party developers to create software and apps that communicate with them.

astroturfing PR or brand comments disguised as user-generated feedback. Attempted use of customer feedback spots to give the impression of grassroots support for a company or agenda.

augmented reality (AR) Live digital imagery or information feed, overlaying real landscape. Coined by Thomas Cowdell (1990).

avatars In computing, the graphical representation of the user; their digital incarnation.

banners The masts on a web page, often used as a platform for an ad message. The horizontal equivalent of *skyscrapers* in online display advertising.

beta Period of time where a technology platform or software is open for use but not fully launched yet.

blipverts Television or computer adverts that flash up unannounced, then vanish. They are usually short 'bumper ads' (promotional spots), approx one second long, that usually fall outside conventional commercials and after programme *idents*. They are most commonly used to plug programmes.

blog Personal online diaries often on personal websites, social network space and internet chat room sites, often used for online discussions. Such sites usually draw like-minded internet users.

Bluecasting An electronic billboard picks up signals from Bluetooth telephones and switches on when you are in range. The medium aims to target digital technology users and *early adopters* (stemmed from Holland).

brand evangelists Customers that choose to be loyal to a brand and are happy to speak up on its behalf. Also called *brand champions* or *brand advocates.*

buzz marketing Information disseminated by *word-of-mouth* as 'must see' content, usually online.

C2C Customer to customer, word-of-mouth *peer-to-peer.*

character migration Brand caricatures or personalities designed for adverts that have a lease of life outside a campaign. When a brand icon – usually a person or cartoon – becomes popular it can represent the brand beyond the frame of an advert.

click-throughs Name given to *the number of* online consumers who click on keyword advertising URL links.

clicktivism Journalistic shorthand to describe the use of social networks during the 2011 Arab Spring protests in parts of the Middle East. Also *hacktivism.*

CMS Content Managing Systems organized to produce a logical flow of information through a website.

communications mix A collection of different types of advertising media coordinated to work in a campaign. Also called multimedia advertising.

constant beta The ability to amend dialogue and content in communications during a campaign, usually based on real-time feedback.

content curator Specialists engaged in collating, editing, grouping, tagging and sharing media news online. *Content curators* distil and circulate relevant content for organizations and online network consumption. Term coined by Rohit Bhargava on *Influential Marketing Blog* (2009).

content snacking Term used to describe browsing internet users dipping in and out of websites and other online spaces.

conversions Term given to customers who *click-through* advertising links and then follow up on advertising messages.

CPC Cost Per Click – the cost charged per click when marketing using the pay per click (PPC) advertising model.

crawling The process that search engines use to identify and update new pages for their indexing system.

CTR Click Through Rate – the percentage of users that see an online advert and then click on it.

digital immigrant/digital native Terms popularized by UK advertiser Maurice Saatchi in 2006: 'Social scientists divide the world between digital natives and digital immigrants. Anyone over 25 is a *digital immigrant.* He or she has had to learn the digital language. The *digital native* learnt it like you learnt your mother tongue, effortlessly as you grew up. The digital immigrant struggles and forever has a thick, debilitating accent.'

direct advertising Materials that target the customer at home, usually by name. The most common forms are money-off vouchers circulated via e-mail, offer letters, magazine inserts and flyers.

DRM Digital Rights Management; a process introduced by music production and distribution firms which controlled access to copy music between formats. Also called Digital Restrictions Management, depending on your viewpoint.

experiential Opportunities for customers to interact, thereby getting first-hand experience of a product, service or brand. The term was coined by Bernd H Schmitt in his book *Experiential Marketing* (1999).

footfall The increased number of people going into a store as a result of a campaign, used as a measure if the client is retail.

full service An agency (usually specializing in advertising) that offers output in a broad range of media, including print, broadcast and web-based content.

full service agency An advertising group offering a complete range of advertising mass media, direct and digital advertising approaches.

gaming Electronic games, which are often generated as *viral* ads or carry adverts within their content.

glocal A global campaign tailored to local (or national) markets.

Google+ Google's social network project (f. 2011).

Google AdWords Google's pay per click advertising platform.

Googlebot Google's crawling technology that discovers web pages and indexes the content ready to be returned when a relevant keyword search is performed in Google's search box.

hatched brand Placement of brands or products in television programmes or films.

hooks Content in advertising designed to motivate the target audience.

IAB MIXX Interactive Advertising Bureau's annual conference during Advertising Week in New York.

ideation Idea generation. A term often used by creative specialists in digital advertising.

idents Mini advert programme sponsorships that are placed between television programmes and an ad break. They brand the program content.

indexing The system used to identify key words on a web page, which are set up by search engines to identify and provide relevant search results.

infographic Graphical representation of complex data.

information age A broad term used to describe the revolution in internet, mobile communications, e-commerce activity. The term is often used to describe what cultural commentators call the post-industrial age.

in-game An online game that has a brand integrated or name-checked within its content. For instance, an advert that appears within the set of the game.

interactive TV Cable and satellite TV services allow viewers to respond to programme content or commercials by using the buttons on a remote control.

IPO Initial Public Offering – when a company raises more capital by floating on a stock market.

junk mail Unwanted leaflets and letters, received online as SPAM or through door drops. Often referred to as direct advertising or direct mail.

Kinect Microsoft Xbox 360 motion sensor for controller-less console gaming.

likes An indication of shared 'thumbs up' or tastes put out to endorse preferred content by users; a form of personal recommendation to a community of friends as seen on Facebook and YouTube.

mash-ups 1. Internet users making their own video content or reusing existing versions and uploading them to websites. 2. A term referring to the fusion of existing programmes with new software to design new interactive features.

MMS Multimedia (digital) messaging.

multichannel Refers to a mix of new and old media formats, on and offline.

narrowcasting Communications – mostly radio or internet – transmitted to a small span of recipients, usually defined by specialist content.

new media A term usually taken to mean digital advertising, but often describes any new platform for communication that does not use *traditional media*.

one-to-one Direct dialogue with targeted consumers, person-to-person messaging, usually practised by *direct advertising* firms to address consumers directly. Also used to describe 'company-to-individual' approaches.

online advertising A term that is used to describe a range of advertising that uses the world wide web. It includes websites, virals, e-mail messages, banners and pop-ups.

online community Social networks of interest groups and personal *blog sites* that correspond over the internet.

organic search Search results that appear after a keyword search and are not paid for by the advertiser. Also called *organic listings*.

p-marketing Permission marketing, where customers receive benefits for receiving commercial messages. Coined in Seth Godin's *Permission Marketing* (1999).

peer-to-peer Passing information on from person to person, *C2C*, word-of-mouth, usually by way of product endorsement.

peripheral add-on Additional hardware that plugs into a games console to enhance the experience.

platform A space or artefact that is used as an advertising medium.

podcast Narrowcast audio transmissions from networks or individuals, in a similar form to that of radio stations. Transmissions can be live streamed or uploaded online.

PPC Pay Per Click – advertising model where marketers can pay publishers every time a user clicks on an advertisement. Ad space is often costed on the amount of *click-throughs* received.

pre-game An advert that appears before a digital game starts, as the game is downloading.

prospects Potential customers targeted because previous consumption habits suggest that they are likely to be interested in the goods advertised.

pull Media that draws in consumers to find out more information. Includes digital and personal modes of communication. A term used to describe the opposite to *push* tactics.

push Media that sends out or broadcasts information to push the consumer. Includes broadcast (TV, cinema and radio), billboards and some guerrilla advertising activity. A term used to describe the opposite to *pull* tactics.

reality advertising Promotional content in a way that is not re-created but drawn from everyday footage, often live and in real time, to communicate in an advert.

relationship marketing Advertising through personal address, establishing a dialogue between advertiser/product and consumer, mostly through digital *platforms*.

rich media Short for *rich* graphical *media* experiences. Often used in the content of *rich media environments.* Also advertising formats that go beyond the banner and button. They create experiences that may include video and some interactive elements like a game.

ROI Return On Investment: the conversion rate of viewers to customers.

search marketing A skill of using search engines as an advertising tool. Search engines are the first point of contact for brands online, so finding listed links is itself an advertising opportunity.

Second Screen (also *dual screen*) Complementary viewing, usually a tablet or mobile phone screen while watching television.

self-liquidating promotion A campaign that has a built-in obsolescence; a project that contains its own end point.

SEO Search Engine Optimization; getting a website/page to the top of search listings. The skill of optimizing website content so that it ranks highly on search engines for specific keyword searches.

SERP Search Engine Results Page – the list of web pages returned by a search engine in response to a keyword search.

serving The search results given by a search engine, organized by relevance and popularity.

SES Search Engine Strategies – search marketing conference first started by Danny Sullivan, now run by Incisive Media.

skyscrapers Paid-for adverts that run up along the side of content on websites. The vertical equivalent of *banners* in online display advertising.

Smart tv Television with built in wifi and internet viewing capacity.

SMS text Short Messaging Service, word-based communications sent via mobile phone. Advertisers tend to add links to text messages which make replying easier.

snacking Viewers' online habits of surfing the internet, flitting through content and sampling short bits of interest. This is often assumed to take place on work breaks.

social network channels Web chat rooms or specialist sites where people with similar interests can share views.

social network spaces Media platforms designed for web users to create their own communication spaces. Such sites attract huge volumes of traffic and are therefore an attractive proposition for advertisers.

SPAM filter Unsolicited junk e-mails containing adverts. Often filtered as junk mail away from inboxes.

SPAMdexing Creating the impression in search engines that a website generates more hits than it actually does. Device used to dupe consumers into thinking sites are more popular than they are because they are towards the top of search engines.

spon Denotes sponsored content, often found on branded tweets and blogs.

subviral Distributed digital video of uncertain origin; footage that conceals if it is authorized messaging.

tagging A term used when adverts are hooked to the end of digital videos. This has become a means of online advertising, via *virals* and *advertainment.*

TED Technology Entertainment and Design conference founded in 1984 and brought alive on the web in 2005 via online video.

tweets A post on Twitter, of up to 140 characters.

Twitter An online instant social network service (c. 2006) enabling users to put out messages to those following their messages.

10-minute snackers The supposed work-break time during a day when people habitually surf the net and check out, tag, play and send online entertainment.

360° promotion Campaign that fuses broadcast and narrowcast techniques in a multimedia approach to advertising.

thru-the-line A neutral approach to advertising, that can use mass media and direct advertising approaches.

traffic manager The name given to someone with the role of managing the advertising process at an agency. They time-manage stages of a campaign and ensure that work is delivered on time. Also a term used to describe the volume of information moving through a communication channel.

transvisuals Large screens carrying silent films or commercials. Usually found in transport stations or mounted onto buildings in major cities (mostly throughout United States, China, Japan and the UK).

UI User Interface; a shorthand term often used by media specialists.

user-generated content 1. Material generated by internet users. 2. Web space that allows people to engage others with similar interests, which currently includes *podcasts*, *blogs* and digital video.

UX User Experience; a shorthand term often used by media specialists.

video advertising Commercials filmed and compressed into various formats for use through a variety of channels including online and mass media.

video on demand (VOD) Online adverts, QuickTime movies or mpegs that can be uploaded at the time of viewers' choosing. Videos are put on website browsers for people to see at leisure.

virals Branded internet commercials or games that are shared on the internet.

virtual reality Also *virtuality* or *VR*. Real and imagined environments simulated by digital software. The term was popularized by Jaron Lanier, then at VPL Research, who produced specialist VR equipment in the 1980s.

Web 2.0 Phrase coined in 2004 to describe websites that had some element of interactivity associated with social media and engagement.

webisode A term that has developed for online programmes put out exclusively on branded websites. Instalments are designed to encourage people register and log on.

web content curator The role of managing, selecting and editing down available web information on behalf of a company for their internal use.

word-of-mouth Messages passed on from person to person by way of recommendation. Such *buzz* techniques are often used to make messages relevant across niche markets.

BIBLIOGRAPHY

Further reading

Battelle, J (2005) *The Search: How Google and its rivals rewrote the rules of business and transformed our culture*, Nicholas Brealey, London

Bogusky, A and Winsor, J (2009) *Baked In: Creating products and businesses that market themselves*, Agate/CP+B, Colorado

Cohen, J (2003) *The Unusually Useful Web Book*, New Riders, Berkeley, CA

Earls, M (2007) *HERD: How to change mass behaviour by harnessing our true nature*, J Wiley, Chichester

Green, A (2010) *From Prime Time to My Time: Audience measurement in the digital age*, WARC, London

Howe, J (2008) *Crowdsourcing: Why the power of the crowd is driving the future of business*, Three Rivers, New York

Jenkins, H (2006) *Convergence Culture: Where old and new media collide*, New York University Press, New York

Ryan, D and Jones, C (2011) *The Best Digital Marketing Campaigns in the World: Mastering the art of customer engagement*, Kogan Page, London

Sinha, K (2008) *China's Creative Imperative: How creativity is transforming society and businesses in China*, J Wiley, Singapore

Springer, P (2007) *Ads to Icons: How advertising succeeds in a multimedia age*, Kogan Page, 2007

Universal McCann (2012) *Wave 6 – The business of social: Social media tracker*, UM, London

Vollmer, C and Precourt, G (2008) *Always On: Advertising, marketing and media in an era of consumer control*, McGraw-Hill, New York

Wang, J (2008) *Brand New China: Advertising, media, and commercial culture*, Harvard University Press, Cambridge, MA

Wiedemann, J (ed) (2005) *Advertising Now! Online*, Taschen, Cologne

Winsor, J (2004) *Beyond the Brand: Why engaging the right customers is essential to winning in business*, Dearhorn, Chicago

Articles

Davis, E (2009) *David Bowie... Godfather of the crunch?* NGN, http://www.thefreelibrary.com/David+Bowie..+..Godfather+of+the+crunch%3F+CREDIT+CRUNCH+CRISIS+Bosses...-a0191935669

Harris, J (2009) Is the recession David Bowie's fault? *The Guardian*, Wednesday, 14 January, http://www.guardian.co.uk/music/2009/jan/14/david-bowie-music-industry

Hoff, R (2011) Online ad spend to overtake TV by 2016. Forbes.com, 28 August, http://www.forbes.com/sites/roberthof/2011/08/26/online-ad-spend-to-overtake-tv/

INDEX

NB page numbers in *italic* indicate figures or tables